The Extraordinary Spirit of Green Chimneys

New Directions in the Human-Animal Bond

Alan M. Beck, series editor

The Extraordinary Spirit of Green Chimneys

Connecting Children and Animals to Create Hope

By Samuel B. Ross, Jr., PhD

Purdue University Press
West Lafayette, Indiana

Printed in the United States of America.

Library of Congress Cataloging-in-Publication Data

Ross, Samuel B., 1928-
The extraordinary spirit of Green Chimneys : connecting children and animals to create hope / by Samuel B. Ross, Jr.
p. cm. -- (New directions in the human-animal bond)
Includes bibliographical references and index.
ISBN 978-1-55753-580-1
1. Children and animals--Juvenile literature. 2. Human-animal relationships--Juvenile literature. I. Title. II. Series.

SF426.5.R668 2011
371.909747'32--dc22

2010045724

Cover design by Mary Jane Gavenda.

Cover Photo: Dr. Ross, Paul Kupchok, and two students participate in a bird release at Green Chimneys. The hawk, which had been injured and rehabilitated, was ready to return to the wild. The bird release has become symbolic of the children's healing through the therapeutic programs at Green Chimneys, acquiring the ability to "go home" wherever home may be for them. Courtesy of Roy Pataro and Jodi Doff.

Author's Photo: Samuel B. Ross, Jr., PhD. Courtesy of Joanne Coates.

I lovingly dedicate this book to my father, Samuel Bernard Ross, MD. Known as "Barney" to everyone he knew, he was a strong figure in my life. He loved to joke with my children that "intelligence had skipped a generation in our family." If he were alive today, I am sure he would make the same statement and think it just as funny. I tell my grandchildren the same joke.

I only wish he could hold this volume in his hands and read the full story.

He would be proud of us all.

◆ ◆ ◆

I also dedicate this book to my wonderful children and to Myra, my "shining star," who has lovingly dedicated her life to me and Green Chimneys.

For Myra and my children there will be no surprises in this book; they lived it.

Green Chimneys . . . is a town for children . . . who may not have experienced "town" or "house" or "country" living. Many of these children may not have had a stable family, school or community in which to thrive. Thus the Town was founded to foster self-sufficiency as well as "citizenship" and belonging. This includes education, leisure, "industry," household chores and "commerce." Everything has a place in the town: a purpose and a structure. Pride in ownership, maintenance, fellowship with neighbors and craftsmanship are evident everywhere. The child has a place, a house, a school, a garden, and animals. The town is familiar, reminiscent of small towns of new settlers of the 19th century. These towns were created and recreated on the hard work and spirit of the citizenry. The difference is these new settlers are children.

-Susan Monserud, Architect

◆ ◆ ◆

While Green Chimneys has an international reputation, almost as well-known is the school's creator, Samuel Ross. This book is not so much a memoir, but a guide for all involved in education, especially those who recognize the value of animals and nature for children. Not only does it document the life of an extraordinary human being, but it is also a guide for child psychologists, teachers, administrators, academic educators, and all those interested in educational policies. Indeed, the extraordinary spirit of Green Chimneys lives on in the pages of this book and in the lives of the children and all who have been at Green Chimneys.

-Alan M. Beck, co-author, *Between Pets and People*

Contents

Foreword

There are some men who have great dreams, and we admire them and marvel at their persistence and determination to pursue those dreams. There are others, however, who have a dream so profound that we are not content to simply watch. We want to be a part of that dream. We want to help achieve that dream, and live within it. And, in the rarest of cases, some very special people convince us that the dream is more real and vital than anything that we have ever touched and experienced. The story that follows in these pages is about such a dream, told in the words of a master dream weaver.

Green Chimneys is a very real place. It is alive with the sights, sounds, and indeed smells of a place that caters to children and animals. Dr. Sam Ross, a.k.a. "Rollo," the founder and force throughout the sixty year history of Green Chimneys, is a very real man. A wander through the bucolic campus in Brewster, New York is restful and life-affirming. If you stay for awhile, listen, and watch carefully, you will see that each and every day at Green Chimneys takes the hard work and dedication of hundreds of staff and countless volunteers and supporters. That is the real magic of Green Chimneys, and the genius of Dr. Ross.

When a young Sam Ross envisioned a boarding school for children on an old dairy farm, it might have seemed a foolish quest. Time and time again, when failure loomed, first Dr. Ross's father, then his grandfather and friends stepped up to keep things going. Early in the evolution of Green Chimneys, Dr. Ross was joined by a most unlikely partner. A young teacher named Myra would become his partner in all things. In years to come they would be joined by many others in this work, including their own children. As much as the iconic green chimneys that tower over the campus, the hallmark of Green Chimneys has been the quality of the people who have joined in this effort.

Scouts and school groups completing service projects and world-renowned musicians and actors have all been drawn to Green Chimneys. Dr. Ross and his wife, Myra, are able to make each and every person who comes in contact with Green Chimneys feel valued and their contribution appreciated.

I would be remiss if I failed to acknowledge the animals at Green Chimneys. They have never been "just ornaments" on the property. They have always been an integral part of the campus fabric. When Green Chimneys was first conceived, the dairy cows on the farm were able to provide nourishment for the children. The animals found there now play a more profound role; they nourish the hearts and minds of the children. I have transported animals to Green Chimneys after they have been rescued from situations of abuse and neglect. I have returned time and again to find these same animals fat and sassy. They have thrived under the care and attention of the children of Green Chimneys.

If Green Chimneys had remained a dairy farm with a boarding school for children then there would have been no real story to tell. It is really the evolution of the Green Chimneys dream that is astounding. Starting first as a school for young children, more grades were added over time as parents wanted their children to stay within the loving arms of Green Chimneys. Eventually it would come to focus on children with special needs. Knowing Sam and Myra Ross, and the history of the organization, I believe that after reading this book, all of us will need to read a volume two, to see where the future takes Green Chimneys.

-Stephen Zawistowski, PhD, CAAB
ASPCA Science Advisor
New York City, September 2010

Preface

For more years than I would like to acknowledge, I have wanted to write a book about my experiences at Green Chimneys. I have had all kinds of advice on how I should complete this task. Each attempt has been more difficult than the previous one. Luckily for me, Myra, my wife of fifty-six years, gave me sage advice. She said I should write the book for myself. It should be what I want to write. No one can do that but me. I have been told that it may only be of interest to those who have been involved in some way with Green Chimneys. There are many people who contact me for advice and help. I know they will be interested.

More than sixty-three years ago I had the original idea to open a school on a farm. It is no secret that I was very young when we started. I was a college student at the time and had never held a year-round job. If my father had said he would not help, there would be no Green Chimneys today. Without his financial support and confidence in me, I could not have gotten started. Without his continued support and the support we received from family and friends of our families, we could not have created the organization.

I had no idea the sacrifices it would entail for me, and later for my wife, and our three children. Our life has revolved around the needs of Green Chimneys. It has been our life's work together. It is still our life's work. And those who know me know that I have been absolutely maniacal when it comes to my work.

Several times over the years, I have wondered aloud to Myra: "Will I ever be anything other than the headmaster of a small private school?" I never dreamed then that we would have grown as we have. I never thought that we would operate more than twenty programs. I never thought that we would have such a large, diverse staff and student body. I knew we would have animals, but not the collection we enjoy today.

I passed the executive director's baton to my successor, Joseph Whalen, in 1996. Joe joined the staff in 1972 fresh from college, and, as Joe tells it, he proposed to his sweetheart, Mary, and she accepted on the condition that he get a job. He landed the teaching job here, and they married. Twenty years later when I was looking for a successor, Joe was an administrator and the logical choice to fill the role of executive director. I think that he showed a great deal of courage in taking over! In 2008, Thomas A. McLaughlin wrote a book entitled *Moving Beyond Founder's Syndrome to Nonprofit Success*. He describes how a founder can remain involved after stepping down from a leadership role, and he adds all the negative possibilities that can occur when the founder cannot adjust to the situation. Joe Whalen takes all my suggestions in stride and with grace.

I must end this statement by saying that my marriage will always be the highest point in my life. Myra has always said that she gave birth to three children and I gave birth to Green Chimneys. Without her, what I did would not have been possible. Myra took care of our children, managed our home, worked in every capacity that she was asked to fill within the organization, and put up with me. Myra is everything to me. On a trip to Purdue University, I was treated to a dinner in a Chinese restaurant. When I broke open the fortune cookie it read: "Your mate in life will be your shining star." All those who know Myra will say nothing could be more accurate. I will never be able to thank her enough.

I absolutely feel invigorated by my work with the children and animals. Green Chimneys will always be an important part of my life, and I will always be involved. I love what I do. Watching the children develop and grow under the watchful eyes of staff members gives me the greatest pleasure. I am indeed lucky to be able to continue following my dream. As one pores over this volume, I can only hope that the excitement of living and working at Green Chimneys comes alive for the reader. I hope that we have done some good for the people whose lives we have touched.

A long tenure creates the necessity to look back and see what is different about the organization today than it was in the beginning. What has changed? What is new and powerful? What has been eliminated and should be reinstated? Who should make those decisions? This book tells of how it was and how it is and what I hope will help keep Green Chimneys of the future true to its original mission of caring for children and animals. I will be honest; it is much easier today to write about what happened than to have lived the experience.

I actually have to catch my breath when I look at the collection of aerial photographs of our Brewster campus—the red barn buildings with green chimneys and cupolas sprawl over many acres. The farm, trails, and gardens—all are surrounded by woods and pastures. Doansburg Road cuts across, neatly separating our main campus—with its multitude of buildings, stable, and upper barn—from our Boni-Bel Farm and the Country Store. How we have grown since 1947 and how good we look!

In the fall the campus explodes with the many-colored leaves of the New York autumn that too quickly turns to winter. Snow, when it falls, brings fresh fun for our children and staff. In the spring trees bloom in front of every building on campus. Flowers are not an exception, but the rule. In-between the business office building and the executive offices it is lush with rose bushes and flowers of every kind. When I leave the office in the early evening and the roses are in bloom, I make sure to walk home that way.

Green Chimneys is indeed a beautiful campus, and although I may be prejudiced, many have agreed with me that walking across our campus in any season is restorative.

With the coming of spring 2011, our children will move into our brand new dorms, and although I know we will always be working on some building or renovation project, the dorms with a private room for each child make me feel complete. Soon some of the older buildings that were dorms will be converted to other offices or torn down and new landscaping installed.

That's how it is at Green Chimneys.

◆◆◆

Recently, Joe told me that I should not work seven days a week. He felt I needed to do other things. After saying that, he paused, looked me in the eye, and said that if I really enjoyed it, he guessed it was alright.

I do. I really do enjoy it.

Acknowledgments

There were many people along the way who assisted me in getting this book to print, but there is someone very special that I want to acknowledge first: Bella Meyer. Bella was my administrative assistant for over forty years. Her dedication, loyalty, and service above and beyond never faltered. At ninety-four, Bella still helps out as she can, and I thank her sincerely for saying yes to me when I turned to her this past year and asked for her assistance in helping to proofread and edit this manuscript.

This manuscript, however, had several editors. At one point I had my wife, Myra, my administrative assistant, Anne Tascio, and my director of fund development, Kristin Dionne, meet weekly in my office to edit the book. You can imagine how I cringed as they sat reviewing together what they thought should stay and what they thought should be cut.

I owe these ladies a big thank you, and I know they made the book a better read. I hope you enjoy the story as much as I enjoyed living it and writing it.

I would be remiss not to acknowledge all the animals, the children, and the staff over these many years. They have brought much joy to my life and more than a few gray hairs.

Chapter I

The Beginning

My Childhood and Its Impact on My View of the World

"When did you first have the idea of opening a school?"

"It was the spring of 1947."

It is a clear, crisp day at Green Chimneys, and I am giving a visitor a tour of the campus. We stop in front of the peacocks, which are strutting about, showing off their beautiful plumage.

"How old were you then?"

"I was eighteen and a junior in college."

"And when did you start the school?"

"After I convinced my father to buy Green Chimneys Farm."

"When was that?"

"In the fall of '47 we purchased the property just two months away from my nineteenth birthday. We opened the school the following June, the day after I graduated from college."

She looked at me in awe.

I had been asked these questions many times before, so I knew what she was thinking: Who would entrust the care and education of a child to a nineteen-year-old? Who would support such an effort, and why? Who would stick with it for so many years?

Many people, as it turned out.

◆ ◆ ◆

Years ago I had visitors from Japan in my office, and they presented me with a wall hanging that pictured the moon and rabbits. I was told that a Japanese fable says that there are rabbits on the moon. I told them that Americans speak about the man on the moon, relating the nursery rhyme, "Hey diddle diddle, the cat and the fiddle, the cow jumped over the moon, the little dog laughed to see such sport, and the fork ran away with the spoon." I suddenly realized we are all the products of our childhood.

◆ ◆ ◆

If one's early upbringing greatly impacts one's later life, my childhood would certainly serve as an example. I had been away at school all my life, so when I got the notion to start a boarding school, to me it seemed entirely reasonable. So the history of Green Chimneys begins, of course, with my childhood.

My Earliest Years

I am a third generation American born in New York City on December 29, 1928. My parents married in 1914, and I came along fourteen years later, an only child. My parents were older than most people having their first child. My father already had achieved success in his career. I know I was spoiled and that I had advantages and opportunities other children of my age would not have had. In addition to sending me to private school, my parents took me to the theater, the Metropolitan Opera, and concerts by the New York Philharmonic. We ate in nice restaurants, traveled frequently, and stayed in some of the finest hotels.

My father, S. Bernard Ross, known to family and friends as Barney, graduated from Columbia University College of Physicians and Surgeons in 1912 and initially opened a private practice at 993 Park Avenue. He carried the designation of general practitioner, but he was also a licensed and practicing surgeon. In addition to caring for his patients, he was a physician in industrial medicine and attended to the medical needs of many corporations' employees in midtown.

In one of life's serendipitous moments while passing the construction site of The Roosevelt Hotel on Madison Avenue at 45th Street in Manhattan one day, he stopped to watch and struck up a conversation with the fellow standing next to him. The fellow turned out to be the hotel's president. Learning this, my father asked him if he would be interested in having a house physician, and the president said that he would. In 1927, my father moved his practice to The Roosevelt Hotel. It was here that he and my mother were living when I was born in 1928.

I went from the hospital to The Roosevelt. The hotel was named for Theodore "Teddy" Roosevelt, and many areas in the hotel, including restaurants and even the child care center, were named after him. I remember especially the Rough Rider Room and the Teddy Bear Cave.

My father's medical offices were on the third floor, and our suite was on the fifth floor, which we called home. I remember sleeping in a crib in their room when I was very young. The pictures that hung in the bedroom and the living room now hang in my home on campus.

My paternal grandparents traced their roots to Austria, Hungary, and Germany. They had a big cuckoo clock over the bed where I slept when I visited them, and hence I called them Grandma and Grandpa Cuckoo. Unfortunately I did not get to know Grandma Cuckoo. She died on New Year's Eve when I was only one year old. Although I was fourteen when Grandpa Cuckoo died and did get to know him, it was my maternal grandparents, Grandpa and Grandma Taub, with whom I became most familiar.

They lived in Forest Hills in Queens, and I spent much of my early years with them. Whenever I was with them I had places to go to and kids to play with and things I could do that I could not do in a hotel. Of course, being with my grandparents was also more fun because grandparents are very good at spoiling an only grandchild. My parents came each evening for a family dinner. Many nights I went back with them to the hotel and then returned after a few days.

When I was five, Grandma and Grandpa Taub were forced to move from Forest Hills back to the Bronx when the man who had purchased their house on the Grand Concourse defaulted on payment of the mortgage. I assume his lack of funds was related to the Great Depression. The house in the Bronx was a three-story brick building with one apartment on each floor. My grandparents lived on the second floor. In subsequent years they moved downstairs. The brick house had a big yard with a separate two-car garage. There was a nice yard with plenty of room for flowers and shrubs, which my grandfather and father enjoyed growing. I had my own room in the front of the house with space for a fish tank, a large bowl with turtles, and my wirehaired terrier, Terry. I had Terry until I was about seven, and then Lassie, a Scottish terrier, became my treasured pet. Whenever I was away from home at boarding school or summer camp, she remained with my grandparents. Then, whenever my parents and grandparents visited me, Lassie came with them.

My earliest memories are of animals. From the very beginning I had a companion animal. My first dog was Sunny, a wirehaired terrier who sat by my carriage, followed by Terry. Then came three Scottish terriers: Lassie, Candy (who I had with me in college until my landlady let her out one day and she ran into the road and was killed by a motorist), and Haggis, who was our first therapy dog at Green Chimneys. Over the years I have had many other dogs and even a few monkeys. Our cairn terrier, Magic, was with us over eleven years. He died in the fall of 2002. Today Spike, a nine-pound Pomeranian, has taken his place. Spike was a gift from our veterinarian Jack Wilson.

School Days Begin

I attended the Kew-Forest School for nursery and kindergarten. This was a private school that is still operating today. I remember the sandbox with the wooden Noah's Ark. I had a picture of my classmates in the sandbox hanging in my office for years, but it has since disappeared. I was accused by my kindergarten teacher of crawling around under the tables just to look up little girls' dresses. I had no idea why the teacher thought that. I did not remember this incident until many years later when sex education was one of the subjects we included in the Green Chimneys' program. It is funny how things remain in one's mind long after they take place.

My first grade was spent at St. Simon Stock, which was just around the corner from my grandparents' home. My grandmother's niece, Rose, taught me to read. The next three grades I spent as a boarder at the Irving School for Boys in Tarrytown, New York. It was not far from home, my parents always came on visiting Sundays, and I went home for a weekend once a month. Yet I was homesick and anxious about adapting to this new way of life. Making friends with the many dogs and cats at the school helped. The headmaster and his family had a few, and the faculty and their families had more. They let me play with them, feed them, and sometimes walk their dogs. Although I made friends with my classmates, there was something comforting about being with the dogs and cats. Looking back, I think my affection for pets really took hold during my time at Irving.

I remember being in our classroom at Irving as we all huddled around the radio to listen to the coronation of the King and Queen of England in 1937. Another historic event was when students and faculty lined up to form the letters "WELCOME" on the football field for the crew and passengers of the Hindenburg to see as the famous German dirigible passed over our school. It was later destroyed by fire at its berth in New Jersey.

Today the school is no longer in existence. Sleepy Hollow High School is on that site. C. William Olsen, whose father was the headmaster, was the president of the People's Bank of Westchester, which many years later provided a mortgage for Green Chimneys. It was at Irving that I met Buddy, a magnificent German shepherd, along with his owner, Morris Frank, from The Seeing Eye in New Jersey.[1] This experience made a lasting impression on me. I had never seen a person who was blind and had a dog to act as his eyes. When I see the dogs at Green Chimneys being trained by students as assistance dogs, I know that will have a lasting impression on them.

During the summer some of my classmates and I went off to Camp Wyomissing in the Delaware Water Gap in Pennsylvania. Here I had my first experience of riding in a sled pulled by sled dogs. The director maintained the dogs as a hobby. The summer sled had wheels since there was, of course, no snow in July and August. It was great fun. Our cabins had a bathtub, which we filled with turtles and small fish we caught on our many trips to the lake. We were not allowed to keep them very long and had to release them back into the lake. I wonder how many times we caught the same fish and turtles.

In the summer of 1938, when I was nine years old, my parents celebrated their twenty-fifth wedding anniversary early by taking a tour around Europe, and they took me along. We traveled by ocean liner and toured Europe by train. On the train from Lausanne to Geneva in Switzerland, we encountered a group of young Americans who had been in boarding school in Coppet, a town near Geneva. We paid a visit to École Nouvelle La Châtaigneraie, and my parents agreed it would be a wonderful place for me to attend school with the added opportunity to learn French. I found it difficult to share their enthusiasm. I would be far from home. I would be one of the youngest at the school. In addition, the headmaster and school founder, M. Ernest Schwartz-Buys, had told me that I would be able to speak English for only one month until I could manage in French. After that, I could speak English only on Sundays. This was not my first experience at boarding school, and my mother's promise that she would come to visit and would spend time nearby probably relieved some of my anxiety. They left me there at the end of our tour.

Thankfully, there was the headmaster's dog Poochy. He was a playful, wirehaired terrier just like my first two dogs, Sunny and Terry. Poochy and I became fast friends on that first visit, and he seemed to remember me when I returned to stay at the end of our trip. I took to stopping outside the headmaster's house to play with him, and he always seemed as glad to see me as I was to see him. After awhile, the headmaster let me take Poochy for walks and eventually entrusted me with his care. I was proud to have this responsibility.

La Châtaigneraie was situated on a farm, and we were allowed to visit the animals, which I did often. The only animals we were allowed to touch, however, were the rabbits, which we could hold. I was fascinated by them. I asked the headmaster if I could help raise the rabbits and he agreed. So every day after school I went to the barn to clean their cages, make sure they had enough water and food, and play with them. I also developed a fondness for cows, pigs, and draft horse wagon rides that year; I already liked horses. One day while I was there, a farmhand offered me a ride on the hay wagon. It was pulled by a beautiful pair of draft horses, and he let me ride up front with him. I went whenever I had the chance.

My schooling in Switzerland was cut short by the approach of World War II. In the spring of 1939, my father ran into John G. Winant, an acquaintance who later became ambassador to Great Britain. Winant asked if I was still in Europe, and when he heard I was, he urged my father to bring me home as soon as possible. My mother left immediately to get me.

When I learned that my mother was on her way over, I expected that we would do some traveling when she arrived. I had no idea what was impending. I knew there was some sort of conflict going on, because we were told to pull down our shades at night so no lights could be seen. I saw Swiss army members on patrol, and I heard planes overhead, but I did not understand what it meant.

When my mother arrived, we packed my things and headed for Paris. We were to set sail from Le Havre on the *Paris*, but a fire on the ship caused us to change our plans. Due to the times, rumors about the cause of the fire were rampant and frightening. Despite the havoc that ensued, my mother was able to book us passage on the *Nieuw Amsterdam*.

It was a long, tense journey. As we boarded the ship I noticed that everyone seemed to be in a hurry. Then a cargo net loaded with baggage broke open and fell to the platform, creating further chaos and panic, leaving us to also wonder if our bags were among those that were lost or damaged. The ship was so crowded that all the ballrooms and lounges were filled with beds. Many of the passengers looked different. They were dressed in black and wore fur caps; the men all had beards. They seemed anxious and huddled together. My mother explained that they were Jews escaping from Europe. Some of my classmates had told me that they had family killed by the Nazis, but I was too young to fully grasp what that meant. I did not realize until I was an adult that this was the beginning of the Holocaust.

When I returned to the United States in the spring of 1939, I had to finish fifth grade, which had been interrupted. I was enrolled at Mount St. Michael's, and the following year I started fresh in the fall as a seventh grader at the Hackley School in Tarrytown, skipping sixth. For eighth grade, my father thought military school would be the best choice for me. The idea was to prepare me for what might turn out to be an eventual war. My parents chose a school in West Virginia about eight miles from the famous Greenbrier Resort in White Sulphur Springs where our family had visited on many occasions and where my parents had many friends. The nearby resort allowed Greenbrier Military School cadets to use the pool.

Greenbrier had a very large farm with all sorts of animals. They raised cows and pasteurized their own milk. They raised sheep and cattle, producing not only enough food to supply the school and a local women's college, but also to sell on the local market. It was at Greenbrier that I really learned how to ride well, and it quickly became my favorite pastime. I rode in the fields and woods for hours on end. I also spent many hours with the farm animals, particularly the calves. Their pen was right next to the stables, and often I climbed over the fence to visit them. From time to time the farm staff would report me, and I was punished once or twice for what was seen as annoying the calves. At Green Chimneys we would not see it as annoying, but as bonding. Times change. The punishment for my transgression was "walking the beat," which was marching around the quadrangle. My time with the calves was worth every step.

The Moment of Decision

After four years of attending the school and Camp Shaw-Mi-Del-Eca, the summer camp operated by the school, I was no better prepared for a career in the military than young people who had not had this experience. When the bombing of Pearl Harbor occurred in 1941, I was not yet thirteen. I was with a group of my friends playing with a set of railroad trains when we heard the news. My two-year stint in the military would not happen until ten years later.

I completed high school during the summer of 1944 at Pennsylvania Military School in Chester, Pennsylvania, and that fall I was registered as a freshman student at the University of Virginia. I was fifteen and a half at the time. The students in the armed services occupied all of the dorms while other students had to seek rooms in town. I found a room in a boarding house a few steps from the university. I had a roommate from Kingsport, Tennessee who assigned me the nickname of Rollo, the blond little mischief maker from the cartoon *Katzenjammer Kids.* The nickname has stuck with me all these years. As a young person among so many older students, I was not part of the drinking scene and did not own a car. But I did get a dog, Izzy, from the pound. Izzy was my companion through college and came to Green Chimneys with me when I graduated. When my roommate joined a fraternity, I moved into a single room at the back of the boarding house. My room was large enough to permit me to raise canaries. This proved to be a good activity for me because I was not really able to be a part of what went on socially. Dating for me meant finding high school girls who would go out with me. I survived, but animals meant very much to me at that time in my life.

During my junior year in college, I began to think about opening a school on a farm with animals and children being raised together. I had been away from home attending boarding schools for most of my life, and since animals had always been part of my life, it seemed an entirely reasonable idea to me. Looking back one might assume that a Bachelor of Arts degree with a major in French and little work experience was not the kind of preparation one would need to organize, open, and operate a school for children of any age. It did not occur to me; it did, however, occur to my father.

It was May 1947 and my father, Grandpa Taub, and I were driving to the University of Montréal where I was scheduled to take a summer course, Intensive French. Along the way, we stopped at a private boarding school for young children in Scarborough, New York. Adele MacDonald, one of my father's nurses, had enrolled her son in the school, and we were to drop off a care package for him. She worried that he was not growing as he should, so every week she faithfully sent him cans of Ovaltine.

We pulled up to the school to deliver the package. As I approached the building, I saw a sign asking visitors to ring the bell, but seeing that the door was open, I just walked in. The dining room was on my right, and the tables were set for dinner with half of a piece of bread and half of a canned pear at each place. Food had been plentiful at my schools, but I had heard stories from classmates who were not as lucky, and here I saw the stories were true. Unopened cans of Ovaltine, sent by Adele for her son, were lined up on the fireplace mantel. I spotted Adele's son, and he was terribly skinny. A woman appeared, I handed her the package, and left; there wasn't anything else I could do. I walked back to the car hoping that there was more for dinner than what was on their plates, and I thought how horrible it was to not give children enough food. It was also wrong, I thought, of the school not to abide by the mother's wishes, yet allow her to continue sending Ovaltine. Children and parents deserve better. And then I thought, I can do better! And in that instant, I made my decision. I had flirted with the notion of opening a school for some months, but now I was sure that it was what I wanted to do.

Back on the road I related to my father and grandfather what I had seen. The ideas that had been germinating for months began to take solid form. Fired up, I broached the idea of opening a school for young children, and I laid out my plans, such as they were: it would be a boarding school for ages three through six. It also would be on a farm, so the children would have animals to play with and care for as I did at my schools. The children would have plenty to eat and a place to grow surrounded by nature. I did not foresee the school going beyond the early childhood years.

From our discussion, it was clear that my father did not think I was on the right track. I am sure when he left me in Montréal and headed back to New York City that he believed I would drop the idea. Throughout the summer, however, I pursued it and remained committed. Whenever we spoke or wrote, I elaborated on my plans. When I returned, we had many long talks.

Finally, in August, my father permitted me to contact a realtor before returning to college for my senior year. I attribute one of the reasons he consented to the enthusiasm of Adele, the nurse in his office who was sending her son Ovaltine. Adele wholeheartedly supported my idea and offered her help. She was to become an integral part of Green Chimneys, and in fact, years later, she married my father. Adele's son was one of the first eleven children we enrolled when Green Chimneys opened.

The Perfect Place

I enlisted the help of Mr. Joyce, a realtor in nearby Mahopac, New York. Over the course of a few weeks, he showed Adele and me several properties in Westchester County, New York. Unfortunately, none of them were quite right for a school. One property sat high on a hill, and while it had gorgeous views, it had very few flat areas for playing. Another one had a beautiful pond at the front of the property, but we were concerned that the pond might pose a safety hazard, particularly with young children. We continued to search.

Mr. Joyce then took us to a farm in Putnam County, which was Green Chimneys Farm in Brewster, New York. With seventy-five-acres, it had a long history as a working dairy farm. I knew it was the perfect site as soon as I saw it. It was only sixty miles from New York City, yet there was more than sufficient space and land for children and animals. I was sure it was an environment that would appeal to families.

It was to be important also that Brewster was easily accessible from Grand Central Station in New York City. Our home and my father's office at The Roosevelt Hotel made this a very convenient place to reach by train. Parents could bring their children to The Roosevelt Hotel and my dad would bring them up to Green Chimneys on the train. When they arrived, we would then pick everyone up in our station wagon.

When my uncle saw the farm, he could not visualize a school on the property. He saw the mess. He worried about rats. He wondered where the children would sleep and eat and learn. He wanted to know if my father, who I had asked to buy the farm, understood the risk he was taking. But most of all, he wanted to know what I knew about running a school. My answer was simple: I had been in school all my life! In hindsight, it was not a very good answer. I was a bit over-confident and a little naïve. But as an only child knows how to do, I wore down their resistance.

I credit my father for allowing me to open Green Chimneys and for providing the finances to make it all happen. Without him there would have been no Green Chimneys.

So, on October 27, 1947, in spite of the many concerns, my father purchased the property for $38,500 from the widow of the late New York State Senator Ward Tolbert. My father would spend much more before the first child arrived.

How Green Chimneys Got Its Name

We had picked the right neighborhood to launch our camp and school, and if we initially had difficulty with staff, it was not so with our neighbors. All our neighbors reached out to help. There were no signs of "NIMBY" ("not in my backyard") when we first opened.[2] This would not always be the case, but initially we were very welcome, and one by one our neighbors came by to meet us. I must admit they probably thought that it was a bit out of the ordinary opening a school on a farm. It helped that the Fresh Air Fund and New Rochelle Lions Club had camps very close to our campus, so the neighbors were accustomed to seeing children walking along the roads. Once people found out what we were doing, they reached out to help.

Today it is hard to understand that the area from Route 22 and along Doansburg Road was all farms in 1947 when Green Chimneys was purchased. The roadway was not a straight road as it is today, but was very winding with a sharp curve. Many drivers missed the warning to bear right and smashed into the wall.

The first farm as one turned off Route 22 onto Doansburg Road was a large dairy farm. It was called Mt. Ebo Farm. Rocky Dell, the next property, was located on the north side of the road. Ms. Brown and Ms. Perrin, two former physical education teachers from Detroit, operated an egg farm. Ms. Brown had a beautiful large horse named Chief. I was able to talk her into selling the horse to me for Green Chimneys. Down the hill from them was Boni-Bel Farm owned by Bella and Mike Meyer.[3] Bella was later to become my secretary. On their property was (and is still today) a cemetery with gravestones bearing the name "Barnum." These were relatives of the famous P. T. Barnum, and they had been circus people too. Actually, many circus people had settled in the area.

Further along the road was a dairy farm operated by the Farrells and the Wallaces. Beyond their farm was a one-room schoolhouse. The road alongside their home was called Welfare Road. The name was given to the road because it led to a piece of property that had been the site of a camp for welfare children. In 1947 the property was used by Camp Coler, a Fresh Air Fund camp on Welfare Road. Another camp nearby that was operated by the New Rochelle Lions Club was on Gage Road, which is now our own Hillside Outdoor Education Center. The next property was owned by the Jackmans. Mr. Jackman was a blacksmith and he shoed our horses. He told us that the elephants for the early circus which was located in the area (probably the Howe Brothers Circus), were housed in his barn. In front of his house he had a large rock slab that was used as a step and had been brought from Vermont and put into place by the elephants.

The property had passed through many hands before my father purchased the farm. The person who gave the name Green Chimneys to the property was Colonel Henry Breckinridge.[4] Before leaving on a business trip, he hired an itinerant minister to paint the chimneys. The minister found some green paint left over from another project and proceeded to use it on the chimneys as well as the cupolas of the barns. This was the talk of the town as chimneys were only painted white, red, or black in those days. Immediately, locals began to give directions to the Dell-Howe Farm by saying, "Go down the road, it's the farm with the green chimneys." When Colonel Breckinridge returned he decided to keep the color, and his farm quickly became simply known as "Green Chimneys." My family loved the story and decided that maintaining the name "Green Chimneys" would help people know where we were located. Six decades later we still tell the story of our name, and all of the chimneys and cupolas on the farm are still painted green.

Making Green Chimneys Green Chimneys

My plan had evolved to include a summer sleepaway camp that would open in June 1948 in addition to a boarding school, which would open that following September. This meant we would have about eight months to make the necessary renovations. At the same time, I needed to complete my last year of college, and my father had to tend to his medical practice. We were wondering how we would do it all when Adele again came to our rescue. As soon as we purchased the property, she volunteered to move on-site and oversee the work that needed to be done, and we gratefully accepted her offer.

The main house on the property was huge: a white clapboard colonial with fireplaces in every room and a widow's walk on the roof. The living room, playroom, dining room, and a large kitchen with high ceilings (which was connected to the caretaker's quarters) were all on the main floor. The bedrooms were on the second floor. In the dining room, a narrow door led to a staircase that took one into an attic room. We stored things there, and I set up the trains I had owned since I was a child. These were the trains I was playing with on December 7, 1941 when the news of Pearl Harbor reached all of us at the military school I was attending.

Today, a painting of this house hangs in the Human Resources and Training Center. One of our first summer counselors, Arlene White from Oklahoma, painted it.

Also on the property were the farm superintendent's house, a small cottage, a large barn, a milk house that included a complete pasteurizing unit, a couple of garages, a machine shed, stables, a dry stock barn, and a bull pen. Across the road from the main house were hay fields that were used for bareback riding by early farmers from circus families who had settled in the area, pasturing horses and cows, and of course, haying. The only animals on the farm were a small herd of Jersey cows. The Croton River traversed the property, and although we did not know it at the time, we could swim and boat in its east branch.

The small cottage on the property has served Green Chimneys well. It was a classroom, a dormitory for a few children, a staff house, and a kindergarten classroom for Nature's Nursery, the community nursery and kindergarten program that is operated on the grounds. Behind the cottage was a one-story building that was built in 1948 to house staff. That building was turned over to my father as a medical office when he retired from his New York City practice and took up residence at Green Chimneys.

In 2009 the cottage was torn down to make room for the new health and wellness center, attached to the building that housed my father's medical office. Today the Henry J. and Erna D. Leir Health and Wellness Center houses an inpatient facility as well as medical, psychiatric, dental, speech, and dietician offices.

The main house was so large that we decided it would suit many of our needs. We would use the playroom as a classroom, and the large kitchen and dining room would be perfect for meals. We would convert the upstairs bedrooms into dorm-like suites by installing bunk beds and small dressers, and we would create a laundry in the basement. Finally, we would add several bathrooms throughout the house.

We planned to use the wing as a staff residence, but it was not large enough. We needed more space for counselors, teachers, and others, so we decided to build a small, two-room residence near the cottage. Adele, Grandpa Taub, and any other visiting family members would stay in the superintendent's house.

At first, it seemed like a manageable plan. However, in addition to running the farm, the renovations proved to be an enormous undertaking. Problems cropped up every day, none of which we were used to handling. If one would like to know what it was really like opening a school in a rural section of New York, one could read *Mr. Blandings Builds His Dream House* by Eric Hodgins. Simply stated, the "city slickers" had a lot to learn.

When the first twenty-six inch snow fell in December that year, the staff told Adele that spreading manure in the fields was now out of the question; it would have to be piled up. So we did. Then, in the spring, they told Adele that the piled manure was unusable and would have to be hauled away. Again, we did as we were told, hiring a bulldozer, a front end loader, and a dump truck. Later we learned that the way to handle manure after it snows is to plow the roadway, pile it in one of the fields, and spread it later. This would have cost a lot less, but the farm staff saw an opportunity to get out of their chores, and they took it.

When we realized that the staff did not have the construction expertise we needed to refurbish the main house and build a new residence, we sought out contractors. As there were few in the area and we were anxious to begin, we hired the first contractor with whom we spoke. He understood what we wanted and was quite knowledgeable. He completed the project on time, and we were satisfied with his work, but later we learned we had paid a premium. We should have taken the time to solicit competitive bids. We also bought supplies we did not need from local merchants who realized they could profit at our expense.

Managing the farm staff was more time-consuming than we had anticipated. Many of them had worked on the farm for years, so we assumed they all got along and cooperated with each other, that they knew what to do, and that they would do it. We were wrong. Rather than take the lead, they waited for us to assign them chores, squabbled among themselves, and even fought with others with whom we did business.

For example, at that time Green Chimneys was a dairy farm known for its rich milk—a brand of milk that was not homogenized and named "Cream Line" because of the "line" that appeared between the cream on top and the milk on the bottom. The farm produced about six or seven cans of milk per day, between fifty to seventy gallons, and every day the staff would place the cans at the end of the driveway where the local dairy would pick up the full cans and leave the empty ones. The empty cans were washed, filled, and put out for pickup the following day. Occasionally, ill words passed between the farm staff and the drivers of the dairy's trucks, and the milk was left by the side of the road where it would sour and have to be thrown out. Acting as mediator sometimes was a full-time job.

Volunteers to the Rescue

Through it all, Adele, my father, and I were in constant communication. Adele would tell us the problems she was encountering, and we would offer ideas and solutions. What she needed most, though, were workers. My father contacted relatives, patients, friends, and employees of The Roosevelt Hotel and asked for help. Many responded and came to clean barns, scrub floors, fix equipment, repair buildings, sand, and paint. Some tackled special projects. One of his cousins spent many weekends refinishing a baby grand piano. Our sing-alongs would not have been the same without the instrument.

Grandpa Taub went up to the farm as often as possible with my father, and after realizing the size of the task at hand, he moved to the farm so he could assist on a daily basis. I worked there on my college breaks.

Many people continued to respond to my father's requests even after we opened. I remember, in particular, the president of Myers's Rum, a large Jamaican rum company, and his wife visiting the farm. They cooked and served meals to the children, washed the dishes, and wiped down the tables. A few years later, Myra and I visited them at their home in Jamaica and noted that they themselves had a large staff to attend to their needs and the daily chores.

To this day, I often think how extraordinary it was that all these folks came to our aid. To a great degree it was testimony to my father—the respect he had earned and the many friendships he had formed over the years. It also demonstrated the goodness of people. In those days, Green Chimneys was a long trip from New York City by car or train; although Green Chimneys was convenient to the Brewster train station, the trains were dirty, made innumerable stops, were poorly heated in the winter, and were without air-conditioning in the summer. Additionally, the work we asked people to do was hard. Yet they gave up their weekends—and in the case of Adele and my grandfather, their comfortable homes in the city for a run-down farm in the country—all to help a college student implement his grand plan. I appreciated it then, but even more so as the years have passed. I received the kind of support I wanted the children of Green Chimneys to know. Perhaps this is where the spirit of Green Chimneys really began.

I credit my mother for my training in giving to others. The Roosevelt Hotel was very close to what was then the Erlanger Children's Home. My mother always had me share gifts with the children in the home. I learned many years later that the home was part of the Children's Aid Society, which is a very active social service agency in New York City to this day. My mother did volunteer work during World War II, and my father constantly sent clothing to collections for people in Europe and here as well. They donated to charity frequently. These are things you never forget. My wife and I have encouraged our own children to do likewise.

Staff and students at Green Chimneys have done their share of giving and volunteering too. It has been a given at Green Chimneys that regardless of what problems our children may have, they are capable of doing good. It is very important to teach the children that "service receivers can still be service providers." This has always been a big part of my life and a big part of Green Chimneys.

Back on Track, Progress is Rapid

After the renovations were completed, we turned our attention to securing furnishings and equipment. We bought bunk beds from a friend of my father's in Tennessee. They were originally army bunk beds and, always resourceful, we had them cut down; young children did not need full-sized beds and smaller beds took up less room. We bought linens, pillows, and green and white bedspreads. We purchased furniture for the various rooms and kitchen equipment from industrial supply houses. We bought a truck, a station wagon, and a tractor. We even ordered a steel wading pool from a company that made boilers. It was an expensive item and we paid extra for quick delivery, but we felt it was important to have for the children. We also brought the farm back up to capacity. We purchased Holstein and Guernsey cows along with ponies, ducks, geese, chickens, pigs, sheep, and goats. We adopted two horses from the New York City Police Department—the beginnings of a tradition of animal rescue for us—and a donkey arrived from Mexico, a gift from a friend. As was typical of a farm, there was no shortage of dogs and cats.

While the physical preparations were underway, I was busy planning programs for our first summer camp. I called it Green Chimneys Farm for Little Folk and anticipated having all the usual activities: arts and crafts, swimming, fishing, games, pony rides, and goat-cart rides. In the spring, I ran an ad in various publications including *Parents Magazine*, *Harper's Bazaar*, *The New York Times*, *Herald Tribune*, *Vogue*, and *Good Housekeeping*, each of which had an advertising section for schools and camps. My ad read as follows:

> Green Chimneys Farm for Little Folk: A child's dream come true! For just 32 children from 3 to 6 years of age. Pets, farm animals, 75-acre farm—everything provided from toilet articles to medical exam. Trained personnel, registered nurses, under supervision of M.D. Near Brewster, N.Y.

For years to come, these magazines and newspapers would be sources of referrals for us even when we were not advertising. Parents would call these publications to ask if they could recommend a school or camp for children, and often the editors suggested the parents call us.

I contacted an employment agency and my father spread the word among his colleagues that we were looking to hire camp counselors, a cook, and housekeepers. We also needed staff to make repairs; tend to the animals and farm; run errands; pick up children, staff, and visitors from the railroad station; and drive the children and staff when they went on field trips.

My father and Adele interviewed many people, and little by little, we hired the help we needed, one of whom was the son of my father's banker in New York City. He was tremendous. Not only did he serve as a counselor, but he helped us with many of the daily chores as well. The last time I connected with Mike Hostage I was happy to learn that he has ten children and thirty-two grandchildren. He could start a Green Chimneys of his own!

When I arrived at Green Chimneys straight from college in June 1948, the site had been transformed—the barns filled with animals, the garden planted with vegetables, and the main house ready for little folk. It was not yet the fifteenth, the day camp officially opened, but a few of our boarders had already arrived. Some parents had called asking if they could bring their children to camp early. We didn't think twice about accommodating the parents' schedules and needs—after all, they were our customers. It has been that way ever since.

We also were expecting a few day campers. Parents from the local area had heard that we were opening a summer camp and called to ask if we would accept their children as day campers. Thrilled that they were interested in the program, I agreed. All in all, we had eleven children for our first summer program.

The Dream and the Reality

I brought to Green Chimneys the best of what I had experienced at boarding schools. The daily regime, the food, the farm animals and pets, the live-in housemothers and faculty, and the program elements could all be traced to my years in boarding school. Some things were not replicated, such as my memories of the harsh punishments given to students who broke rules. Those I did not think belonged at Green Chimneys. The worst thing I remember in some of the schools I attended was allowing older students to discipline younger students. Letting older students use a gun sling as a tool for discipline frightened me even though I was never subject to this punishment. There is a difference between consequences and punishment, and my personal practices have provided a recipe for success here.

Green Chimneys started with the dream of raising young children together with animals. This remains a primary goal despite the fact that the young children are now older children and adolescents. The practice of raising poultry, beef, lamb, and pork for the kitchen table has long since been abandoned. More than two hundred animals live out their lives here naturally. Milk from our own herd of dairy cattle was never realized. Vegetables for consumption and flowers for the table remain in place today.

I learned many things on the job. I learned early on that it was not in the American tradition to have a boarding school for very young children. I learned, too, that parents who are experiencing problems cause stress and anxiety for their children. Young children away from home show problems that must be addressed. The staff and I addressed these problems, earning the respect of those who referred children to us and laying the foundation for our future work with emotionally fragile children.

◆ ◆ ◆

Staff Notes

> A. T. is bright, bubbly and talkative. But as a toddler her tantrums turned to such deep depression and self-destructive behavior she had to leave home, then later, school. Soon after a stormy adjustment to Green Chimneys, (caring for) Rosie the rabbit, horseback riding and visual arts gave her confidence.
>
> A. T. now comes out of bouts of distress and interacts with other kids. An exceptional rider and hard worker, she's beginning to show signs of trust. Now a caring, concerned child, A. T. feeds, grooms and handles Rosie with considerable skill. She likes to talk about Rosie to any interested listener. A. T. has told the staff that being with Rosie relaxes her so that she can do her schoolwork better.

Notes

1 Still in existence today, The Seeing Eye in Morristown, New Jersey continues to provide assistance dogs for the blind. For more information, visit www.seeingeye.org.

2 It also helped to have friends in high places to smooth rough roads for us. Bishop Fulton Sheen, who was a former patient of my father, put in a good word for us with St. Lawrence O'Toole Church in Brewster, which was of immeasurable help down the road when I was running for school board.

3 The property is now owned by Green Chimneys and is designated the Ingemar and Rudolf G. Sonneborn Nature Preserve. It provides space for the community-supported organic garden program, which is operated by students and staff.

4 Colonel Henry Breckinridge had served in President Wilson's cabinet and was married to Aida de Costa Root. For more information on the history of our property and area, visit www.historic patterson.org.

Chapter II

The Fledgling Program

Staff Has Always Been Important

As much as we had our ups and downs with our original farmhands, we had the same ups and downs when we tried hiring local people. Our first housekeeper found our checkbook and wrote herself a check, which the bank cashed.

However, our luck began to change when Helen Scherer came in to ask for a job. Mama Scherer was one of many Germans who had settled in the nearby Putnam Lake community before the war. There did not seem to be anything she could not do, and she recruited other German women just like her. Together they cooked, baked, cleaned, and cared for the children. Martha Fiebach was one of her recruits. She came in for a temporary job and stayed over thirty years. Another of her recruits, Gertrude Drost, taught nursery school and kindergarten. A few years later, when our oldest son, David, was in Mrs. Drost's class, he reported to us that he was "veaving." When we explained it was "*w*eaving" he replied, "If Mrs. Drost says it's veaving, it's veaving!"

Josephine Gagliardo, also of German descent, was another cook for the children. Frieda Sparr helped raise our own children while we worked. She cooked on weekends for the entire school. We found Frieda through her husband, my father's patient. In addition to the women, their husbands were also talented and came in to do things for the school. These strong and good-hearted women all lived in the Putnam Lake community, and to get them to work for us we agreed to pick them up since many did not drive and there was no public transportation at the time. Mama Scherer retired in her late seventies after more than thirty years of work.

In our early days, all of our children lived in dormitory rooms with bunk beds lined up in a row. We employed staff at night who stayed up to take care of the children. I slept in the dorms at times when my help was needed. Our own children loved to sleep in the dorms and play "coast is clear." They would run around after lights were out hoping not to get caught by the person who was on duty. Uncle Fred, Uncle Larry, Grandpa Mattes, and Mrs. Rush performed this night duty. Those of us who toiled in the evening until the children went to bed worked very hard to get the children to go to sleep. When the night staff arrived, we were pleased to report that everything was quiet. For some reason, when Mrs. Rush, who had been a nurse, would arrive for her night shift at 11 p.m., she would yell at the top of her voice: "You better be quiet or heads will roll." She always anticipated problems, but the children knew she meant well. In the early days, the night staff shined the children's shoes. Some children always volunteered to help and were rewarded with a late night snack.

Grandpa Mattes (my father-in-law) was a true asset. When he stopped working in the hat factory in nearby Danbury, Connecticut, he joined our night staff. He spent many years at that job. After my mother-in-law died he gave up his apartment and moved in with us. He was a real grandpa to all the students. Our own children and their friends share tales of their experiences with him. He loved to garden, and when he could no longer bend down to raise the tomatoes he cherished, the students felt it was a privilege to help him.

Farm help continued to come and go unsteadily. We had a terrible turnover problem. Finally, we recruited farmers through an employment agency in New York City as well as from a local employment agency. We also hired family who had emigrated from Estonia. They had not been farmers before, but they needed jobs and were willing to learn. However, the real solution to the problem of hiring farm staff was taken care of when we decided to get rid of the dairy cows. Without the milking to attend to, the chores could be handled by a very small staff and the children. The resident teachers and the children were more than pleased to accept the responsibility for the animals. We were lucky to have a staff member to handle the horseback riding. The children knew they had to do their chores if they wanted to ride.

The Children Arrive—the Program Begins

Hosting preschoolers that first summer required us to rethink our ambitious planning. There were only so many things they could do. They took naps. Some went home at the end of the day, and the rest went to bed early. Running a camp proved to be more strenuous than I expected. There were counselors to train, clothes to wash, groceries to buy, meals and snacks to prepare, staff to manage, and a fall term to plan. That the youngsters tired often and early gave us some badly-needed breaks.

I had continued to run ads in magazines and newspapers throughout the spring, and by early summer I had received hundreds of inquiries from parents for the fall term. Some telephoned, others wrote. To everyone who inquired, we sent a brochure and invited them to visit, which we tried to make as easy as possible. We sent them directions if they were driving, picked them up at the station if they were coming by train, and even offered to drive them up if they would meet my father at his office.

When parents arrived, I gave them a tour of the children's classroom, dining area, and bedrooms in the main house. I showed them the animals and the play areas. Over lunch or coffee, I explained that Green Chimneys was more than a camp in the summer and school in the fall and spring. It was a year-round home on a farm. Housemothers attended to the children's needs, giving them baths, combing their hair, tying their shoes, cutting their nails—in short, doing anything that the children could not do for themselves. Mrs. Davies, who was a grandmother, took care of the youngest children. Marjorie Emery worked with the older children. Both were on staff for quite a number of years.

Our night staff made snacks, brushed teeth, tucked the children in, told bedtime stories, and once the children were asleep, shined their shoes. If the youngsters woke during the night, staff members were there to help them to the bathroom or comfort them from a bad dream. Adele was the school nurse, and my father was the physician who looked after the youngsters' health.

In addition to the requisite preschool academics, we planned activities for the children just as their parents would, including horseback riding, music instruction, and dance lessons. We took children to church or synagogue. We made sure they got a lot of fresh air and exercise. We even gave every child a job, such as picking up paper or putting away toys, and since we were located on a farm, there were always farm chores where they could pitch in and help. My philosophy was that a boarding school must do more than provide a place to live and traditional academics. Caring for children meant we had to act and do as their parents would to raise healthy, well-rounded, responsible youngsters.

I envisioned that parents would see Green Chimneys as an ideal environment for their children because we paid such close attention to all aspects of their growth and development, their care and well-being. How ironic, then, that parents saw it simply as a nice, warm spot for their children.

The parents were largely middle-class or upper middle-class Caucasians of Christian or Jewish faith who, for one reason or another, could not care for their children. Some were diplomats or entertainers who traveled extensively and either could not take their children along or felt that life on the road was not suitable for children. Others were parents who both worked or single parents. Men and women who found themselves raising children alone as a result of separation, divorce, or the death of a spouse often found it overwhelming and had difficulty juggling work and parenting. Still others had all they could do to cope with the illness of a spouse or another child. It was these situations that led the parents to consider boarding school during these early years, and their relief when they saw Green Chimneys was a safe, healthy place.

Because we were a young school, recruiting was constant. We were flexible and would see people at their convenience. I was always impressionable and got excited when I felt that the student and the parent would be a wonderful addition. On one particular occasion a well-dressed woman who wore a Persian lamb jacket arrived in my office. Her son wore a Little Lord Fauntleroy suit with a black velvet jacket, short pants, and white-laced collar. Because his mother was slim and attractive, I assumed she was a dancer. I was impressed. I told everybody that I could not guarantee it, but I felt she must be a prima ballerina. After repeating this story often, one of the other parents came to me and said, "Don't you know who she is? She is one of the best strippers you will ever see," though when asked, she described her profession as "fire eater." Suffice it to say, she was a wonderful parent and her son was a great student.

◆ ◆ ◆

From the very beginning there were children of foreign nationals enrolled. The majority enrolled for both camp and school. The parents either worked at a foreign consulate or were with the United Nations. Then we enrolled students from families who wanted their children educated in the United States, which required federal approval for Green Chimneys to admit students who were foreign nationals.

The first foreign child we enrolled was living with her parents in an apartment in New York City. She was the daughter of the ambassador of Iran to the United Nations. Her parents had many diplomatic obligations to fulfill, which necessitated hiring a babysitter often. One evening when they were out, the wife became ill and returned home early to find their child alone and the babysitter missing. Panic ensued. The babysitter had been going out in the evening and returning before the parents came home, which led to her instant dismissal, and the child was placed at Green Chimneys. Following her placement, several more Iranian families sent their children to the school. Our contact with the Iranian community in this way brought us a gift of a Caspian miniature horse, Mehregan, a wonderful addition to our stable. He was easy to train and was able to be ridden and driven. Like most horses of his breed, he loved to stand on his hind legs, which is a stance often depicted in movies. Of course, we did not allow the children to permit this behavior from Mehregan when they rode.

One child enrolled in 1948 was the son of a German national, a member of the Nazi party, who was in the United States under the protection of our government working on matters in Washington. We also had children of diplomats and business owners in Colombia and Venezuela. Some families had three children enrolled. A former student whose father was on the United Nations staff visited us a while back; she is now a college administrator in South America.

We had the daughter of former Haitian President Paul Magloire as a camper after he had been deposed and was living in New York. Myra and I met the president while in Haiti during our honeymoon, so we were not surprised that he sought us out when he moved to New York City. We met the president of Haiti after becoming acquainted with an important Haitian woman who shared a room with my aunt when she was ill at the Roosevelt Hospital. When Myra and I arrived at the Haitian airport during our trip, we saw troops lined up and flags flying. I inquired in French what was happening and was told they were expecting the arrival of a couple from New York. You can imagine our surprise and pleasure to discover that we were the couple. We were whisked away in the government limo. That evening we were entertained at a reception at the president's home. It was a very memorable visit.

◆ ◆ ◆

Nursery school began that first year, in September 1948, with all of the children who attended camp, plus a few new boarders. My plans had been exclusively for a boarding school, but the local parents whose children had attended Green Chimneys as day campers asked me to accept their youngsters as day students. We were a new school. It was the ultimate compliment.

As headmaster, I felt it was my job to make the children feel welcome. For those who had camped with us, this was easy. But for the newcomers, the prospect of leaving their parents for a day or longer was something many had difficulty accepting. When it came time for parents to say good-bye, the children often cried and threw temper tantrums. I tried to comfort them as best I could. I would hold their hands and describe all the wonderful things we were going to do, all the fun we were going to have. It was a tough sell.

Then one day I took a crying child to see the animals. It was pure instinct. It was where I went as a child myself during trying or lonely times. Perhaps by that point in the day it was as much for me as it was for the child.

It worked like a charm then and every time thereafter. Petting the ponies or feeding the goat was enough to calm children, stem the tears, and help them decide Green Chimneys might not be such a bad place after all.

I remembered distinctly what it felt like as a six-year-old enrolled in the second grade at the Irving School for Boys in Tarrytown, New York. I had faced the same anxieties that my young boarders faced.

I had been lucky that my school (and subsequent schools) owned pets and animals, and I had found them to be fun, wonderful, comforting companions. All that was still fresh in my mind when, as headmaster, I watched children become mesmerized by the ducks waddling around the barnyard. Animals had helped me through many periods of adjustment and anxiety; it would help them, too.

Now I know I greatly underestimated the impact the animals could have on children.

◆ ◆ ◆

While my focus was on comforting the children, Adele continued to oversee the business operations of Green Chimneys, which also freed me to attend New York University to pursue a master's degree in early childhood education. It confirmed my career choice, and I learned a great deal, although much of my education took place outside the classroom.

One of my earliest lessons happened one afternoon when I stopped by to see a couple of young staff members to discuss the schedule. They were just out of school and living on their own for the first time. Walking into their room, it showed. Clothes were strewn across chairs, tables, lamps, beds, even the floor. Wet towels hung from doors and fixtures. The beds looked like they had not been made in weeks. I insisted that they clean their room and keep it neat. The children were in and out, and they had to set an example. If they threw their clothes on the floor, so would the youngsters.

That was just the beginning. For years to come I would remind staff of all ages that we must lead by example. If we wanted the children to dress, act, eat, speak, and behave properly, we must do so as well. It was up to us to show them. I learned that not everyone is cut out to be a role model twenty-four hours a day, and over the years we lost many people to other jobs with less exacting standards.

Perhaps one of the biggest lessons I learned during this time was that not everyone pays their bills. Some of our parents were well-off, but many struggled. They could not afford the tuition, and yet they could not keep their children at home. Often illness, separation, divorce, or death took a financial toll.

We were sympathetic. We were patient. And soon we had difficulties paying our own bills. We counted on tuition payments to fund the camp and school.

Sometimes grandparents realized that payments were in arrears and paid a child's tuition. More often, however, parents simply tried to avoid us. They would arrive on visiting Sundays, take their children out for lunch or a drive, and then drop them off at the end of the driveway so they could leave without seeing me. Those who were separated or divorced often blamed the other. Still others found fault with the food, the rooms, a teacher—anything to justify not paying. It would be an ongoing problem we would struggle with in the coming years. At first, it was parents who were the delinquent payers; later, it would be government agencies. If it had not been for my father, I do not know what we would have done. More times than I can count, he paid the bills when we were in a bind.

The most difficult and heartbreaking lesson happened many months into the school year when I was escorting the children home for a weekend. All was arranged in advance: the parents knew the train we were taking, the time we would arrive, and the place to meet. If they ran late, as one or two inevitably did, they knew to come to my father's office. I would be waiting there with the children. At my father's, I would do my best to keep the youngsters busy. We would read, play games, and tell stories, but after a few hours a plaintive voice would ask, "When is my mom coming?" or "Where is my dad?"

As the hours dragged by on this particular day, I could not help but begin to share the child's angst. Would they come? After many hours and several unanswered telephone calls, I had to tell this child that we should take the train back to school; his parents were not coming. When he asked why, I didn't have an answer. I didn't know why parents would build up a child's hopes and then not show.

This continued to happen to children. Sometimes it was for a weekend; other times it happened for a holiday. Seeing the toll it took on the children, I began insisting that no-show parents come to the school. I didn't want the children to be disappointed over and over. Only when the parents arrived would I tell the children they were going home. Occasionally, it was years before parents would come pick their child up for a visit home.

Growing the School, Expanding the Family

> "This is Maria, Joey's little sister. She's only two, but could you take her, too?"
>
> -A parent of a Green Chimneys student

I never anticipated having children younger than three or older than six. Yet as parents re-registered their children for camp and school, they began asking if I could take a younger brother or sister. At the same time, parents of children who were nearing the end of their preschool days asked if they could stay on for first grade. I obliged, only to be asked a year later about second grade and then third. Through the 1950s and 1960s, we grew largely by accepting younger children and then adding grades for them as they grew older.

◆◆◆

To accommodate our growing student body, we renovated the large dairy barn. The New York State Education Department and the Department of Health had frowned upon us having a small dairy and serving the children milk that was high in butterfat. Wanting to be in their good graces and realizing we could use the barn for other purposes, we closed the dairy, sold the herd, and began buying milk for the children. It was a great way to save money; operating a small dairy herd that required staffing by others was very expensive.

This was the second time in our brief existence that the Education Department made a request. The first was just a short time after we opened. The Department asked that we change our name from "Green Chimneys Farm for Little Folk" to "Green Chimneys *School* for Little Folk." We complied then, too, although in hindsight I wish I had thought to name it "Green Chimneys *Farm School* for Little Folk."

We converted the barn's downstairs into a large, open classroom. This suited our fluctuating enrollment. Usually there were several children at each level; however, occasionally we had none or only one. One alumnus, Kenneth Wilkoff, loves to recall the year he was the smartest student in the class, and voted the best looking and most likely to succeed. Then he readily admits he was the *only* child in his grade that year.

Open classrooms did not become popular in the United States until the 1960s, so although we were ahead of the times, I cannot claim to have had any advanced insight. Perhaps having a little red schoolhouse, which one passed on the way to Green Chimneys, was an inspiration. In any case, I simply did what worked. An open classroom meant we could have all the children in one place. We could rearrange tables, chairs, and desks to suit our needs. We could have a sandbox and some small animals in the classroom, including ChiChi, our resident monkey.

Chi-Chi did cause problems, however. The children would walk by with a sandwich, and Chi-Chi would jump down and grab it; crying would follow. When outside on a chain in the willow tree, he would jump down and pull artificial flowers from ladies' dresses. Once, during a cold spell, he escaped and spent the winter living with the pigs in the pig pen. When finally caught, he reclaimed his role of children's pet and pest. He was a real performer and knew how to grab everyone's attention with his tricks. Today one of the staff in our adolescent psychiatric unit visits with a monkey who has been specially trained as a therapy animal. He is very popular.

With an open classroom we could work with some children while others worked or played on their own. It let older children help younger children. But most of all, leaving the room open gave us time to think about how best to arrange the classes.

Having a small school meant many of us—Adele, the teachers, some of the other staff, and I—knew the children very well. We not only knew their academic strengths and weaknesses, but we knew their favorite animals, what jobs they liked and disliked, and what foods they could not bring themselves to eat. We knew what made them laugh and cry. We knew what held their interests, how they would react in situations, what corners they would cut, and what fears they had. No two children were the same.

What we began to realize was that some of our children had special needs. They were here because their families could not care for them. But why they could not care for these children was more complex than we initially believed.

In many upper-class families, children grew up expecting to go away to school. That was what their parents or older siblings did, and that was what they would do. But sending children to boarding school was not common practice for middle-class American families. Parents felt guilty to be even considering the option. They were embarrassed that they could not care for their children. They saw boarding school as an admission of failure, and they were angry at themselves and their situation.

Often by the time the parents came to terms with sending their children to boarding school, the families had experienced turmoil for some time and the children had been affected. They came to Green Chimneys with a range of behavioral, social, and emotional problems. A few had learning disabilities. Even youngsters who were bright, perhaps gifted, weren't exempt.

We took the children's problems to heart. The other teachers and I spent time with the children individually, trying to improve their academics, but other staff members also became involved. Knowing which children were having difficulty, the cooks would spend a little more time with them when they were helping out in the kitchen, or my dad would ask them to help him water the plants. Given our small size, this was possible.

What we learned was that a little extra love and attention went a long way toward boosting their spirits. And when children felt valued, they began to blossom. In addition, accomplishments in one area carried over to others. They were willing to work harder at spelling if they were having some success in riding or art or math. Ensuring that each child continually had small accomplishments became one of my goals.

Many children overcame their difficulties, and by the mid-1950s, we had acquired a reputation for helping such children. We began to receive referrals from family physicians, psychiatrists, psychologists, and school districts. We accepted children other independent schools turned away. It was an easy decision. I asked myself, "Who will help these children if we don't?" Many times the answer was no one, and we made a spot for them.

While some parents recognized that their child needed help, others didn't or didn't know where to turn; they were overwhelmed by their circumstances. That is when professionals familiar with the situation usually intervened. They would recommend that the family consider boarding school, and they would suggest Green Chimneys. Then the professional would call to let me know, so I could expect the parent's call, and so that the professional could explain why they hoped we could find room for the child. Not every family was pleased with this help. Many felt their problems were private matters and professional intervention wasn't necessary.

As the number of referrals grew, we became more skilled at dealing with these special issues, which in turn drew more referrals. That we were willing to help children was another reason why we grew during the 1950s and 1960s.

◆ ◆ ◆

Just as we got two years under our belts and were feeling a modicum of comfort with running a farm, a school, and a camp, I was drafted. In December 1951, I reported to Camp Kilmer in New Jersey for induction, and then I was sent to Fort Jackson in South Carolina for sixteen weeks of basic training. I was assigned to the Army's Medical Corps and transferred to the hospital at Fort Jackson, where I worked in the Neuropsychiatric Section as a social worker. This left Adele shouldering most of the burden through a particularly tough patch.

It was during this time, in February 1952, that a short in the furnace caused a fire that swept through the main house. I was on duty in the company office when I received a call telling me that the main house had been lost in a fire. No one was hurt, but with the exception of a wing, the house burned to the ground. We were shaken and devastated by the loss of all the time, effort, and money we put into renovations. I immediately applied for emergency leave, which was granted, and arrived in Brewster to see what I could do to help.

After getting over the initial shock, we discussed rebuilding, and the idea quickly gathered steam. We had architectural plans drawn up, arranged for the site to be cleared of debris, and contracted for the work to begin. Luckily, we could build again on the same foundation. The location of the front door was maintained in the same location. It was decided not to add a second story. A dormitory wing attached to the main building was all that was saved from the fire. Part of the dormitory wing included the one-story two-car garage that was part of the original buildings on the farm, which had been renovated as living space. Replacing the building required town approval. The fire completely changed what we were doing. With the main house gone, every available space on campus was needed.

We made temporary sleeping arrangements for the children in the cottage and superintendent's house. We used the kitchen in the superintendent's house to cook meals, and we rearranged the open classroom in the former dairy barn to include a dining area. After the fire, the second floor of the barn was renovated as an auditorium/gymnasium. Offices and classroom space was constructed in the entrance to the building where the large panel truck was originally kept.

After suffering such a staggering loss, some might have suggested that we consider other options, perhaps even close. However, my father and Adele were nothing if not resilient.

Within the year, the new house was up and ready for use. We gained additional dormitory space, a modern kitchen, a larger dining room, and a storeroom in the basement, all of which we were grateful for as we grew.

After eighteen months at Fort Jackson, I was transferred back to New Jersey and assigned to the Mental Hygiene Clinic at Fort Dix. Now I could drive to Green Chimneys and help out on weekends and holidays, sometimes even during the week. When I was discharged in December 1953, I had been at Green Chimneys full-time for two months; I had been entitled to leave, but since I had not taken any I was released from duties early.

I was home only a few weeks when I met Myra Mattes. I was on a blind double date and did not click with the person I was with that evening. As it so happened, Myra did not click with her date either, and we began talking. Among other things, I learned Myra was a teacher at a local public elementary school in Danbury, Connecticut; I told her about Green Chimneys. We shared a few stories and some laughs about our early teaching experiences.

A few weeks later I received a postcard from Myra while she was vacationing in Atlantic City. When she returned, I called her. After a few dates, I brought her to the farm. Many years later in an interview with *Biography Magazine*, Myra described that visit:

> "I was scared to death of animals. . . . The first time I visited Green Chimneys a monkey came over to me and I nearly had a coronary . . . and then Rollo/Sam took me to the stables and there were cows and horses and I thought; what am I doing here?!"

Yet when I proposed that May, Myra accepted. When the pigs got loose before our engagement party, Myra laughed, and in her good clothes helped me chase them back into their pen. Despite the risk of having uninvited guests, she agreed to have the wedding at Green Chimneys. On August 22, 1954, we were married with family, relatives, friends, and all twenty-seven students (but thankfully no pigs) in attendance. As Myra often says of that day, I married her, and she married me and Green Chimneys. She truly did. "We didn't analyze things in those days like you do today," Myra recently told someone who asked why she would marry a person who lived on a farm when she was so fearful of animals. "We accepted things as part of life and coped with them," she continued. "I decided to marry Rollo, and the animals were part of his life at Green Chimneys. I suppose I tried to ignore them for a while, but little by little you learn to adapt."

That September Myra joined the faculty as a teacher and became a member of the Board of Directors. She pitched in wherever she was needed: preparing meals, doing laundry, putting the children to bed, driving to the Fulton Fish Market with my father to pick up supplies, or bundling up on a cold winter night to help me check the brooders and make sure the chickens were warm.

In Myra I had someone who knew what was needed, and she initiated many program elements as well as bringing to us her knowledge and gift of working with children.

One of her biggest sacrifices was foregoing a salary. New York's education laws, under which we were incorporated, stipulated that only two members of the Board of Directors could be paid employees of the corporation. The board at the time consisted of my father, Adele, Herman Levine (our accountant), me, and Myra. Since my father and Herman had incomes from their practices, Adele and I had been the two members drawing a salary. Myra graciously agreed to let that continue; it would be twenty years before she received another paycheck.

When Myra joined me at Green Chimneys, it was like joining a large extended family. Many relatives and close friends of the Ross family regularly came to help or worked at Green Chimneys full-time. Some of the students were relatives of the Ross family or children of Adele's close friends. We often hired teacher couples, some of whom lived in the dorms as houseparents, and others who lived on the grounds with their families.

Myra extended the family even further. Her parents, Julia and Ben Mattes, were warm, wonderful folks. He was a hatter, she was a bookkeeper, and they lived in Danbury. After we were married, relatives of the Mattes family began attending the school and camp, and Julia and Ben often came on weekends to help. He loved to garden and spent hours caring for his flowers and vegetables, taking special pride in his tomatoes. This was a nice complement to my dad who took special pride in planting and nurturing the trees. Between the two of them, they kept the grounds blooming.

We all ate meals together in the dining room—the faculty, staff, and children—and we took to celebrating holidays and birthdays together with a special meal or dessert. I enjoyed the family atmosphere, and it was good for the children. Parents noticed the warm environment as soon as they arrived.

In keeping with the informal atmosphere, Myra was known as Myra, and the children called me Rollo. Not all staff were on a first-name basis with the children, however. The German women were not used to such an informal situation; they were called Mrs. Scherer, Mrs. Drost, and Mrs. Sparr. My father was called Dr. Ross. But there were others like Adele whom the children were so fond of that they took to calling her Mommy Mac, and later, when Myra's father came to live at Green Chimneys, he was known as Grandpa Mattes.

◆ ◆ ◆

In 1954 we acknowledged our changing population by revising our mission to be an independent boarding and day school for children ages two through ten, with academic instruction from nursery school through fourth grade and a sleepaway and day camp for the same age group. We had always promoted Green Chimneys as nondenominational, and we began emphasizing that we were interracial as well. While initially the children had been largely Caucasian, many non-white children came to be enrolled.

Having gone to all-white male schools and camps, I planned for us to accept girls as well as boys and children of all faiths, but enrolling children of diverse ethnicity never occurred to me. And yet many parents from outside the United States, such as Iran and South America, began requesting we admit their children. My reaction was, of course! My concern, however, was for the children. Would we be able to teach and care for them as we should? Everything for them was different—customs, language, religion, food. How would we be able to make them feel at home? I accepted the children and met regularly with the faculty and staff to express my concerns and give them guidance: "Remember that the children might not understand what we are saying; English is not their first language. We must be careful not to impose our values and beliefs on them. We should make ourselves aware of their traditions and holidays, and ask them which ones they would like to observe."

Food was always a hot topic at these meetings, not just in terms of what to prepare for foreign students, but for Americans as well. I insisted that we serve meals that were healthy and appealing to the children. Menus designed to please the children, however, often did not please the adults, leading to complaints. But I had little sympathy for the adults. They could drive off campus for meals; some went home at the end of the day and could eat what they liked. The children had no options. It was clear to me that we should prepare meals with the children's needs, likes, and dislikes in mind, not the adults.

Catering to the children sometimes took unexpected twists. In the spring of 1955, one child, Henry Sheinkopf, was completing fourth grade, and his mother wanted him to continue. He had been the only child in the fourth grade because two children withdrew at the last moment, and he would be the first and only child in fifth, a grade that did not yet exist at Green Chimneys; I wasn't sure that was good for him. Yet Henry had been with us since first grade and was doing well; he loved school, camp, and the farm. I talked with Myra about having him live with us and attend the Brewster public school, and she agreed. We often had children stay with us for weekends and holidays when they couldn't go home; a full year was just a little longer than usual. His mother gratefully accepted our offer.

Looking back, this solution had its pros and cons. Henry was blossoming at Green Chimneys, and it was best for him to stay with us. It was a bit of a shock, however, for him to transfer into a class where he was one of thirty after being one of, at most, seven children in a class. But we kept a close eye on him, and he made it through; the following year, he attended sixth grade at Green Chimneys. By then we had recruited older children and added fifth and sixth grades to our program.

While Henry lived with us, our own immediate family expanded. On December 3, 1955, Myra gave birth to our first son, David, and our lives became even busier. Thank goodness for Myra's parents. They came every day while we adjusted to our new arrival and then kept coming so Myra could return to teaching. This was unusual for a woman in those days, but Myra is a gifted and an unusual woman.

Actually, that Myra attended college and planned on a career was uncommon. Being a child of the Great Depression with a working mother, however, she grew up having summer jobs and expecting to work. She, like other children who lived with very little, looked forward to getting her first job and felt lucky to have one. Her parents encouraged her to pursue her education so she would be able to have an even better job. She knew, however, that they could not afford to pay for tuition. As it turned out, that would not be necessary. Myra's heart yearned to teach, and she enrolled in Danbury State Teachers College to pursue her bachelor's degree. After her first semester, Myra discovered that the College sponsored an unusual financial aid program. Having made the Dean's List, the school informed Myra that no payment was due; the college's policy was to absorb the semester's tuition for any student that earned this recognition. Thereafter, Myra was on the Dean's List every semester; her education didn't cost her or her parents a cent.

Through the years, Myra has given generously of herself to our children, our Green Chimneys' children, our program, our friends, our family, and the community. At Green Chimneys she has been Director of Admissions and Director of Quality Assurance. She was the Clinical Coordinator, and it was she who was responsible for the development and implementation of the policies, procedures, and manuals we were mandated to follow. Myra created the structure for the treatment forms, requirements, and protocols for necessary documentation of what we do here. Her hardest job, I am sure, has been trying to keep me on track. After fifty-six years, I think I am more in love with her today than ever, and my love continues to grow.

Myra's achievements would fill a book by itself.

◆ ◆ ◆

Henry Sheinkopf is our 2011 Gala Honoree. He was eight years old when he came to Green Chimneys along with his two younger brothers. He wrote me the following many years ago:

> June 1995. I find myself in the White House. Upstairs in the residence of the President of the United States. Looking at his personal library, and gazing through the window in front of me, looking at the Great Lawn. Thinking of the greatness that has been in this room, and wondering for a quick moment before the President's entry—and before the beginning of a seventeen month adventure as part of the creative team which will re-elect the first sitting Democratic President in more than 50 years—how I got here. . .
>
> . . .A young boy—the product of a union between a 15 year-old girl and a 19 year old boy—arrives at a farm, whose apparent only outstanding

features are the chimneys, all painted green . . . Emotionally ripped to the core, dropped out of the lives of his parents for their own convenience. His brothers, one an infant who is not even toilet trained, are dropped along with him. You (Rollo) and Myra take this boy into your home . . . The boy is a member of a family, something he has never known before. My life proves that every child's life is worth saving. And can be saved.

Chapter III

Meeting Children's Needs Outside the Classroom

> "Our stable has been enlarged during the winter and we have more space as well as horses. This means more riding. Riding and swimming are always the things during the summer."
>
> -"The Green Chimneys News," Summer 1956

Horseback riding and swimming were our campers' favorite activities. Every morning they greeted their counselors with the cry, "Are we swimming today? Are we riding today?" The answer was, of course, "Yes!"

Offering horseback riding had always been a part of my plan, and we had horses and ponies from the beginning. That we were able to offer swimming was a stroke of luck. It was only after we bought the farm that we discovered a swimming area on the east branch of the Croton River, which flowed through our property. There was a shallow end that was ideal for the little ones to wade in, and a deeper area that could be used for swimming. We cleared the shoreline of branches and debris that had accumulated after years of harsh winters, dug up the grass and weeds, and created a beach. Then every June, in preparation for camp, we trucked in sand and spread it on the beach. We constructed a dock from which the children could jump and dive. We also had rowboats tied up along the shore that we used to take the children boating and fishing. Every day unless it was raining, the counselors and I walked down to the river with the children, the dogs running along beside us, and we would spend hours there. It seemed to provide endless fun.

Not everyone knew how to ride or swim. One of the reasons many parents sent their children to camp was to learn. Naturally, many were apprehensive. The other instructors and I did our best to encourage the beginners, but usually it was the enthusiasm of their peers who knew how to ride and swim that helped to boost their confidence, or at least persuade them to put their fears aside and try it. The desire to be part of the group, part of the action, and do what everyone else was doing was a far better motivator than anything the counselors or I could imagine.

Learning to ride was particularly intimidating. The horses towered over the children and once mounted, they felt high above the ground—even if they were on a pony. There was the fear of falling off and the worry of what a skittish horse might suddenly do.

I was very young, probably three, when I first rode a donkey at the amusement park at Rockaway Beach and was treated to neighborhood pony rides by my grandparents. When I was about four or five, my parents visited friends in Bermuda and indulged my frequent requests for a ride in what I recall to be a beautiful horse cart with a canopy pulled by two black horses. I also had a donkey cart, and hanging in my home office is a picture of me in a donkey cart in Bermuda. The donkey has a blue ribbon, which we won together in a show.

These were wonderful first experiences and ignited a lifelong interest in horses. I also knew, however, what it was like to have a horse gallop too fast for me to control and to have a saddle come loose because the girth wasn't tightened properly. These and other frightening experiences made me sensitive and sympathetic to the children's concerns.

I probably pushed the children more when it came to swimming. After weeks of giving lessons to a group, the day would come when I would announce, "Today's the day!" They all knew what it meant. I would toss them into the water, jump in after them, and we would swim to the float. Some of the children thought it was fun; others who were more timid were anxious. Because I had been swimming for as long as I could remember and never had any bad experiences, I didn't realize how long it could take before some children felt comfortable.

Those children who were fearful of riding or swimming felt an immense sense of pride and accomplishment once they succeeded. I could see it on their faces. I would overhear them proudly tell Adele or their housemother of their triumph; they would blurt it out to their parents as soon as they arrived. As I watched the youngsters over the years, it was clear that there was another benefit to their learning these sports: the children gained a self-confidence that was long lasting. Since that time, many studies have been done and books written that proclaim riding and swimming as two of the best ways to build a healthy self-confidence in children. Swimming is also a safety skill. If you go for a ride in a boat and fall overboard, you need to know how to swim.

In addition to riding, swimming, fishing, and boating, we had arts and crafts, games, biking, barbecues, camp fires, Indian dances taught by Native Americans who were recruited through the Bureau of Indian Affairs, and movies. We made sure the children always had things to do whether it was hot and sunny or cold and rainy, and no matter what their ages. I loved camp as a child, and I wanted to make sure Green Chimneys' campers had as much fun as I did.

Writing letters home was a weekly activity at all of the camps I attended, and I had our campers do likewise. I broke with tradition, however, when I instructed the staff not to read the children's letters or correct them unless the children asked for help, and even then they should exercise great restraint. I felt it was important that the children be able to communicate freely with their parents. If they complained, so be it; we should not influence what the children wanted to write. This was my policy for letters written home during the school year as well.

In the late 1950s, a neighbor named Eduard Wallach, or Edi, offered to put on a fireworks display for the Independence Day. It became an annual event that officially kicked off the summer camping season. Edi's intent was to have a display for the children and their parents. But as we were to learn, fireworks are not something you can do on the Q. T. The following year neighbors called inquiring if we were having fireworks again and if they could come; many others just stopped along the road to watch. Every year the display was better than the previous year and soon folks came from all over Putnam County; cars were parked along Route 22 for a mile in each direction. It was wonderful of Edi to do this for us, year after year. Words were insufficient to express how much our campers enjoyed the tradition.

I was glad to have the community join us. Many people had misconceptions about Green Chimneys and the Ross family, and any opportunity for them to get to know us was a good one. I had joined the Rotary Club of Brewster to meet area businesspeople and professionals, and I become involved in local events. I also served on the Board of Education of the Brewster Central School District and was active in Temple Beth Elohim. Having residents share this event with us was another step in the right direction.

◆◆◆

On September 20, 1957, the New York State Board of Regents granted Green Chimneys an absolute charter. We had been operating under a five-year provisional charter granted to us in 1952. A permanent charter meant that we had successfully met the organizational and educational standards set by the Board of Regents. It was a good feeling. With their blessing, we updated our mission once again to reflect our growth: to maintain a private boarding and day school for children ages two to twelve, providing instruction from preschool through sixth grade, and a summer camp for children of the same age.

Now in my tenth year working with children, I felt even more strongly about the benefits of a private boarding school education. First, there was the academic advantage of small classes. Fewer students meant teachers could spend more time with each child. In addition, small groups assimilated material more quickly, leaving time for extras such as music instruction, dance lessons, plays, and class trips.

But it was much more than that. Being responsible for children's care and development as well as education meant that we had something quite unique: complete pictures of the children. We could make the experience much more relevant and fulfilling when we were with children the entire day. Teachers could tie health and science discussions to the children's daily routines, such as washing their faces and hands, and brushing their teeth. The teachers could associate math lessons with number problems the children encountered feeding the animals or baking in the kitchen. The gardener could help them relate planting seeds to the foods they eat. The farmhand could explain the many ways animals play a role in our lives. Few if any instructors in traditional schools had complete pictures of the children or spent as much time with them as we did. For our students we were *in loco parentis.*

For the children, the advantages were more than academics as well. They had the full attention of a professional staff that was aware of their academic, social, or family problems, attuned to changes in their moods, attitude, or behavior, and ready to help. They learned not only how to get along with others, but how to live together, which takes much more work. It's one thing to learn how to share, cooperate, and be considerate of others for six or seven hours a day. It's another to learn how to get along with classmates all day, every day.

It may seem contradictory, but at the same time we fostered a sense of independence. Early on we taught the children how to present themselves and how to express their thoughts, opinions, and feelings whether they were in the classroom or on the playground. They learned how to ask questions, analyze information, evaluate situations, and reach a conclusion. They learned how to make individual contributions to a group as well as work on their own. In some cases, without their parents to lean on and speak for them, the children learned to do these things for themselves.

By way of illustration, a friend recently related a story about when she and her sister invited their two nieces and a nephew on a ski vacation. The children were young—five, eight, and twelve years old—but they loved to ski and were good for their ages. On Sunday morning my friend and her sister picked up the children, and by late afternoon they had checked into the hotel. Without being asked, the children unpacked their bags and put away their clothes. Then, for the next two days, the children got themselves up, showered, and dressed. A little help was required to get them into their boots, but they carried their own skis to and from the car. All day long, during stops for snacks and lunch (for which they ordered milk), they kept track of their belongings. After a long day on the slopes, they changed and got ready for dinner without any help. They even went to bed on time so they would be ready for the next day.

On the third day, the children's mother arrived and everything changed. They relied on her to get them up, help them dress, find their hats, gloves, and mufflers, carry their skis, eat right, pick up their clothes, and get them to eat right and go to bed. All the things they did competently and willingly the day before they suddenly could not do. The children perceived that their aunts expected them to act a certain way and they did, whereas they knew they could get away with different behavior with their mother.

The Green Chimneys faculty and staff were in the unique position to be both the parents and the aunts, so to speak. As substitute parents, we provided the children with the help, encouragement, and the extra care that they needed. At the same time, like their aunts, we had expectations. Naturally, it is a balancing act, but because we were with the children constantly and consistently, we managed well. I watched the students change, and this was confirmed by others. Parents and professionals who recommended children to us saw low achievers become high achievers, disruptive students begin to listen, and reclusive students begin to participate. An alumnus from these early years recently said, "One of the things you always knew was the pride [Rollo] had in you . . . you knew he felt you could rise up and be somebody." It's true. That's how I felt and the children responded.

To further develop their independence, every day the children were allocated some personal time. Some read, took a walk in the woods, or went for a bike ride. Others teamed up for a game of baseball or basketball. No one planned these hours for them; no adult told them what to do. It was a time when they got to make their own fun. In addition, the children had jobs and the opportunity to raise a pet, which imbued them with a sense of independence and responsibility while they contributed to the overall welfare of the group or the animal. Many of our students would never have had a pet otherwise, for it wasn't feasible for their families.

The school continued to grow and change, as did our immediate family. After the birth of our second son, Donald, while David was still a toddler, Myra felt it was time to have dinner together as a family in our own home.

I agreed, but it was hardly ever the family dinner hour she envisioned. I sat during dinner with a two or three button phone on the floor to one side of me, and an intercom on the other side. Any time was a good time to call the headmaster in most parents' minds.

For me and my family, it sometimes felt as if we were living in a glass house. Children, teachers, and staff stopped in at all hours during the course of a day. Most of the time, we didn't mind, but there were occasions when we felt as if too little consideration was given. On one occasion, the father of a wonderful boy walked in our front door without knocking, and upon seeing Myra, he said, "Oh, don't mind us. I just want to show these folks the headmaster's house." He then proceeded to give his companions a room-by-room tour. Another time a mother called in the middle of the night after dreaming that something was terribly wrong with her daughter and she wasn't breathing. I pulled on my coat and boots and went to check. After finding her sleeping peacefully and breathing normally, I called the mother back and reassured her that her daughter was fine. It was only a dream.

◆ ◆ ◆

Although we had achieved some recognition for our work with children and were enrolling more children in a broader age group, we could not rest. I began taking additional graduate courses in elementary education at Yeshiva University; Adele was completing her master's degree in education at New York University; and we all sought ways to expand the list of extracurricular activities for the children. We began offering ballroom and acrobatic dancing in addition to lessons in tap and ballet. We expanded our music instruction to include the accordion. We worked with the children on more plays. We encouraged the children to draw, paint, make collages—follow their artistic instincts. Then we organized recitals, performances, and exhibits so the children could demonstrate their hard work, talents, and accomplishments to their families, teachers, and friends.

I continued to emphasize sports and outdoor activities, for I thought they were an important part of raising well-rounded, healthy children, and if burning off a little energy caused them to be more attentive in class or ready for bed at night, all the better. Unlike other schools, however, Green Chimneys did not have team sports. I wasn't particularly athletic as a young child and wasn't drawn to traditional sports, such as baseball, football, or basketball, so it wasn't my inclination to offer them to the children. In addition, when I considered what I wanted children to take away from their experience, my intent was to build confidence, to teach them skills they could use for life, learn about themselves and the world around them, and make activity part of their lives. This dovetailed with some practical considerations, mainly our limited athletic facilities; we didn't have the gymnasium and ball fields available at other private schools. It made sense to take advantage of the farm and our rural surroundings.

Many of the activities we offered during camp, such as horseback riding, boating, fishing, hiking, and biking, also were offered during the fall and spring. In the winter, we showed the children how to build forts and took them sleigh riding or for rides in a horse-drawn sled with sleigh bells. Every winter the river would overflow and turn a pasture into a wonderful ice-skating rink.

The river's tendency to rise wasn't always welcome, however. On two occasions it caused local officials to worry that it would break through the dam at Putnam Lake and flood the campus, and we had to evacuate all the faculty, staff, and children in the middle of the night.

The first time it flooded, not only did we have the children to worry about, but Myra was very pregnant with David. We took refuge at the firehouse, where the firemen gave the children turns sitting in the engine, and luckily Myra did not go into labor. The second time the local Chinese restaurant came to our aid, feeding and housing all of us for forty-eight hours. Each time while we anxiously awaited news of possible damage, the children had a grand old time. To them, it was an exciting adventure and that helped to lighten our mood.

One young couple who had emigrated from Czechoslovakia showed up on both of these occasions to make sure their daughter was fine. That meant driving up from the city until the roads became impassable from the flooding waters, then wading through the rest of the way with the water up to their chests. They took it in stride; they experienced much worse situations before coming to the United States.

Despite the many extracurricular activities, there were always a few children who never seemed to shine. Searching for a solution, I remembered being given a pleasurable assignment by my first housemother, Mrs. Grimes, at the Irving School for Boys. I say pleasurable because I do not remember complaining about it, and I do recall a certain amount of self-satisfaction having accomplished the task. Every week she had her charges memorize certain lines of poetry that each of us would recite. It occurred to me that poetry might provide children who had not been able to make their mark with a few minutes in the limelight. I revised our program so that all of our children were introduced to poetry.

More children were excited about this than I ever dreamed. Some, particularly the younger ones, memorized poems. Others tried their hand at writing original verse or poetry. No matter how poorly they wrote or spelled, we told them that if they brought their poems into class, we would read them, help them correct them, and work with them on their style. We explained that poetry can be simple, and were thrilled when one five-year-old wrote, "Run little bunny / You are so funny."

She understood, and it was a wonderful example for all the students. Many children offered to recite or read poetry to their class. We began to have poetry exhibits at our art shows, and many volunteered to recite their poems at school assemblies.

By 1959 poetry had attracted so much interest that we planned a "Poetry Festival," coordinated by a faculty member named Ms. Blanche Leiby, an avid poetry fan. Finally, the youngsters who were not used to shining—who were never chosen for leading roles in plays or picked first for the kickball team—were the stars. They performed before a large audience of appreciative parents who moved their lips in sync with a child's recital or quietly chuckled as a child delivered some nonsense phrase or silly word.

No sooner was one festival over than Ms. Leiby bombarded the faculty with ideas for the next one. During the year, she kept everyone enthused. She suggested poems to teachers and students. She painstakingly went over every poem the children brought to her and helped them to express themselves. She attended classroom poetry sessions, listened to the students recite or deliver their poems, and read selections to them. She arranged for visiting poets. Through her efforts, poetry became part of assemblies and English classes, and original poems were published in the school newspaper. She even worked with music teachers to set poems to music. To her and the students, poetry never seemed like schoolwork.

The reason for learning poetry was not for performance alone. It was to encourage the children not only to think, but to feel and perceive. Through poetry, children become acquainted with a range of emotions, such as pleasure, gaiety, sadness, sympathy, fear, and love. It also was to provide them with another means of expression. If we encouraged children to communicate through art, dance, music, and prose, we could not forget that poetry, too, had its place. Today poetry is still part of the cultural landscape of Green Chimneys. In the winter of 2010, our students performed in an evening event entitled "The Spoken Word," which was a great success for our children, and an enjoyable evening for staff.

During the 1960s, the number of children at Green Chimneys who had emotional, social, and behavioral problems, who came from destructive home settings, and who had learning disabilities swelled, as did the severity of their problems. Increasingly, they arrived unable to identify their feelings and without the right words to express them. Many acted out, others withdrew. For some, poetry proved key. Whether reading it or writing it, they found verse to be therapeutic. To encourage them, we assured them that if they described their work as a "confidential poem," no one would see it except those with whom they chose to share it. For those children who had trouble writing, teachers had them dictate their poem and transcribed it verbatim.

Alison Wyrley Birch, a poet who lived nearby in Kent, Connecticut, visited with the children in their classes, attended one of our Poetry Festivals, and later made this comment in her column in a local newspaper: "One thing was clear. These children aren't pressured to accept poetry, nor is it taught prosaically as 'good for them' because it's a part of literature. They enjoy it, they understand it, and they live it. They will, then, most certainly grow up into adults who have access to the extra dimension that poetry creates."

Preparation for the World of Work

> We have become two societies—one of arms and backs, one of suits and laptops. We send our children to computer camps so that they may learn how to gain access to information instantaneously, but most of us would never give our children a shovel and gloves and send them to dig weeds for a month so that they develop a sense of what it is to get dirty and tired for someone else.[1]
>
> -Victor Davis Hanson

While our extracurricular activities were important, teaching children the value, importance, and satisfaction of work was something we had always emphasized. It improved their self-esteem and self-confidence, and instilled a sense of responsibility, all of which was necessary for them to one day return to their homes and pursue higher education.

We also began to realize that teaching children about work was important in order to prepare them for the future. Many children talked about getting a summer or after-school job when they went home; others might be working full-time in only a few short years. As much as our goal was to return the children to upper grades at their schools, we had to acknowledge and anticipate that not all would stay. Some might drop out, or if they did get a diploma, might not go on to college. I felt strongly that we should begin preparing them for the working world.

We instituted a prevocational program that had several objectives: to introduce the children to a range of potential occupations; to provide realistic work experiences; to acquaint students with the physical, emotional, and social demands of a job; to teach them the skills required by various occupations; and to help them identify their interests and talents.

The prevocational program went beyond the farm; the children could choose jobs anywhere on campus—in the kitchen, maintenance department, classroom, library, gym, or office. As we encouraged them to try different areas, we realized that many times it was not the work that attracted them to a particular job. As one alumnus confessed years later, "I signed up to paint with Norman Plue (maintenance department) not because I wanted to be a painter, but because his job was so quiet and tranquil, and all the stuff in the back of his truck was neat. Norman's wife also always packed extra stuff in his lunch for us kids." Whether it was the quiet or the goodies, this student found a mentor in Norman, and eventually the student went on to own his own painting company.

One of our current young students, who has been with us about three years, enjoys being around the maintenance staff. He particularly shines when Joe Shay in the maintenance department takes him under his wing. When this young student recently went through an extremely emotionally wrenching time, his pre-established relationships with staff like Joe and Jackie Ryan (administrative assistants in the executive office) helped ease the pain.

Interestingly, the more we prepared children for the working world, the better they did in school. Suddenly, they were applying what they learned and saw the connection between school and work. They realized that to succeed at work they had to listen more closely in school, but they did not mind so much anymore, because they were using what they learned. Work gave them new experiences, ones they were able to draw on during class discussions. Participating made all the difference. One student relates:

> When I work at my job with Mr. Johnson, we work hard! First I think I came a long way. When I came here I did not know how to paint. I did not know what a pig, falcon, vulture, golden eagle was. When I talk[ed] to Mr. Johnson, he said there was a farm and stuff and if I behave I could be on the highest level . . . and I could do a lot of good stuff with him and with the farm and with other people too. Ms. Taylor and Mr. Johnson brought me a long way. I did not know what respect was. They told me to never be nasty to people and treat people how I want to be treated.

We also discovered another benefit: the more work the children did, the less damage and destruction they caused. Weather and aging always took a toll on our buildings, but the majority of damage at the school was caused by the students. By helping to repair and maintain the buildings and grounds, the students became less destructive.

In an article in *The Nonprofit Times* from September 1994, in describing the programs operated by Green Chimneys, it was pointed out that making money is only one reason for venturing forth into business activities. It was indicated that sometimes the chance to provide students with the opportunity to learn and earn is in itself a good reason to undertake the business venture. The commercial projects that involve animals, plants, and the outdoors provide community visibility and gain both revenue and public support for the program.

Green Chimneys cannot correct all the ills of society, but it can be held responsible for the standards we have on campus—in the way our young people are prepared for daily living and in the way they are trained for work. The farm program offers them some extraordinary vocational opportunities.[2]

The service industry is the place where additional jobs will become available in the future, and Green Chimneys offers sound practical training in real work. In addition to the day to day chores the students perform while caring for our animals, there are other opportunities to experience a true work environment. They can work on our organic farm, can do grounds maintenance, or can make things through our woodworking program. Our students can also gain retail experience at our Country Store, which sells our farm produce as well as gift and food items. In our culinary program, Green Cuisine, the students become chefs complete with jacket and chef hat. Chef Mark Kaplan wanted to start a restaurant with the students, and I wanted them to have more vocational opportunities. With the generosity of Waldy Malouf, Wolfgang Puck, Joe Essa, Mike Severino, and my son Donald, we started this program in September 2008. The participating students are troubled, requiring some help transitioning between school and dorm. Each semester is five months long, and Chef Kaplan concentrates on one subject per semester. They have studied Italian and French cuisine as well as spending a semester on baking. When we dedicated our school complex in June 2010 as "Newman's Own Education Center" (in recognition of the wonderful, longstanding relationship between Paul Newman and Green Chimneys), it was our Green Cuisine students who prepared and served the food to our distinguished guests. It was professionally presented, and I was so proud of the students as I heard them describe to the guests what each dish contained. The students learn general kitchen skills as well cook fine cuisine. They learn how to properly present the food and serve it; clean up is also part of the job.

◆ ◆ ◆

S. K.: "I went to work to feed the animals at the farm. My job is to feed all the animals at the farm. . . . Dutch, a cow, was waiting to eat. She must have been very hungry and excited to see me because she kept jumping on her cage and licking her tongue at me. I thought this was so funny and I was cracking up laughing. Dutch kept licking her tongue at me and every time she did it and I kept laughing. I fed Dutch and she calmed down."

Notes

1 Author, classical scholar, and farmer. http://www.victorhanson.com/.

2 I am not trying to train all our students to be farmers, but I believe that caring for the animals, being in touch with nature daily, and doing chores helps our students build character.

Chapter IV

Children and Animals

> If we want children to flourish, to become truly empowered, then let us allow them to love the earth before we ask them to save it. Perhaps this is what Thoreau had in mind when he said "the more slowly trees grow at first, the sounder they are at the core, and I think the same is true of human beings."[1]
>
> -David Sobel

Helping Children, Helping Animals

When I had instinctively combined a farm and a school in 1948, I intended us to provide much of our own food. We no longer raise our own meat and poultry, however. We do not eat our therapists! I had no idea that we would become internationally known for being pioneers in animal-assisted therapy. That was all to come as we developed and as the world around us saw its benefits too.

In 2001 when President Bush signed the "No Child Left Behind Act," this concept also was not new to us at Green Chimneys where we were concerned daily with the lives of children of varying abilities and backgrounds. We accept only those children we believe we can help.

It is difficult to know which children can be helped and which cannot. When it comes to youth committing serious offenses, we as a society need to come up with a means for children to perform an act of repentance. A serious transgression is something we must seek to reverse. My experience has shown that many children have not had the proper role models. They have had limited direction. It is essential that all of us practice and teach respect for all living things.

The current rapid growth and global interest in the field of animal-assisted learning, animal-assisted activities, and animal-assisted therapy has been a credit to all those who have worked hard to provide a carefully thought out approach in the field. No one should suggest that education and training in the field is unnecessary. The thought that any cute, warm, fuzzy animal in combination with any willing adult is all that is required to engage children and adults in an animal therapeutic or learning experience is badly mistaken. This new adventure for a growing number of people has emphasized academic and practical experience. I shudder to think about the dangers that can result if those delivering the service do not understand animals or people. It is not enough to be trained only with animals *or* to be trained only in human service; the combination is essential.

Fortunately for me, I am pleased to have played a part in the growth of animal-assisted learning, animal-assisted therapy, animal-assisted activities, equine experiential learning, equine-facilitated psychotherapy, therapeutic riding for the handicapped, horticultural therapy, organic gardening, the City and Country Farms movement in the United Kingdom and Europe, 4-H in the United States, outdoor education, and adventure education.

We decided to go public with our farm and outdoor education program in the 1970s. Our gardening program at Boni-Bel Farm was expanded, and we spoke about our families "getting back to their roots." In fact, the animals gave the parents and children something they could share together, which was pleasurable. Our idea of mainstreaming was to bring the community in to share with us as many activities as we were able to offer. In recent years, the garden has been expanded to four acres. It follows all organic practices and is listed in various publications as an example of community-supported agriculture.

In 1974 *The New York Times* ran an article about the farm program entitled "Troubled Children Touch the World Through Animals."[2] Healing takes place every day at Green Chimneys for animals and children alike. It is the restorative contribution of Green Chimneys that warrants its very existence. It is something that involves the children in residence, the day students, special populations from the local community, and indeed it includes all those who come for an extended or brief moment. It is the intergenerational, multipurpose, intercultural aspect of the farm that attracts people to Green Chimneys. We stress the importance of cooperation and encourage innovation. We support the idea that work is a means of bringing people together. We value the participation of many and see much that exists on the campus as opportunities for learning. Striving to give each student a chance for rebirth, the program provides a somewhat different approach to the care of young children and adolescents with special needs.

Our program, which emphasizes contact with animals, nature, and the environment, seemed like a good prescription for reeducation. As local farms have disappeared, the animals at Green Chimneys become so much more important not only to our students, but to the greater community. It is safe to say that what has been constant throughout our history has been animals, plants, and the outdoors. Years ago we were required to obtain licensure as a behavioral health care hospital. A major achievement was the approval of animal-related activities without any reservations. Gaining approval for animals in living units, classrooms, and the wildlife center opened the way for others to gain similar approval for their animal programs.

Green Chimneys has achieved worldwide attention because it has fostered the effort to bring children into contact with the natural world. Edward O. Wilson, in his 1984 book *Biophilia*, defined biophilia as the "innate tendency to focus on life and lifelike processes." Green Chimneys planned for this in 1947. For all people, contact with nature has the ability to reduce stress. For those with special needs, the presence of something living has proved itself to be an important element in the healing process. It is not only the animal, but it is the open space and the views that one can experience that completes the restorative quality. We are very accustomed to get children to work together on an animal or garden project. We feel that as they work together they may develop a friendship and overcome loneliness.

For children who may have always experienced urban blight, the power of the campus vistas may be greater than one can imagine. It is therefore important to help the young people in care to accept responsibility for their home neighborhoods since not all people will be able to come to Green Chimneys and may spend their entire lives in the urban environment.

In the beginning, the idea of "a home away from home" for very young children seemed as an end in itself. The curriculum was similar to what one might find in an early childhood program, but the enrichment, which came from animal-assisted activities, added to the excitement of learning.

Gradually the program expanded and older children became part of the students in residence. The intensity of the animal and outdoor education experiences became more and more important. The success with children brought requests to handle children with more difficult learning and emotional problems. Year-round schooling in combination with intensified animal contact proved to be a very strong attraction for those seeking services for children.

An animal can serve as an object for love. When a child craves a close, cuddly, affectionate relationship, companion animals can provide this in a non-judgmental relationship on call twenty-four hours a day, if necessary. Animals will respond with love if they are well treated. Indeed, loving and caring for a companion animal may be the first step toward developing what ethologists call the "human ethic," a concern for other people derived from the opportunity to give love and be loved. In many cases in our work at Green Chimneys, we have seen how the companion animals of our staff have helped a child work through difficult feelings. Dr. Boris Levinson, child psychologist and the first to document the beneficial effect the presence of animals can have with children who are experiencing emotional and mental challenges, expressed interest in our population at Green Chimneys. We developed a good friendship over the years, and I always enjoyed listening to his expert opinions. He felt that companion animals can aid children in accomplishing important developmental tasks. It was his opinion that when children are able to express many feelings toward animals, they can better see these feelings in themselves, and this has been confirmed by our own experiences here.

The children at Green Chimneys do not have pets, but our staff do, and they are encouraged to bring them in so that there are many dogs on campus to which the children can respond. When I am out walking, I usually have my Pomeranian, Spike, at my side. I know the children are happy to see me, but honestly, Spike is quite the draw. Companion animals give the shy, awkward, immature child easy conversational openings or may bring about interest in an otherwise uninterested, underachieving youngster. The child begins to open up often during the caring of a companion animal, farm animal, or wildlife.

Pet or farm animal care may help teach responsibility in a child. It is generally agreed that a child can begin to take some responsibility for an animal at a young age with the guidance of an adult. As the child gradually becomes able to assume more responsibility for the animal's care, the adult can exercise less guidance. Being close to and responsible for the partial care of a companion or farm animal may improve the child's self-concept and self-confidence, may teach a child to be a better person and reporter of observations, and may provide a dress rehearsal for later life experiences that relate to sexual behavior, birth, and death.

Levinson also found the use of an animal as a "social lubricant" to help the child be more relaxed and interested during therapy. The presence of his dog, Jingles, helped lower the anxieties of children and made them easier to test and treat. Children's hospitals, institutions, and our farm have given us continuous evidence of this.

We try to find out if children who come to Green Chimneys have ever owned a pet. We want to know also if there is a history of cruelty to animals, because we recognize such behavior as a precursor to cruelty to humans. We are appalled when people say, "Isn't it better that the child has hurt an animal rather than another child?" For us, this is not acceptable. We must not ignore animal cruelty, for a child or adult that would deliberately mistreat an animal may very well mistreat a person. Additionally, a child's persistent cruelty to an animal may be a distress signal within a family.

That raises question: do we accept children who have abused animals in the past? It would depend on the frequency and the severity. If we feel that the child is a danger to our animals, we cannot accept them for admission. There are other programs without animals that can work with the child. If the history of abuse is not severe, and we believe being with animals could help, we will consider taking the child.

In our case, an attempt to establish a program that would serve to change children's trouble situations occurred when Green Chimneys was founded. The original idea was to surround the children with animals for the betterment of both. Over the course of each year, the campus welcomes over twenty thousand visitors to the farm and wildlife conservation center where over three hundred animals are housed, including many rescued injured birds of prey. The program stresses antiviolence, and through its various activities, the program provides students with service learning opportunities as a means of allowing the students to improve their self-concept, to develop internal controls, and to gain social recognition. Having adolescents provide assistance with horseback riding for very young children is just one example.

An annual student survey coupled with documentation of the student's performance serves as a means of evaluating the outcomes of this human-animal integration approach. Our students are actively involved with the Roots & Shoots program spearheaded by Jane Goodall.

◆ ◆ ◆

Over the years I have come to understand just how serious a task we have undertaken. Not all the advocates can agree on what is best for the animals. Human–animal integration requires great knowledgeable about the needs of both. It is not enough to have a casual interest. It is, instead, extremely important to be very passionate about the proposed program.

While there have been modifications and changes at Green Chimneys, the overall model has always called for the integration of children and animals in an atmosphere beneficial to both. Some people are concerned and confused about the tenets of our program. Some wonder whether we are involved in a program related to animal welfare or child welfare. Many question our serving both animals and children and wonder if we can serve both well. Some speak about the innate cruelty of children and the fear that the animals are therefore in constant danger. Others see the animals as a potential danger to the children. There is some validity regarding anxiety and fears surrounding children and animals. However, observing the healing potential of the animals for the children and the healing potential of the children for the animals is a constant personal reminder that we are fostering something that is important to those we serve.

The cry for a gentler, calmer society comes at a time when the world has become a more violent place. We read about unbelievable cruelty to animals, and fortunately there is a trend to connect violence to animals as an indicator of future violence toward people.

It is especially important to understand that the population of children and families with whom we come in contact are a microcosm of the society in which we live. It is not unusual to see reference in children's case records to such problems as family violence, physical, spousal, and sexual abuse, drugs and alcoholism, death from illness, critical and/or terminal illness in family, suicide or murder, incarceration in a prison, admission for care in a long-term psychiatric hospital, divorce, separation, or custody battles, homelessness, lack of family resources, and absent family members. Children often feel powerless to impact positively their environment. Working with animals is a win-win for our children.

In caring for the animals and interacting with our staff's companion animals, we create many opportunities to interrupt previously learned negative behaviors, and introduce and substitute new, more acceptable conduct. We know that we cannot cure all the ills our children and families have faced or will face. We hope that through contact with good adult role models and an accepting, warm environment where children and animals coexist for the betterment of both that we can provide new hope and new goals that previously were considered unattainable.

Today, thankfully, there is an awareness of our natural resources that was not prevalent several decades ago. Being "green" is part of the vocabulary of school children, the public, corporations, and government. Having our children participate as caregivers in a wildlife rehabilitation program and/or in the maintenance and conservation of domestic animals that are in danger of extinction is a valuable way to show our children that their efforts make a difference.

Without the animals, we might be very much the same as many other programs. The animals make us different. With children and animals under foot, there needs always to be a degree of patience and understanding. We are ever mindful that the children, families, and animals with whom we come in contact depend on us for protection, safety, and care. There has to be a collaborative effort by staff to make it work. What does this mean? It means we have to be extra protective of the children around livestock, and we select tools, equipment, and tasks that are appropriate for the child.

In order for animal-assisted therapy to be effective there are several criteria that must be met. The therapist must have respect for the animal and can make a choice in his or her interaction with the client to assign or project human emotions onto the animal or not. Regardless of approach, animals are not "used" in this form of therapy, but build a corner of the AAT triangle relationship—therapist, client, animal. The therapist serves as facilitator and must be as cognizant of the animal's temperament, capabilities, history, and reactions as they are of the child's. Safety issues for both animal and child are the priority for a successful therapeutic session. Neither the animal nor the child should feel at any time threatened. Rather, there should be a natural progression of trust learned by responding to the animal. The goal is to have the child's experiences with the animals generalize to their interactions with people. This is the essence of how AAT works. As one child wrote:

> I was scared when I first went to the farm. The animals were big. They made funny noises and I did not know much about them. Now I am not scared at the farm because people told me why they make funny noises; the animals may want their food or to say "hello" or "good-bye." I feed the animals sometimes and it makes me nervous and happy. I am not afraid to pet them any more because they won't bit me. They are soft to pet. I like to go to the farm now because I can pet and feed the animals and it makes me excited!
>
> -T. H., age 8

Animals—Rescue and Loss: The Story of Romeo

On March 15, 2001, the local *Journal News* reported on an abused horse, Romeo, which was rescued, brought to Green Chimneys, and given a new lease on life. Found starving to death in a Brooklyn stable, the animal was rescued by workers from the American Society for the Prevention of Cruelty to Animals (ASPCA). Rescuing horses for our students brings about dramatic changes in youth and persons at Green Chimneys.

Here are items about Romeo taken from an intern's diary:

April 7, 2001—Observation

I decided to observe Romeo because I am in awe of his spirit and his will to live and I wanted to observe his progress here at Green Chimneys.

What I saw on this first day was a frail horse. A tender body being held up by skinny, tired legs. Ribs sticking through skin and old scars peeking through nutrient depleted hair. Unsure feet on new earth never before walked on. Ears perked to listen for unfamiliar and scary sounds. A body that was tensed and ready to receive any hurtful action. I saw no relaxed stance, I saw no big proud breast of a powerful beast thrust forward, and I saw no strong neck held high with confidence. As I laid my head on the fence to look at this burdened and broken animal, I spoke softly to him. I told him he was in a good and safe place now, surrounded by people who loved him and would care for him. I did not reach out to him because I wanted to let him know that a human could be close to him without touching him for selfish reasons or to gain something from him. I tried to do what we have been taught. Really see the animal. Send positive thought and energy out to the animal. Not think of "I" or "ME" or what I want and need from the animal.

It was only his eyes that lifted my heart. Deep, deep inside, past the scared part, there was a glimmer. A spark. A message that said I am still here. Try to find me because I have not given up yet. Those soft eyes watched me. They followed my every move. Maybe because he was nervous about who I was or whether I would hurt him, but maybe because he was communicating to me. Telling me with his eyes that he was working on his comeback. I was looking forward to our next meeting.

April 14, 2001—Observation

Today Romeo looked a little sturdier on his feet. Again his eyes followed my every move but he seemed more alert and "present" in his body. I decided to touch him today and did so while talking soothingly to him. His ears communicated that he was very interested in my ramblings.

I decided to give him some grass. After sniffing loudly he ate the whole handful in one gulp. I gave him some more. When I would walk away to get some grass he would walk and follow me. This was a good sign that he was interested and not withdrawn. He had gained some weight and I was happy to see someone had put a braid in his mane. I added my own braid and after some more stroking I left. As I was walking away I turned and saw that he was watching me walk away. He wants to connect.

May 12, 2001—Observation

Romeo got a bath today. He had been infested with flies and since his immune system is still so weak he had no natural resources to fight them off. What I got to watch however was a horse really enjoying a luxury he was not used to getting.

His legs were spread evenly apart at a stance that appeared solid but relaxed as if he were not going to move for anything—he was going to enjoy this. He never flinched or moved away from the washing. While being washed on the face with a washcloth and scrubbed under his mouth, his eyes were half closed and he looked so relaxed. His ears were up and alert and listening to the women who were washing him. He would move to face the girl holding his rein almost to get reassurance from her that he is all right. His eyes would move and follow what was going on around him.

While being sprayed down with the hose he moved his head up and down trying to shake off the girl holding his rein. He walked forward but not wildly—sort of slowly as to not frighten his washers. After a few minutes of a scared look on his face he stopped trying to move away and let them hose him down. Eyes were forward, ears were alert, calm stance.

When he was finished he walked almost proudly as they led him to some grass for a treat. He pulled quickly and hungrily at the grass and then let a big puff of air out of his nose as they led him into the barn. It was a happy scene to watch.

Sean, one of our residents, played a major care-giving role in Romeo's life. He was discharged in the summer of 2001 and wrote this note after he returned home:

To Romeo and Dr. Brooks,

Hi. How are you two doing? I am doing fine. My new school is fine. My new school is I.S. 88 and my teacher's name is Mr. Forker. My grandmother drives me there and my grandmother or my grandfather pick me up. I've enclosed a picture of me, you and Romeo. I miss you very much. When I come up I will put money in a envelope for Romeo's food and supplies on a desk. Well I love and care for you ~~boy~~ Romeo and I told you I'll write to you soon. Bye.

From your favorite, Sean

I state over and over again that rescuing animals makes a big difference in the lives of the rescuers. In the case of Romeo, the care he needed and received, the story of his rescue, and his recovery because of the care we gave him had a great impact on the students. They saw a team of caring, generous adults, which was in sharp contrast to the previous owners who had let Romeo suffer and decline. In addition, Romeo gave back to us as generously. We now had a wonderful horse for the children to ride. When Romeo had to be put down in 2009 because of his inability to stand, the children and staff celebrated his life after he was gone. It became another teaching opportunity on how to grieve, that life inevitably includes losses. For our children, the lesson teaches we can go on and make a difference in the next person / animal.

Animal losses are comparable to human losses, and children are particularly vulnerable as it is frequently a first experience with the death of a loved one. They go through the normal stages of the loss process—denial, anger, and finally, acceptance. Grieving is expected after such a loss, and most children return to an emotionally stable state after a period of grieving. However, several researchers report occasional depression or school phobia resulting after the loss of a pet, and suicide may be contemplated by a child who finds the emotional pain overwhelming.

The farm and social service staff at Green Chimneys form groups with the children to discuss separation from or loss of an animal. Throughout this process the support group is available to help the children through the transition period of losing an animal and accepting a new one. We allow the children, whenever possible, to participate in or observe the arrangements being made for an animal. They may feel they must help the animal until the end, they may want to provide comfort, or they may not want to be involved at all. It is important to keep communication open and be supportive.

Additionally, the response of children and staff to animal suffering and need for euthanasia are part of the life cycle, lessons from which all of us can learn. A staff member at the farm wrote about the experience:

> We had to euthanize, kill in mercy, our, my beloved llama, Angel, yesterday. She is 14, has had a bad back for years and has been in the final stages of arthritis recently. She couldn't get up two weeks ago without a lot of difficulty and yesterday when, again, she did get up, she fell and her back legs took a long time to support her. She was shivering, which means she was in pain. I just said, it's time. So we had a big meeting where everyone said what they needed about anything regarding Angel and the HUGE process I will have to plan. We decided to euthanize her yesterday at 4:00 PM and I will collect my team and we will tell the children Monday. I will go to class with social workers and we will treat each classroom like a group therapy session. The children will have a chance to face and begin grieving this loss and, of course, whatever

> else gets triggered for them. I will notify the school principal, the dorm supervisors, staff and all the social workers. The farm staff will be ready for the onset of cards and poems and pictures that will be hung adorning Angel's stall. The transition team will get a list of high risk children (as far as we know), . . . and life will go on . . . sigh, this has to be known on my way out . . . anyway, Angels' death was beautiful. We transported her down to our other farm, loaded her up with hay, extra food and bute (an intense aspirin) and at 4:00 PM our vet came. The whole barn staff came to be with her. Some of us sang. I sang "Ave Maria," Lois sang "Shalom Haverim," and Miyako sang a Japanese children's lullaby. We sat while the relaxant was given and while the meds were given that would stop her heart. Very slow, very calm, very beautifully. It took about an hour and a half. It was snowing intensely. We thanked her in many ways; we cried and supported each other as we sat around her. Because she was one of my sweeties, I also felt very supported by my colleagues and we all came more closely together. Today she is dead . . . then there is Monday.

The following letter, written from one student to another, who helped care for Jagger, a horse who died, illustrates what the horse care program means:

> Dear R. D.,
>
> I'm sorry about Jagger. He was a special horse. We all loved him. If there is anything I can do to make you feel better, I will do it because I know how you feel. I am upset myself. I know you will miss him for I will miss him too.
>
> Your friend, M. P.

◆ ◆ ◆

Many animals that we have here have been rescued and some have been gifts. In 2001 we were privileged to have former New York Senator (and current Secretary of State) Hillary Rodham Clinton visit us and donate two Icelandic horses that had been a gift to her from the government of Iceland. After her visit, she wrote the following:

> Dear Sam and Myra,
>
> Thank you for a memorable visit to Green Chimneys, and, even more, for your lifetimes of service to children. I look forward to working with you to ensure that you reach as many children as possible. Thanks too for taking such good care of "my" Icelandic horses.
>
> The enclosed check comes from the proceeds of my book, It Takes a Village, which spotlighted the ways we all share responsibility for the

well being of our children. You exemplify what I believe the "Village" should be—animal too.

All the best for a Happy New Year—Hillary

Through the Eyes of Visitors

What do visitors see when they visit the Green Chimneys campus today? It depends on the day of the week and the time of day. If they see children playing with or walking a dog on a leash, then they are witnessing the dog providing companionship to the child. If they see an adult, child, and an animal together, then they can surmise that psychological, social, or educational assistance may be underway. It may be animal-assisted *therapy* if the person is a credentialed therapist, or it may be an animal-assisted *activity* if the adult is not a therapist. Although all animal / child interactions may be therapeutic in terms of healing, for it to be AAT, the adult must be a certified therapist.

What else might a visitor see? Children may be participating in the therapeutic riding program on campus with instructors who are all certified by the North American Riding for the Handicapped Association (NARHA). These instructors know how to provide one type of program for our students who are not physically challenged and another for children who may have physical challenges.

If the staff and children are in the process of loading animals on a van as a part of our mobile educational animal awareness program, entitled "Farm-on-the-Moo-ve," our visitors will see another effort being made to allow our students to provide service to others. In prior years, service opportunities occurred when our students conducted farm tours for younger schoolchildren, and Farm-on-the-Moo-ve took the animals to schools, hospitals, and agencies within an hour and a half drive from Brewster. We worked for many years with all the elementary schools in District 8 in the Bronx. We would also take Farm-on-the-Moo-ve and visit residential institutions for children, and our students developed real sense of importance by bringing some joy to the kids.

Although today we have cut back on the amount of trips we make, Farm-on-the-Moo-ve still goes out about five to six times a year, and the aspect of student service remains present. Additionally, by working in the garden and greenhouse, the problem behavior of troubled youth has been harnessed, interrupted, and changed.

If visitors observe a group of students, each with a dog in hand, training the dog to perform certain tasks, they will learn that the dogs are being trained as service animals for children and adults who are wheelchair-bound or in need of assistance because of physical challenges. In a recent survey of all the student trainers there was unanimous agreement that this was a worthwhile experience for the young trainer and that the goal of preparing dogs to be service animals was something they would be willing to do over and over again.

One young student who had resisted wearing his hearing aids began to wear them consistently without prompting from anyone. He was asked by staff why he had his hearing aids in place after so many repeated requests. He replied that he was afraid he would not hear correctly, and as a result, would be unable to train his dog.

Another young adolescent at a service dog graduation ceremony revealed a secret about himself that he had never shared. He stated that he had never loved anyone and had never felt that anyone loved him, but he had come to love the adult trainer and the program aide. He loved the dog, and with tears in his eyes, he spoke about how difficult it was to turn over the dog at that time. He further stated that he was thrilled to have reached his goal and felt very good about knowing the dog would provide the help the recipient required. There wasn't a dry eye in the audience when he finished his remarks. In this and other similar cases, the young trainer became a "giver," a powerful lesson.

◆ ◆ ◆

A walk along the nature trails adjacent to the farm area provides the visitor firsthand contact with wildlife. The collection includes foxes, deer, emus, and birds of prey. Large cages display permanently injured or imprinted animals. Some of these animals have successfully bred in captivity, and the young return to the wild. In two large flight cages there are birds being exercised for their planned release. These are the birds that will be used in the special bird release ceremony that is held to coincide when a bird is ready to be returned to the wild and a child is being discharged. Wildlife, in a good educational program, becomes great teachers. As long as the quality of life of the animals is excellent, no one should decry the fact that the animals are being maintained with physical limitations. The chance for the young caregivers to provide nurturance and care can be a very important means of teaching about preservation of wildlife and can improve the ecological concern of the young people. In the case of imprinted animals, the young person learns how important it is to not try to make pets of animals that are meant to be free.

In addition to saving individual animals, we have rescued dying breeds through our rare breed program. Some of these near-extinct traditional breeds date back to pre-Roman times and some of these animal species are unknown. They need to be brought to the attention of the public at large so that people will continue to raise them. Some of the breeds have lost their commercial value to the larger modern breeds, but that is all the more reason that these animals must be maintained. With the advent of mad cow disease in Britain, one can understand why we might be very grateful that the older breeds were preserved. Paul Kupchok, the farm director at that time, pointed out to me that we must maintain a happy balance between the number of rare breeds we retain and the domestic animals we rescue. We have to save spaces for rescued animals, because their care and rehabilitation are equally important lessons for our students to learn.

It is very fortunate that Green Chimneys has taken the attitude that these animals—wildlife and rare breeds—are worthy of our concern. They serve effectively to educate the students at Green Chimneys and serve as part of the educational program offered to the thousands of children and adults who visit the farm or enjoy a visit from Farm-on-the-Moo-ve. What better way is there to learn about wildlife and rare breeds than to have the opportunity to care for the animals? What better way is there to teach than to show people the results of cruelty to wildlife and the value of rehabilitation to permit the potential release of animals and birds of prey? What better means can be found than to exhibit rare breeds of domestic animals that people can handle? They can empathize with the wildlife and rare breeds and will be able to relate to stories they see on television or read about in newspapers and magazines.

Green Chimneys Farm and Wildlife Rehabilitation Center has been home to hundreds of animals. A cooperative arrangement existed for years between Green Chimneys and the Wildlife Conservation Society in New York City, and the arrangement made possible the exhibit of rare breed domestic animals in the children's zoo in Central Park. A number of birds and animals in our collection have come from the Bronx Zoo.

The wildlife rehabilitation program operates its main center on the campus in Brewster and has successfully bred barn owls in captivity using a pair of permanently injured owls. Releasing the young owlets has been a very exciting and meaningful experience for the children in residence. Barn owls are birds of open terrain, hunting in fields, meadows, and farmland. They are known to spend their entire lifetime in close proximity to humans. The rehabilitators believe that through the barn owl project they are replenishing the number of owls in the area. Many other birds have been successfully bred and released also.

The animals in the classrooms provide the opportunity to enrich the curriculum and to find practical opportunities to introduce and reinforce learning. Aquariums are excellent additions to the classroom, or for that matter, to any space where adults and children come into contact. There are ways to integrate the excitement of working with animals into every aspect of the school curriculum. Reading, writing, mathematics, social studies, geography, science, art, and music are all available. One cannot ignore the fact that there are career opportunities related to animals, plants, and the environment, which may too often be overlooked or seem beyond the capacity or interest of urban youth. At Green Chimneys the Learn & Earn Program provides valuable work experience opportunities.

Visitors hopefully take away with them a new way of looking at children, especially troubled children. They become aware that the protection, health, and safety of child and animal must not be overlooked or underestimated. They see that these children can contribute to the community. They also express concern for the animals and the children, and they interact with the staff who are willing to listen and discuss their concerns. They watch the children and the staff work together. They see impediments to the process, and they see examples of successful collaboration. They hear the children express their fears, their joys, their frustrations, and their accomplishments.

◆ ◆ ◆

Staff Notes

> N. N. is a heavy-set, robust 12-year-old who has been at Green Chimneys for 18 months. Before that, he'd spent four years in special ed classes due to disruptive behavior and lack of academic progress. A pattern of acting out in class and truancy landed him at Green Chimneys. Not only have his grades gone up, N. N. is on Green Chimneys' football team. He no longer overreacts to teasing about his weight. He's shown his rabbit, Tiger, at the 4-H County Fair and he won the blue ribbon for best buck rabbit, which gained his friends' respect and made him quite proud of himself.

Notes

1 Sobel, David, *Beyond Ecophobia: Reclaiming the Heart in Nature Education* (Massachusetts: Orion Society, 1966).

2 Hammel, Lisa, *The New York Times*, April 14, 1974.

Chapter V

A Time of Transition

"Opening a milk bottle and sipping the cream off the top . . ."

"Finding the big peanut in a treasure hunt . . ."

"You and I delivering the baby pigs and foals . . ."

"Being bathed in the kitchen sink because I was so muddy from playing . . ."

"Riding our ponies, Peaches and Billy . . ."

"Sleeping over at your house to take the laundry back the next morning . . ."

"Driving the tractor and baling hay . . ."

"Hiding kittens in the laundry room . . ."

"The way Mommy Mac would smile and put her arm around me . . ."

"Singing our song . . ."

"Green Chimneys Farm for Little Folk
The place that we all know
Whenever we go out
We love to yell and shout
Green Chimneys Farm for Little Folk!"

-Green Chimneys School Song

It is interesting what children recall. Over the years, adult alumni have written or called and told me what they remember most. I have to admit that, at first,

I expected them to mention the big class trip we all worked so hard to organize, or the class play for which we sewed costumes and rehearsed endlessly. I have learned that the students remember those events, but the things that stand out, that spring to mind first, are often a lot simpler—and unpredictable. A former student called and during the conversation asked me if I still drink coffee milk (half coffee, half milk) out of a glass, and I told her I did, but now I use a plastic mug. She laughed and said, "There goes my image of the father figure." Forty years later she remembered my custom. I knew children watched adults closely; it was a good reminder of just how closely.

Whenever these alumni reminisced, I also was reminded of how much simpler things were in the beginning. Not that supervising eighty-six boarders and fifteen day students—which was our enrollment by the end of the 1950s—was simple. But what the students were happy doing, what intrigued and entertained them, was a lot simpler than today—picnics and barbecues, sing-alongs, playing tag, checkers and chess, exploring the woods, digging up worms for bait and going fishing, riding bikes, climbing the willow tree. It was healthy fun. And as it so happened, just what Benton & Bowles wanted to see when it contacted *Parents Magazine* in 1959.

Benton & Bowles was a New York City-based advertising agency, and one of their accounts was the Florida Citrus Commission. When the Commission decided to sponsor a popular television quiz show called *What's My Line?*, it asked Benton & Bowles to create the commercials. One of the concepts involved children, and the agency asked *Parents Magazine* if it knew of a boarding school where it could film children—not child actors and actresses, but real children—in action. The magazine recommended Green Chimneys.

The agency paid us a visit, and in early February 1960, arrived on campus with a camera crew in tow. The *Patent Trader*, a local newspaper, reported on the event and ran a wonderful photo of children peeking in the windows of the building where some of the filming took place. The building was the machine shed, although it no longer looked like one. A few months earlier we had finished converting it into a classroom for fifth and sixth graders, and it looked like new. In addition to plenty of room for desks and chairs, it had a small kitchen area with a stove and refrigerator so we could include cooking in the curriculum. On visiting days it doubled as a canteen, and parents and friends had lunch and refreshments there. It was behind the kitchen counter that Myra stood. The producer wanted her to be in the commercial; however, she was five months pregnant, which was not part of the script. The counter served to hide the evidence.

While the children on the outside wished to be on the inside, the thrill for the children on the inside quickly waned. It was a long shoot, and the predominant activity was waiting, which is not children's forte. About halfway through, the children asked if they could drink water; they had had their fill of orange juice.

Within weeks of the shoot, the commercial began running on national television, and we received calls from friends and family who saw the ad and recognized the school. One caller was the owner of the hatchery from whom we were buying several goslings; he was happy to see where they would be living. It was our few minutes in the spotlight, and we were still enjoying it when Lisa Ellen arrived on May 30, sixteen weeks after the filming of the commercial was completed. Our family was now complete; we had three children—and a lot of people telling us how to raise them.

Our parents, in-laws, some cousins, and other relatives either worked at Green Chimneys or frequently came to help. All the women we employed as housemothers, housekeepers, cooks, and preschool teachers were mothers. Raising three children with so many to approve or disapprove was difficult to say the least. They constantly reminded Myra and me that they were older and knew better. Perhaps if they had all agreed it would have been easier, but usually they each had their own ideas and methods, and we struggled to find a middle ground with which we felt comfortable.

It was a little easier when it came to running the school, but not much. Because the school and camp were my idea, and I was the headmaster, they expected me to make the final decisions. But everyone lobbied hard for their positions.

I knew it was important to receive input from others; no one has all the answers, after all. I also felt that I had an obligation to listen to others' ideas and opinions. Whether family or staff, a headmaster should invite everyone to contribute and then give their input careful consideration. On the other hand, when it came to running a school we were all novices. Subjects could be debated endlessly if allowed. I often thought of the sign on Harry Truman's desk that said, "The Buck Stops Here." I, too, was responsible, and I could not shy away from making decisions. Looking back, I know I was a bit of a dictator in some regards and a pushover in others. Others might have chosen to be more lenient where I was strict and stricter where I was lenient. That is always to be expected. Besides, I was young; my instincts were not theirs. But ultimately, it was up to me.

One might wonder how we not only worked together, but remained a close family in spite of this. I think it was because we all shared the same goal—to have a wonderful school and camp—and we tried to keep that uppermost in our minds. We recognized that if someone was forceful with an opinion or idea, it was because they only wanted the best for the school, the camp, and the children.

Having clearly defined roles also helped. Everyone continued to pitch in wherever we were needed, but we respected and worked with whoever took the lead in that area. Adele was the school nurse, did a great deal of the cooking, and ran the business office, a job that she found most distressing. Between parents not paying and creditors demanding their money, she was in tears almost on a daily basis. I was the headmaster and a teacher. Myra was a teacher and the guidance counselor. My father was the benefactor, physician, and chauffeur of parents and children to and from New York City. We all worked long and hard, shared happy moments and sad moments, and the bond that formed was strong.

One of those sad moments was the death of my maternal grandfather, Jake, in 1960. He was ninety-one. Having stayed with him and my grandmother as a youngster, Grandpa Jake and I were very close, and we remained so through the years. He often accompanied my parents when they visited me at school, and of course, he was an integral part of the launch of Green Chimneys. After my father, I admired him the most.

After Green Chimneys opened and we were on our feet, Grandpa Jake moved back to his home in the Bronx but visited frequently. When my parents separated in the early 1950s, however, he took the news hard and no longer made the trip. He was worried about my mother and angry with my father; he did not want to see him, which he would have had to do if he visited. Much to his credit, my grandfather did not let my parents' separation and subsequent divorce get in the way of our relationship. He stayed in touch, and Myra and I would visit him at his home and later, at the nursing home. He was thrilled whenever we brought his two great-grandsons, David and Donald, with us.

To this day, I am not sure why my parents divorced; I believe they drifted apart. I do not remember them ever arguing or yelling. They did many things together. But my mother was less social than my father and maintained few friends and little, if any, contact with relatives other than her parents. Looking back, it seems to me that she was an unhappy person and suffered from insecurities.

I think my mother and father's parting was particularly painful to my grandfather because he and my father enjoyed such a wonderful relationship for so many years. They saw each other frequently—when I was staying with my grandparents, we were all together for family dinners almost nightly—and my father often took my grandparents with him on trips, even when my mother did not go. They worked together in my grandfather's garden, and the three of us often went fishing together.

Shortly after my parents' divorce, my father closed his New York City practice, moved to Green Chimneys, and married Adele, whom he had known for many years. We turned the staff house into his medical office, adding a wing so he had room not only to provide medical care to the children and staff, but also to the local residents. Adele and he continued to live on the grounds and be as involved as ever in the school and camp. To better serve the school and the community, my father became affiliated with Mahopac and Danbury Hospitals. By that time he had practiced medicine for almost fifty years.

My children remember my father as a loving but stern grandfather. He was always telling them, "Sit up straight"; "Pull your shoulders back"; "Take your elbows off the table"; "Help your mother." He was always warning the students and staff, "Don't walk on the lawn!" But despite his gruff manner, he was caring and thoughtful. When we began Green Chimneys, many people came to our aid largely to repay the help, kindness, and friendship he had given them. While he was at Green Chimneys, he often took David with him to medical meetings, which I am sure influenced David's decision to become a doctor, and took children into his home. One student tells of developing an affinity for Guy Lombardo[1] after spending several New Year's Eves with my father. This child had nowhere to go, no family with whom to spend the holidays. When this child was older and again in need of a place to stay, he lived with my father while he attended Brewster High School.

Bella Meyer still tells of my father's help when her husband, Mike, died suddenly. Bella was my secretary. We had known Bella and Mike for several years and had become friends. It was Bella who had encouraged me to meet Myra. Bella had been working for me only a short while when Mike passed away, and as she tells it, was left penniless with a daughter and three sons. Well-meaning relatives told her daughter, Bonnie, who was a freshman in college, that even though she was on a scholarship, she would have to leave school and take a job; her mother needed her help.

When my dad heard that, he said, "Oh no. She's going to finish school!" He drove Bella and Bonnie to the school where he met with the dean and explained the situation. He made sure the college understood the circumstances and that Bonnie's scholarship would continue. After getting Bonnie settled in, he and Bella drove back and stopped at the social services office to inquire about benefits. Bella learned that each of the children was entitled to receive a monthly social security payment. "I was shocked that he took the time to help me, but I was so grateful," Bella says. "I wouldn't have known what to do had it not been for him." Bonnie graduated, became a teacher, and secured a good job, and Bella finished raising her three sons, Johnnie, Jeff, and Bobby, while she continued to work at Green Chimneys. I was not surprised at my father's generosity. The Meyer's were a second family to all of us. Indeed, I taught Johnnie to read, Bobby to swim—and Jeff asserts that because of my insistence on him eating his peas at dinner, that I taught him to hate peas! Bobby still comes on campus. He has a floor cleaning business, and he takes care of our carpeting. Bella is an amazing, warm, wonderful person who is very dear to us. Words fail when I try to describe Bella and all that she has done and continues to do for others. She retired in 2003 after forty-two years of working for me. At ninety-five she still comes to volunteer whenever we need her, and that includes helping to proof the volume you are holding in your hands.

So, in spite of his gruff manner, my father's concern and care for others ran deep. A year or so before Grandpa Jake died, he fell and broke his hip, and my father took it upon himself to attend to his medical care and then visited him in the nursing home. It was an unfortunate accident, but it brought them together again, and I would like to think that it gave them the opportunity to reconcile ill feelings.

Often I would visit my mother in New York City. She had been diagnosed with cancer, and on one of my regular visits I was shocked to see how ill she looked. I called Myra from my mother's home and explained the situation. Without hesitation Myra told me to bring her home to stay at Green Chimneys. My mother agreed, and Myra and I helped her move. Despite the strained relationship between my mother and father, he and Adele offered to care for my mother. It was a wonderful gesture on their part, and a courageous decision for my mother. In addition to their care, my mother received almost daily visits from her three grandchildren. To see my parents and stepmother together gave the children, Myra, and me a wonderful memory, and it brought solace to all our lives.

◆ ◆ ◆

By 1960 we had reached capacity. Every bed was taken, and we had to squeeze in an extra one here and there to accommodate a late arrival. For a young private boarding school and camp, it was a tremendous achievement.

Yet as any parent of a large family can tell you, what you do for one is not done just as easily for five or eight, and certainly not for eighty. Catering to a larger population required that we expand our faculty and staff. In addition to more teachers, houseparents, and camp counselors, we hired a director of physical education, a director of admissions, an after-school staff, a chef, a night staff, and a dentist. It fell to Mama Scherer to be the "clothing supervisor." It was no small feat keeping tabs on what the children had and what they needed; checking for name tags and replacing iron-on tags with sewn-in labels (the former would come off in the laundry and then there was no telling whose socks were whose); and helping the houseparents make sure each child received the right clothing.

More children meant more work, and it meant more wear and tear on our facilities. I used to tell our accountant that our children "accelerated the rate of depreciation." It was impossible to keep up with all the chores and repairs.

Having expanded our faculty and staff to accommodate a larger population, we found ourselves having to maintain our enrollment level in order to have the money to meet our overhead. In hindsight, it was the beginning of a vicious circle, and it was not easy. Some of our advisors suggested that we raise the tuition. As they correctly pointed out, while we could boast a full house, unexpected expenditures—a washer, boiler, or tractor breaking down—were a hardship and a source of much anxiety. I was opposed to increasing tuition. Our families were largely middle-class and many were struggling to pay the current rate; increasing it might force them to take their children out of the school, and it was clear that these children needed our help. I also was proud of the care, attention, and education that the children received, as well as their achievements. We had a good reputation among physicians, psychiatrists, psychologists, schools, and social services agencies for helping children, and continued to receive referrals. I told myself that as long as we were helping children, that is all that mattered. It was true that we could not provide many frills, but the basic needs were in ample supply. Our equipment was modern. The dormitories and classrooms were bright and cheerful. The food was appetizing, and the children were encouraged to eat; we provided three meals and snacks. Surely, these things were more important than the manicured lawns and baseball diamonds that other schools boasted.

However, I could not deny that we needed more money and that we were operating without a buffer. Often Adele and I didn't take a paycheck. If it had not been for my father's continued support, we would have had to close the school.

I had always asked parents to make donations so that we could provide more extras. Many made non-cash donations, and we received books for the library, an aquarium for the kindergarten, a practice piano and chimes for the music department, a typewriter for the office, a stopwatch for the athletic program, stuffed toys for the preschoolers, a television, furniture—even a brand new Wurlitzer piano, a most generous and overwhelming gift from an anonymous donor. Corporations sometimes sponsored an afternoon of movies. All was needed and greatly appreciated, and the movies were a wonderful treat. Unfortunately, however, it did not solve our financial dilemma.

Then one day I received an offer of a donation contingent upon the school becoming a nonprofit organization. Some weeks later I received another. Our accountant and lawyer advised us to become a nonprofit school. They told us that private schools need donations to operate, and it was unlikely that we would receive any sizeable ones unless they were tax deductible for the donors. I began to see that they were right, and on March 25, 1961, Green Chimneys School for Little Folk became a nonprofit, 501(c)3 corporation retroactive to March 25, 1960. The children would benefit greatly from these gifts.

I was glad to make this decision for another reason as well. I had been concerned that as a for-profit school, parents, donors, state officials, and others might question our intentions. Were we running the school and camp for the money or the children? This ensured there would be no question of our priorities.

A Period of Rapid Change

> Nineteen members of the Advisory Committee met. . . . The Headmaster . . . asked the committee to boost our enrollments and to look around for people who are philanthropically inclined and who will make contributions. "We need new classrooms, the kitchen and dining room must be enlarged to accommodate 7th and 8th grades and a large sum of money is needed. The State Education Department wants the school to go through the 8th instead of 6th grade and parents would also have it so. This can be done BUT . . ."
>
> —"The News," June 1962

I was feeling the weight of meeting our ever-expanding payroll and basic needs when the New York State Education Department expressed its wish for us and other private schools to add seventh and eighth grades. Many private schools had discontinued these grades, offering only first through sixth or ninth through twelfth. Increasingly, parents' only option was to send their children to public school for seventh and eighth grades until they could send them back to private high school. Many parents had asked us to add these grades, but we had resisted, having neither the staff nor the facilities to accommodate their requests. The faculty was stretched thin because of their increasing responsibilities as teachers, advisors, and coaches for after-school activities and sports, and sometimes as houseparents; the living units and classrooms were crowded and showing signs of fatigue; and despite providing only the essentials, we still were not making ends meet.

Yet, I couldn't help but think that this was an opportunity. If we were somehow able to accommodate seventh and eighth grades, we would please parents; we would get a leg up on other schools if we acted quickly; we would offer parents a complete elementary education; we could retain current students for another two years; it would give us a bigger pool from which to attract candidates; and more parents would likely register the older children for camp, all of which would increase our bottom line. And of course, responding to a request from the New York State Education Department was always a good thing to do whenever possible.

I turned to the Advisory Committee and the Green Chimneys School Association for help in raising funds to add the new seventh and eighth grades.

The Advisory Committee, formed in 1956, was a way to enhance the school's prestige. I hoped that a committee of knowledgeable professionals, businesspeople, and politicians would push us forward. I had begun to realize that if we were going to progress, we needed the ideas, input, and experience of outsiders.

The Green Chimneys School Association was the parents' organization. Early in 1961 I had encouraged the parents to form a group that would unite them and the staff on behalf of the children. I envisioned that the parents' association would work with the staff to plan educational, cultural, and recreational activities for the children on and off school grounds. I anticipated that it would host speakers to educate parents on topics such as child behavior and development, and easing a child's separation from home.

I had formed both of these groups at two different times but with the same intention; I expected that in addition to other benefits, they would raise funds for school programs and capital projects.

I hoped that if I presented both groups with a clear objective, raising funds to add seventh and eighth grades, that they would organize to support the cause. It was wishful thinking. Initially, both groups seemed willing to take on the challenge. However, as the months passed, I began to realize that I could not rely on these organizations to raise the necessary funds and would have to find another way.

These organizations were to prove to be critical to our success. Although not able to be an effective fund-raising tool, each group was to prove beneficial to Green Chimneys.

Parents of prospective students and those who made referrals reacted favorably when they learned of the Advisory Committee and Green Chimneys School Association, and many individual members proved to be assets. One member from the New York State Department of Education kept me abreast of what was happening in the public schools and helped me secure materials that private schools did not ordinarily know were available. It was a wonderful gesture on his part to alert us so that we could order these items. Several others were local merchants who not only aided us with various projects, but obtained good prices on school materials as well. Another was an architect who drew up plans for several remodeling and construction projects. Many others lent an ear and were generous with their time and advice whenever I had a business problem or a legal question. It was not the outcome I had wanted or expected, but it was invaluable. Little did I realize that some of their biggest contributions were yet to come.

The push toward seventh and eighth grades did not happen at a convenient time, but I had already begun to realize that change was necessary and had taken steps in that direction. Despite our impossibly tight finances, it was time to take the school and camp to the next level.

Raising the Bar for Ourselves

I registered the school as a member of the New York State Association of Independent Schools and the Independent Schools Education Board, which would merge with the National Council of Independent Schools in 1962 to become the National Association of Independent Schools. Every year, many of the faculty and administrative staff attended the annual conferences of these organizations. Staff also attended conferences of the American Association of Children's Residential Centers, which stressed the important role that houseparents, cooks, maintenance men, housekeeping personnel, and others play in the day-to-day care of residential children. If we were going to be responsible for the care, development, and education of children and do it well, we needed to stay informed of what was happening in our field, avail ourselves of the latest thinking and methods, and learn what other schools were doing. Attending these conferences was a step in the right direction.

We also needed to learn more about the children themselves. I began having the Admissions Department give all new students I.Q. tests and speech evaluations. In addition, at regular intervals throughout the school year, I had the teachers administer achievement and diagnostic reading tests. If the tests showed any weaknesses, we began working with the children immediately to correct the deficiencies. For the sixth graders nearing the end of their stay with us, I implemented the Independent Schools Education Board Exams in English and math. They were going on to other schools, and it was important for them to have a standardized test score in their file; although new to our school, such testing was fairly routine at others. At the same time, we also expanded our annual medical checkups to include dental examinations and tests for hearing and eyesight.

I introduced a Headmaster's Honor List and a Headmaster's Penalty List. The Honor List was to recognize students' accomplishments, and the Penalty List was to pinpoint bad behavior, incomplete homework assignments, or poor recitation. I altered our reporting system, now mailing detailed reports to the parents apprising them of their child's performance and inviting them to discuss the results with the Headmaster or teacher after they had reviewed them. I also implemented departmental teaching for fourth through sixth grades and uniforms for all grades; the uniform consisted of a green blazer with the Green Chimneys emblem, white shirts, gray skirts for the girls, and gray pants for the boys. No longer were Myra and I called by our first names; we were known as Mr. and Mrs. Ross.

We improved our science and music programs, and expanded after-school activities to include a student newspaper, sewing club, student orchestra, and camera club. We arranged for our religious program to include not just services, but also religious instruction for Catholic, Protestant, and Jewish children.

We expanded camp activities to include more sports, such as softball, kickball, badminton, tetherball, spaceball, and miniature golf. We arranged for inter-camp softball games. We hosted Hobo Day, Circus and Carnival Day, Wild West Day, and the Pan Fish Derby. We increased the number of class trips for all grades and arranged for trips to local farms, factories, businesses, and historical sites. We even had special events for senior campers, such as a Record Hop and an outing to a night softball game of the Raybestos Cardinals in Stratford, Connecticut, an amateur softball team that competed nationally in the Amateur Softball Association and more than once won the ASA Men's Major Fast Pitch National Championship.

We were becoming more structured and sophisticated. In some regards, it was necessary to compete with other private schools and camps. But mostly, preparation is necessary with an enrollment of one hundred children. To keep one hundred children engaged all day, every day takes extensive planning and coordination, and it is important to have rules and procedures that can be conveyed clearly and quickly. Our student population was now filled with children with more serious learning disabilities and emotional, behavioral, and social problems than before; they responded well to more structure. However, often more challenging than the children were the parents.

In almost every issue of "The News," and later "The Green Chimneys News," there was at least one note—and sometimes a whole page—devoted to parental reminders: please answer your children's letters; pick your children up and drop them off on time; do not send cakes, boxes of cookies, and bags of candy—they ruin the children's appetites and attract mice and ants; please arrive on time for plays and performances; do not take your children off the grounds without notifying us; visit on visiting days; let us know if your phone number or address changes; smoke in the designated smoking areas; remember to provide extra mittens; do not litter; park in the parking lot; and on and on. Sometimes I went so far as to remind them that they were setting an example; if they didn't follow the rules, neither would their children. What seemed like common sense was not.

On more than one occasion I found a parent napping on his or her child's bed and had to explain that visiting days were for visiting. I also pointed out that while they slept, their child was playing outside unsupervised, which was unacceptable. When parents who were separated or divorced couldn't put their differences aside for a few hours, or insisted upon bringing their latest companion to parade in front of the other, I suggested that next time we arrange to have them visit at different times.

Not all aspects of our development and growth happened under my tutelage. Every spring, without any advice from me, the horses, rabbits, sheep, geese, and ducks contributed to Green Chimneys' expansion by bringing forth little ones of their own. The children and I often helped deliver the babies, and then we waited and watched for the piglets to suckle, the foals to stand, and goslings to swim. It was a sign that spring had arrived, and it was something we all looked forward to every year.

◆ ◆ ◆

With no funds for renovations but wanting to add seventh and eighth grades, I did what had become an unofficial Green Chimneys tradition: I innovated, reevaluated my plans, and scaled back my expectations. Building a new dormitory, expanding and remodeling the dining room and kitchen, adding classrooms—all that would have to wait. I asked myself, "What is most important? What is absolutely necessary?"

Moving forward was still my goal, and I took stock of our current plans and contemplated alternatives. Remodeling of the school farm to have a classroom in the farm area was already underway. This was important, as it would let the fourth, fifth, and sixth grades begin school-year-long projects in the raising and care of animals. We also had plans to construct a new horse barn and paddocks, as well as to create a campsite for sleep outs. These projects would enhance our sports and recreation programs, benefiting all the children. They could not be delayed.

Perhaps we could add *one* grade while I worked to fund these renovations for the following year. I decided what we needed to do was innovate, working with what we had. To alleviate some of the overcrowding in the short term, we added on two bedrooms for seventh grade girls to the current dormitory. We enlarged the foyer to hold additional tables and chairs for a study area. By reassessing existing classroom assignments, we made a room for the seventh grade students. With these things accomplished, we accepted seventh graders for the coming fall semester.

When the doors opened in September 1963, we had a record enrollment of 120 boarding and day students, 10 of whom were seventh graders. We had our work cut out for us.

By this time, the parents in the Green Chimneys School Association had planned trips for the students to the Bronx Zoo, Museum of Natural History, and Central Park Zoo. To raise money, they held a country fair with games, pony rides, and an art show, and sold paintings, ceramics, jewelry, homemade food, books, household articles, antiques, and plants. They also hosted the King Bros. Circus on the school grounds, a big hit with the children. Yet to come were a rummage sale and a theatre party.

In the spring of 1964, we were honored with a benefit by Thelonious Monk, the famous jazz pianist and composer. His daughter was one of our students. I still recall when he and his wife, Nellie, dropped off Barbara the previous September, arriving in a Rolls-Royce. Although it was late at night when they arrived, they still sat and visited with me in my office. When they were about to leave, I asked Thelonious Monk if he would play for the children sometime. He replied, "That will open up new horizons," after which Nellie leaned over to me and said, "He means that the children will get a lot from the experience."

Thelonious Monk did more than he promised. He not only played for the children, but he gave a concert at the Palace Theatre in Danbury, Connecticut, to benefit Green Chimneys. Then the following year he wrote a song called "Green Chimneys," which was released by Columbia Records a couple of years later. We couldn't adopt it as our school song, because the children couldn't sing it; it was Monk jazz. We framed several copies of the sheet music, however, and hung them where everyone could appreciate them. You can imagine my delight recently when someone alerted me to a video of Wynton Marsalis, a famous jazz musician, playing Thelonious Monk's "Green Chimneys." I dropped a note to Marsalis, inviting him to come see the Green Chimneys that inspired Thelonious Monk.

Some of the projects that I had hoped to get underway in 1963, plus a few new ones, began in 1964. After completing the new stable, which made it possible to house the ponies and horses adjacent to the riding paddocks, we remodeled the old horse barn to provide space for an art studio, a photography shop, and a storage area for athletic equipment, bicycles, and sleds. We paved the old paddock and made it into a parking lot. We installed a new septic system and dug new drainage ditches. We completed a new baseball field, freeing up the old field for soccer, football, and other sports. Knowing that our new baseball diamond wouldn't be in constant use, I approached the local amateur men's softball league and asked them if they would like to play their evening and Sunday afternoon games on the field. It would be a treat for the children to watch and a new field for them. They were delighted with the idea, and the children were thrilled.

That summer, we also finished the dining room, the kitchen, and completed the dormitory, which we dedicated to my father, named Ross Hall. With fifteen rooms and one faculty apartment, the building could house thirty students and a teacher couple. In addition, we purchased thirty acres on the opposite side of the river; we now had 105 acres at our disposal. The extra thirty acres gave us room for additional pastures, bridle paths, and hay fields; and it allowed us to greatly expand the area for swimming and boating in the summer, and ice skating in the winter. But mostly, it gave us peace of mind. The happy shouts and screams that go with outdoor fun that are music to camp counselors' ears, could be unwelcome noise to others. Because of the additions, there would never be neighbors within earshot who might object to our activities. Some years later we discovered that the thirty acres were wetlands, and therefore, it would have been unlikely that any builder would have bought the land and put up homes. Still, we were glad to know it was ours rather than live with the uncertainty.

After all the construction, renovations, and a busy camp season, we were ready to offer a complete elementary education to our students. We had barely caught our breath when our first eighth graders arrived in September 1964. Our enrollment stood at 115, with 88 borders and 27 day students.

◆ ◆ ◆

Staff Notes

N. R., an energetic, bright-eyed, 10-year-old boy, has been at Green Chimneys for one year. His depression, anxiety and self-destructive behavior made a traditional group home impossible. His learning disability led to failure in public school. At Green Chimneys, N. R. is thriving socially and academically. Still impulsive and easily distracted, he's become an affable, well-motivated child, who easily engages other children and particularly the staff. A sponge for adult supervision, N. R. is enthusiastic and tries hard at everything he does. N. R. is fond of all the animals and can be counted on to work with anyone assigned to him. Somewhat awkward with his peers, he gets along famously with the four-legged creatures (the rabbits are his favorites). The satisfaction he gains is starting to rub off in his budding friendships with other kids.

Notes

1 Guy Lombardo and his orchestra played every New Year's Eve broadcast from 1930 until his death in 1976. Perhaps my father had a special interest in him because Lombardo and his orchestra first played "Auld Lang Syne" on New Year's Eve, 1929, at the Roosevelt Grill in the Roosevelt Hotel where we lived.

Chapter VI

Diversity and Constant Change

> I remember in our early years a grandfather who was the guardian of a young girl, who was a candidate for admission, called up and asked if we admitted "niggers and Jews." When he was told yes, we expected he would not register the child, but he did. The child did well, and the last time I heard was living in the Rochester area and working in a bank.
>
> -Samuel B. Ross, Jr.

In 1948 the population at Green Chimneys was mostly Caucasian. That changed almost immediately, and over the years there was a more diversified population with Asian, Hispanic, and African-American students and staff. During the 1960s there were increased numbers of minority and at-risk students. Today we continue to include children from all backgrounds—privileged, middle-class, and disadvantaged. Attendance for all is tuition-free through payment from individual school districts. Racial issues with children, families, and staff have never been a serious problem.

The challenge we faced when we first opened is one we continue to face today: having sufficient enrollment to generate the income needed to provide services. In most private boarding schools, enrollment was a simple matter. The boarders registered by a certain date after which day students were accepted to fill the remaining classroom spots. Few exceptions were made; schools were careful to control class sizes and keep them small to maintain one of the primary benefits of a private education. Once a class was full, a school closed it to admission.

For us, enrollment was never so neat. As a young school, rarely did we have all our beds filled by the fall. We began recruiting early, but we seldom had a full house when school opened. Luckily, parents, doctors, school districts, and others would call all year and ask if we could take another child. Requests trickled in, and by May we always had more children than we began with in September.

I was pleased we received referrals and could accommodate families. And as it turned out, accepting children during the year had its benefits. Green Chimneys acquired a reputation for being flexible. When children need help, at Green Chimneys it would not be delayed simply because of an academic calendar.

Practically speaking, the additional revenue helped, and these children tended to stay for at least another year. Youngsters who were referred to us not only were the right type, but had parents who were convinced in advance of the value of the program, and these enrolling referrals brought additional ones. From all perspectives, accommodating latecomers made sense. It never occurred to me to weigh whether they were boarders or day students.

As we grew, however, I slowly acknowledged what other headmasters already knew: a school needs every bit of revenue it can generate, there are only so many spots available, and boarders generate more revenue than day students. Since we knew we would always receive some referrals of late boarders, for every empty bed, we should reserve a desk. If there were still classroom spots available after that, then we could accept day students.

This was not as easy to determine as it sounds. While I could estimate the number of latecomers based upon previous years, there was no pattern for their grade level. It was impossible to determine how many desks should be reserved in each classroom.

It proved a fruitless exercise for another reason as well. I simply couldn't bring myself to turn away day students who sought our help when I knew, at that moment, we could accommodate them. Who would help these children if we didn't? Would another semester—or an entire year—pass them by? I told myself that if and when a late boarder arrived, we would find another desk.

For many years things worked out. However, during the 1964-1965 school year, we had more requests than previous years, and the number of children jumped 30 percent to 149. Never before had we experienced such a large increase in that ten-month period. We were squeezing desks into classes and beds into dorms, and I had to admit that I had accepted a few too many students. Yet as it turned out, overcrowding was the least of our worries.

As our enrollment swelled, so did the number of children with emotional disturbances, social and behavioral problems, and learning disabilities. In addition, we found ourselves being asked to describe the type of children we would accept. After considerable thought and discussion, we were able to clarify criteria for admission. We said we preferred children who had a minimum I.Q. of one hundred and that we were prepared to work with youngsters who were mildly withdrawn and feeling aggrieved or friendless; students who misbehaved by clowning, fidgeting, and talking out of turn; or more seriously, those who often scrapped with others and might be aggressively discourteous. We would accept children whose manner or appearance was mildly eccentric or so considerable that it might cause them to be rejected by their peers as well as brain-damaged children whose problems were due to some type of neurological impairment.

The term "brain–damaged" is no longer used, however. Many parents objected to it, because they thought their children would be perceived as mentally retarded, which they were not. Eventually doctors renamed the problem "minimal brain dysfunction," but that was no better in many parents' minds. It then became known as "hyperkinetic impulsive disorder," and more recently, "attention-deficit disorder" (ADD), both of which more accurately described these ailments. Today it is known as "attention-deficit/hyperactivity disorder" (AD/HD).

As the population of children changed, patterns emerged. One was that more and more children had difficulty adjusting to the summer camp program in June and readjusting to school in September. This wasn't new; we had noticed it before but thought them isolated instances for it was a few children among many. Now that was no longer true; it was clearly more prevalent. Most children welcomed days spent playing outdoors and slipped effortlessly into that schedule, but children with special needs and challenges did not respond similarly. The change made them agitated and disagreeable for weeks. The social and behavioral problems we thought were beginning to fade suddenly resurfaced. Gradually, the children adapted, but when it came time to go back to school, their attitudes and behavior again took a turn for the worse, and it took a lot of time to settle into the new routine.

This was not completely unusual; most children had trouble settling down in the fall. In addition, some forgetting always occurred during the summer vacation. That was why our teachers—as elementary teachers everywhere did and still do today—began every September reviewing rules, good habits and practices, and subjects before beginning the new year's lessons. But unlike the neurotypical children who regrouped fairly quickly, some of our children did not. And unlike the neurotypical children whose memories we could jog, other children had regressed emotionally and intellectually. During the fall of 1965, we spent more time bringing these students back up to speed than ever before.

I realized that this had serious implications. Every day we spent recovering lost ground was a day not spent on new work. To make matters worse, the troubled children were already behind their peers, and they required more time to learn the same lessons. By the end of the year they would be even further behind. If this went on year after year, how would they ever catch up?

I began to question our program in light of these youngsters. What could we do to prevent these children from regressing? Here they were in the same surroundings all year—school in the winter, camp in the summer—with many of the same adult guardians and teachers, and still they suffered setbacks. Something wasn't working; we needed to explore alternatives. Because it was summer, did that necessarily mean that children must be on a drastically different schedule? That they must play outside every day from dawn until dusk?

With doubts about the benefits of the traditional school program for these children, I registered for classes at the Postgraduate Center for Mental Health in New York City to learn more about their disabilities. At the same time, Myra enrolled in Danbury State College, now Western Connecticut State University, to pursue a master's degree in education and psychology. We were intent on finding an answer.

What's Wrong with Summer Vacation?

In November 1965, I received a mailing from the New York State Camp Directors Association. It urged camp directors to send for a booklet, "Economy and Increased Educational Opportunity through Extended School Year Programs," which described "five plans for trimming the summer vacation period to between four and seven weeks." Then I received an announcement from the American Camping Association for a meeting on camping in New York State; the speaker would be Consultant for Rescheduling the School Year of the State Education Department Dr. George I. Thomas. In 1963 the legislature had directed the Education Department to determine the educational, social, and additional effects of lengthening the school year, and Thomas was hired to design and implement an experimental program.

I sent for the booklet and signed up for the meeting, but a heavy snowstorm prevented me from attending. So in February 1966 I wrote to Thomas and requested his help in changing to a twelve-month school from a summer camp and winter school. Thomas responded and arranged to visit the campus in April. He was interested in learning why we, a small, independent school, would consider adopting a program where we would have classes throughout the year.

When the staff and I met with Thomas, I described what we had observed and said that after reading the booklet, I began to wonder if some type of combined school and camp program could be the solution. Something that provided more structure than the present camp program but less than the regular school year, so children could transition between the two with less difficulty. While that was my main objective, I explained that there might be other benefits as well. I envisioned having time to cover more subjects and make them more meaningful for the children, and enable the children to learn without so much pressure. I also thought this would be welcomed by the gifted students who often complained they were bored by the typical camp activities.

Dr. Thomas agreed wholeheartedly and after his visit wrote:

> It was a pleasure to visit Green Chimneys for Little Folk. I found your interest in the problems of boys and girls most heartwarming and just wish that more educators would be as sympathetic to their needs as you and your staff were while I was there.
>
> As a result of our discussions I hope that you will proceed with plans to lengthen the school year with a combined school and camp program.
>
> In view of your wonderful setting and the splendid facilities available, the combination of camp and school experiences can go a long way towards furthering the natural development of good work study patterns.
>
> Your tentative plan should go a long ways towards alleviating the problems pupils and teachers have to cope with each September due to their extended break with a guided series of learning activities. The program we outlined could decrease the forgetting curve for most pupils, but more important it will allow children to acquire knowledge and skills with a minimum of pressure since your concept of the Extended School Year is based upon offering a combined enriched and broadening program to all with a minimum of acceleration except for gifted pupils.

With support from Thomas and other officials in the Education Department, in September 1966, Green Chimneys became one of six pilot schools in New York State to test the extended school year concept. We now had the equivalent of 223 school days[1] versus the standard 180, which was less than most other countries according to a study by the United Nations Educational, Scientific and Cultural Organization (UNESCO). In looking at 51 countries, UNESCO found the median length of the school year was 210 to 212 days. In Germany, Denmark, and China the norm was 230 to 240, and children in the Soviet Union attended school 228 to 234 days. The U.S. placed fiftieth with 180 days, just ahead of Italy, which was ranked last, averaging 154. This study confirmed many educators' contention that the 180-day school year was an outdated relic from our agricultural past when all hands were needed on the farm; in order for American children to compete in an increasingly global world, more of what had become their free time must be spent in school.

We revamped our program, dividing the year into three semesters: September through December, January through June, and July through August, each punctuated by a two-week break. The children needed more structure, but they also needed time off.

The daily schedule for the fall and spring semesters remained largely the same, but beginning in July 1967, the children's summer days were now divided between school and camp. We still blew whistles and wore T-shirts, but now, Monday through Friday, children pursued academics for three and a half hours every morning. After lunch there was an hour for special projects. Then the rest of the day was spent on camp activities, which, in addition to a long list of sports and recreational activities, included: art, jewelry making, ceramics, leather work, singing, dancing, dramatics, gardening, farming, animal care, and nature lore. Camp activities always went on well into the evening with everything from after-dinner swims to bicycle rides, movies, and overnight camping trips. So despite the new schedule, most children did not feel deprived.

The extended school year yielded the benefits we anticipated and then some. The summer term, it turned out, was an excellent time for new students to begin. They found it easier to adjust to their new surroundings with only a half day of classes, especially if their prior school experience had been unpleasant or difficult.

The longer school year also significantly reduced the amount of tension, anxiety, and frustration students experienced. Children with emotional issues found comfort in the academic continuity and more readily adjusted to camp activities, experiencing little or no regression. Academically challenged students had the opportunity to do remedial work at a steady pace, which brought improvement and gave them the confidence and encouragement they needed to press on. Neurotypical and gifted students liked being challenged and felt a sense of accomplishment when they learned something new. The teachers and administrators reported fewer social and behavioral problems among all the students. But best of all, when September rolled around, the children were relaxed and ready to learn.

Perhaps the most telling data came from my father and Adele who, as the school doctor and nurse, ran the clinic. They often saw children try to avoid class (among other activities) by coming into the clinic and complaining they did not feel well or had mysterious stomach pains. By the end of the first combined school and camp session, however, the clinic had no such cases to report. Not one child had tried to skip a class.

The extended year proved equally satisfying for the teachers. In prior years, many stayed on during the summer months and served as camp counselors. While they enjoyed this, teaching was their first love and what they knew best. The prospect of spending more time in that role thrilled them and enticed other teachers who had previously worked elsewhere for the summer to remain at Green Chimneys. It also proved helpful to new teachers joining the faculty; they found it easier to adapt during a period that required less daily preparation and was somewhat less demanding than a full teaching day. But it was the students who ultimately were the real beneficiaries. The new schedule inspired the teachers to make the most of the extra time, and they built creative learning activities around summertime events.

While Thomas and the Education Department supported our efforts, they were unable to provide us with funding to make the transition. Changing to a year-round school meant hiring additional teachers and recreational staff, and purchasing equipment and materials in order to design and create a new curriculum. But I was optimistic that a single, annual enrollment that combined school and camp would smooth our cash flow. So one year later, in September 1967, we formally adopted the extended school year program and became the first New York State nonprofit, independent boarding and day school to do so. I do believe that part of my optimism was based on our experiences over the years. Many times the outlook seemed impossible and dismal, but we always had come through.

In subsequent years, some public and private schools in various states implemented the extended school year program as well, but the National Education Association's prediction that all schools would include some type of extended year plan by the 1970s never came true. Today, the majority of American children still have ten months of cramming followed by a ten- to twelve-week hiatus.

When the booklet on extending the school year was released by then Commissioner of Education James E. Allen, the *Long Island Press* wrote, "Allen suggested lengthening the school year several years ago. At that time he was besieged by protests from resort owners who saw their businesses jeopardized. The department is braced for a similar onslaught in the event it recommends any of the plans now under study."

As the department anticipated, it happened again. Resorts and other vacation businesses lobbied heavily against extending the year for fear they would lose money. However, they weren't the only ones against the plan. The United Federation of Teachers opposed it for fear it might create conflict between teachers who taught in the extended year programs and those who did not. Superintendents and principals predicted staffing nightmares. And some child care experts and parents were against it for fear that children would be subject to pressure eleven months of the year rather than ten, and eventually compelled to complete in eleven or twelve years what they currently did in thirteen.

While their fears were not unfounded, the opponents concentrated on squashing the plan rather than exploring potential solutions to address their concerns. This was too bad, for they missed what I thought was the real opportunity: curriculum reform. Many assumed that extending the school year into the summer simply meant more of the same, but that did not have to be true. School districts, administrators, and teachers could have seized the opportunity to rethink their programs and create a more balanced schedule of innovative programs that educated the whole child. A mix of academic programs plus opportunities for recreation, culture, arts, work, and prevocational experience would have given children the chance to learn steadily and grow into well-rounded adults.

This would have been a boon for all children, but especially for those with troubles, as our experience proved. The extended school year let us bring to bear whatever remediation was necessary and ensure that it was done continually and without pressure. No longer was the summer a period during which the children regressed and forgot so much of what they had learned. For us, it became a period during which many students continued to make steady progress while maintaining important skills and work-study habits, and others learned simply for the sake and joy of learning.

Innovative Ideas: Creating a Better Future

> What an exciting time it was! . . . The phones rang sometimes daily around the country with hurried consultations about what happened when children arranged pictures to "tell stories," or shot pictures and used them as a basis for talk. . . . Thanks to Sam and Myra and their responsive staff, "we" learned that a child whose tongue is locked for emotional reasons, even for weeks or months, may suddenly talk about a picture story he has made. "We" found that a child categorized as dull, using verbal tests, may be bright and expressive when using pictures.
>
> -Jack Debes, "Visual Literacy Newsletter," December 1977

In the fall of 1966, Milton Willenson, a parent of one of our students, who knew I was always on the lookout for new methods, approached me with an idea. A founding member of the National Academy of Photography and director of the Germain School of Photography in New York City, Milton suggested giving the children cameras and letting them take pictures. Photography, he explained, will direct the children's attention to one subject at a time, require them to focus, and thereby make them more perceptive of the world around them. It is also an art form—just as some children have taken to dance, music, or poetry to express themselves, some might find their voices through pictures. And it will help the children's teachers and caretakers to better understand them; looking at their photographs, they will see the world through the children's eyes.

I was intrigued, so Milton arranged a meeting with two other members of the National Academy of Photography: Director of Program Development at the W.E. Upjohn Institute for Employment Research Dr. Herbert Striner and Photography Editor of *The New York Times* Jacob Deschin. They, too, saw the potential benefits and felt they were too great to ignore. They encouraged me to develop a plan for an experimental photography program, which I did with their help. Then, with the plan in hand, they took me to meet Advisor of School and Youth Services Jack Debes, from the Consumer Markets Division of Eastman Kodak in Rochester, New York.

Debes was impressed with our work and said that he would support a pilot project. It turned out that he was doing research on something he called "visual literacy." He theorized that if youngsters learned how to interpret images, it would improve their ability to read.

With Debes' help we secured enough cameras and film from Eastman Kodak and General Aniline & Film (GAF)/ Ansco for all of our second and third graders, plus a commitment from Arax Photographic of Poughkeepsie, New York, to develop the students' pictures. With materials in hand, we launched the pilot in July 1967 just as our first combined school-camp session was getting underway. We taught the youngsters how to use the cameras and then turned them loose; they were free to photograph whatever they chose. Since one of the reasons for the pilot was to assess if photography appealed to the children as a creative outlet, we decided not to establish goals, set parameters, or suggest subjects. We didn't want to influence the results; we wanted to see what the children would do on their own.

What an education it turned out to be—for students and faculty alike. The photos spoke volumes without the children saying a word. A high percentage of students photographed the animals, which made me realize how important the farm was to them and inspired me to expand it in subsequent years. Some took pictures of only inanimate objects or people's backs. Others focused on their friends and teachers. Still others concentrated on the landscape or vehicles and machinery.

Yet when asked about their photos, the children could hardly contain themselves. Hands waved in the air, "Me! Me!" a few called out. They all wanted to be first. We went around the room, and they all talked proudly and at length about their photos when their turn came. When their classmates were describing their photos, they listened intently and then commented in great detail. In the following days, they returned to their pictures over and over again; photography let them study their subjects at their leisure.

It was the excitement of one child in particular, however, that convinced me that this pilot should be adopted and made a permanent part of the curriculum. He had been depressed and uncommunicative ever since arriving months earlier. But without my prompting, he eagerly described the mallard duck he had photographed. If photography could reach him, I thought, perhaps it could reach others.

That fall, Eastman Kodak conducted photography workshops at Green Chimneys for the entire faculty, and by the summer of 1968, the photography program was in full swing. It now included all grades and a motion-picture camera with which we encouraged the children to experiment. Again, the results were both rewarding and revealing. One boy had a friend film him as another friend pushed him on the merry-go-round, slowly at first, and then faster and faster, producing a vivid flash of color and movement. When asked about his film, the child explained that it showed how he feels when things begin to close in on him.

The children weren't the only ones experimenting; the teachers did so as well. They devised tests for the younger students, such as asking them to arrange their photos in some order or sequence so as to evaluate their logical abilities or how well they understood their subjects; they gave some of the older children photo-story assignments; and to the eighth graders, they assigned the production of a full-length film as a class project.

Myra was the brave one who agreed to be the advisor on the movie project. An experienced teacher, she also had some experience in filmmaking. Yet despite her experience, early on in the project even she was a little overwhelmed by their excitement. They constantly peppered her with ideas and questions ranging from the topic they should pick to story line development and production techniques. She made suggestions here and there, but mostly she pushed them to talk things through, evaluate options, and make decisions as a group. That was just as important for them to learn as how to write a script or operate the camera. The children had worked in groups before, but usually someone—a teacher, counselor, farmhand—was directing their work with a particular outcome in mind. This was different. What they did, how they did it, and when they did it were completely up to them.

The subject they chose was the experience of a newcomer, and the film began with a boy arriving at Green Chimneys carrying his bags and his hostility. It then depicted him acting out his resentment by refusing to do his homework and getting into trouble. At one point the students staged a fistfight, and the simulation turned into the real thing. The movie ended showing the student at a crossroads, which was symbolic of the children's realization that they have choices—their futures are in their hands.

Over the years, I have come to realize that while we may not cure, if we can interrupt what is happening that may be enough to see the child accept a new path, a new direction.

I am not sure who was more proud—the children or me. They tackled the project with great enthusiasm. They selected a topic that hit home for everyone at the school. They pulled together and worked as a team from concept through production; every eighth grader had an important role. They applied themselves, learning the technical and creative skills required to make a film. They even turned the fistfight into a positive experience by participating in a productive soul-searching session. It was evident that they felt special and privileged for having been chosen and wanted to do their best in return. When the movie was finished, they showed it to their peers, teachers, and parents, and their self-worth seemed to rise with every viewing. They now knew the satisfaction that comes from turning an idea into reality, the pride of being part of a great team effort, and the joy of being able to share a special accomplishment with others.

In August 1968 Jack Debes invited a group of people who were interested in visual communication to Rochester to plan a conference on visual literacy. I was honored to be among those he invited and pleased that he asked me to be the executive secretary of the conference. Seven months later, in March of 1969, three hundred and fifty people from various disciplines convened and presented papers that discussed their theories of visual literacy and suggested potential applications. It was the first national conference on visual literacy, and it was such a success that we immediately initiated plans for a second conference to be held the following year. With this unexpectedly large gathering we had launched what in 1975 formally became known as the International Visual Literacy Association.

As Debes remarked in the *Visual Literacy Newsletter* many years later, it was an exciting time. Photography was now a part of our curriculum, and the teachers and children were pushing the boundaries. We began to accept visual essays. We encouraged the students to use art materials, typewriters, and other tools to enhance their written assignments. No longer were the children solely passive recipients of information. They were becoming active participants in its creation, and with that there was a noticeable change. Children who time and again displayed impatience or the need for immediate gratification would spend hours planning their projects, painstakingly arranging and rearranging their photos, and critically assessing their work afterward, adding the finishing touches. They expended great effort to make it just right. In addition, children who seemed incapable of working with others managed to find a way when the assignment involved pictures.

It was an exciting time for another reason as well: Green Chimneys' faculty was becoming more attuned to the individual learning styles of the students. Teachers, administrators, local and state education officials—we all knew a great deal about learning, but we had been ignoring the fact that not all children learned the same way, at the same rate, at the same time, or with the same motivation. Understanding how different children learned, it seemed to me, was a step in the right direction.

I became convinced that there was no one approach that could educate all children. If we were truly interested in having all children reach their potential, we would have to explore alternative methods to find the ones that unlock their abilities and talents, that encourage them—inspire them—to participate in their education, which should happen as early as possible. Nursery school was not too soon.

In May of 1969 I had the privilege to discuss our programs and my conclusions with the Executive Office of Education in Washington, D.C. I also began speaking on these topics at various conferences and seminars, and had articles published in *Audiovisual Instruction and School Media Quarterly*. But, in fact, I still had a lot to learn.

As we continued our photography program and assigned more challenging projects, it became apparent that the children couldn't always or automatically convey what they had in mind. Often, what they were trying to "say" with pictures wasn't "heard" by the viewer. It was evident that we needed to teach them how to express what they wanted to communicate. In addition, a misunderstanding on the part of the viewer was not necessarily the fault of the photographer; some children had difficulty interpreting images. Just as we taught children how to read, we needed to teach them how to see, and we also realized that we had to help the children learn how to discriminate.

This brought up another point: while many images were meant to stand alone, more often they were part of something else—articles, advertisements, cartoons, books, television shows—and accompanied by music, sound effects, and words, whether written or spoken, to convey an idea. Photography brought visual literacy to my attention, and I quickly realized that visual literacy was more than the ability to take and understand photos.

I introduced classes that studied and critiqued movies, television shows, commercials, and advertisements, and examined how different mediums were used for different messages. When we gave assignments or engaged the children in creative projects, we began asking them to consider not just the content of their messages, but the medium as well. Posters, mobiles, short films, sculptures, recordings—what would best convey their messages? Finally, we abandoned visual literacy as a separate subject and made it a part of every class. Math, science, history, English, health—visual literacy applied to all, for it seemed to me that we were fast becoming a multimedia world, and it was for that eventuality that we had to prepare the children.

As we encouraged the children to work with combinations of elements in different mediums and in all their classes, their work became more creative. For those who were known mostly for their faults, this was often the breakthrough they needed. Classmates, teachers, parents, and others began to notice them for their talents, and they gained some self-confidence and self-esteem. Their interest in school began to grow, and their relationships with others improved. For the first time, they were having a worthwhile experience at school.

Today we have SMART Boards (interactive whiteboards) and computers. Our students and teachers have worked with advisors from the Jacob Burns Film Center and Media Arts Lab in Westchester County to learn animation, prepare cartoons, and make videos. At the thirty-ninth annual Putnam County 4-H Fair, Jerry Newell's class debuted their animated film, *Now Playing: Green Chimneys in Motion.* According to the judges, "We were blown away by the work you all did. Amazing!!! Movie was educational and entertaining. We loved it!" Hitachi and the Jacob Burns Film Center made it all possible by their support of the project.

We reached out to corporate friends and personal relationships, welcoming creative concepts that we could bring to our children. For example, recently, through our relationship with Nokia, our students and selected teachers got to experience The Mobile Institute, a creative program designed to make mobile handheld devices—like cell phones—valuable classroom learning tools. Through Nokia, the Pearson Foundation trained our teachers and then our students, teaching them how to make video stories right in the palm of their hands. The student films had a red carpet debut at our school, and the children beamed with pride.

Visual literacy, as we know today, is the ability to create visual images that communicate to others and interpret visual images that others create. The visually literate can comprehend the ideas conveyed by images, put them in context, apply critical thinking, and draw a conclusion. This ability, as we discovered, is not necessarily innate.

◆ ◆ ◆

While visual literacy was innovative on our part, it paled in comparison to Green Chimneys' being in the forefront on sex education in the schools. Very often at the center of the controversy was Dr. Mary Calderone, president and executive director of the Sexuality Information and Education Council of the United States (SIECUS), an organization she co-founded in 1964. Its purpose was to address what she saw as widespread ignorance of sexuality. Having been the medical director of Planned Parenthood since 1953, she was eminently qualified on the matter.

Under her direction, SIECUS took a practical and sensible approach to sex education. One of its precepts, for example, was that sex education should not be used to force sexual standards upon its students, but rather to give them the information they need to make their own responsible decisions. It was the approach I took when I introduced a sex education class for the older children around the same time, so it was gratifying to have an authority on the topic express the same opinion.

In 1966 the National Association of Independent Schools held their first Institute on Sex Education. The purpose of the conference was to examine various approaches to effective sex education and explore the role independent schools should play in teaching the subject. They invited Calderone to be the keynote speaker and sponsored workshops that focused on what educators should teach, how, and when, in order for young people to make choices with wisdom, responsibility, and respect for others.

I attended and found Calderone's address and the conference on sex education highly informative. Afterward, I made the literature available to the rest of the staff and decided that other faculty members besides me should learn to teach sex education. Adele, Myra, and Eddie Gross, a science teacher, agreed to undertake the effort, and I had them attend an intensive, week-long seminar sponsored by the National Association of Independent Schools at the University of Maryland. I also began exploring ways to educate the public; I felt it was important for parents to understand why schools should assume at least partial responsibility for this type of instruction.

A year later, in May 1967 and in cooperation with Dr. Norman Vincent Peale and Ruth Stafford Peale's Guideposts Associates, which had offices in Carmel and Pawling, New York, Green Chimneys sponsored the conference "Sex, Morality, and Ethics During the Formative Years." I asked Calderone to be the keynote speaker. More than three hundred people attended the meeting on our campus, including medical, legal, and education professionals as well as religious and community leaders. They came from New York's Putnam, Dutchess, Rockland, and Westchester counties, and Fairfield County, Connecticut. Everyone listened with interest as Calderone urged attendees to discuss sex frankly at home, in school, and in the community to eliminate fears and misinformation, and to begin this discussion at an early age and not wait until the children were in ninth grade.

The debate did not end there, though I did think, perhaps naïvely, that such forums would help the majority of people conclude that sex education was needed in schools. Instead, the debate ensued locally and nationally for years to come.

In the meantime, we continued to offer classes. I was sure that to exclude sex education was to foster concern, uncertainty, insecurity, and confusion among the children rather than provide them with logical answers to logical questions. I did not want to usurp the role of the parents and religious authorities, but as an independent boarding school, we had a unique obligation. We were the children's teachers, but more importantly, we were *in loco parentis*, a role that made special demands. If we were to oversee their growth and development, and instill everything from manners to values, surely we could not overlook educating the students about sex. Besides, it was simply unrealistic to think we could ignore the subject. We lived on a farm. The animals brought forth little ones on a regular basis, and the children wanted to know how that happened.

◆ ◆ ◆

> L. R.: Green Chimneys is a lot of fun. You can play with the animals. You can ride on horses. We get to go to school and play with toys. You can play with toys when your school work is done. The people make me feel good. They take care of me very well. We go on a lot of trips. I am happy to be here.

Notes

1 Today we have 210 school days as opposed to the standard 180 days.

Chapter VII

Fiscal Challenges, Politics, and Policies

> Just in case you think the founder of Green Chimneys got any preferential treatment around here, Bella and I had our offices in the old milk house. We were there for many years. The milk house had no bathroom, and I was told that it would be impossible to add one. Bella and I had to run out to other offices all day long. I laugh because no sooner had Bella and I moved into a new office, than somehow a bathroom was able to be added to the old milk house. Thank goodness, as it has been used for a multitude of purposes over these many years.
>
> -Samuel B. Ross, Jr.

Seeking Sources of Income

I had planned to build a new dormitory, construct a new classroom building for kindergarten through third grade, and renovate the old one to be used by the administrative staff who was severely hampered by their working conditions. By 1966 administrative staff offices were spread across two buildings with the mimeograph and copy machines in a third; both offices were crowded, and neither had space for the staff to spread out and work on large projects, such as the school newsletter or bulletin; business records were in one office and student records were in another with many floating in between, making record keeping, mailings, and purchasing frustrating, complicated, and time-consuming. Even the phone system did not work correctly.

As the year continued, our needs continued to mount. With our rapid growth and more than 160 students, we were straining the limits of our water resources; we needed a new well and a new water-storage system. We had outgrown the library, and we needed a gymnasium-auditorium that we could use during the day, not just after 3 p.m.

Years before we had taken the largest space we had—the second floor of the big barn—and made it into a gym. We thought it an excellent plan, for not only would it provide enough room for physical education classes, indoor sports, and dance lessons, but also for three hundred chairs; it could double as our auditorium.

What we had not anticipated was the noise. Below the gym were classrooms, and soon the teachers found themselves shouting to be heard above the clamor of children running, jumping, and bouncing balls overhead. It was an untenable situation, so we banned activity in the gym until classes were over for the day. It was a tolerable compromise in the beginning, but as we grew, and particularly during the winter months, scheduling became a nightmare. There were simply too many children and too many activities, and they couldn't all be squeezed in after 3 p.m. It also didn't completely solve the problem. Along with classrooms, some of the administration's offices were downstairs, including mine. Every afternoon, around 3:30 p.m., I would begin to hear *click click click click click click click*—slowly at first, then faster and louder. It was the sound of girls and boys tap dancing above my head. Believe me, it was more than anyone could endure.

So to the original list of major projects I added a well, water-storage system, library, and gym. There also were a myriad of smaller renovations needed as well, such as installing new lockers, expanding the bathroom facilities, buying a walk-in freezer, replacing laundry and dishwashing equipment, and painting the buildings. Many independent schools billed families annual capital improvement charges of several hundred dollars to meet such needs, but with so many of our parents struggling to pay the tuition, I wanted to keep contributions voluntary.

When we were not within sight of our goal by May, I began to seek funding from foundations. What I learned was discouraging. Grants for private elementary schools were practically nonexistent as many foundations considered them a luxury and, therefore, something for which parents should pay. In those days, where children went to grade school did not determine where they went to high school. This was not the case with independent secondary schools, however. They often paved the way for students to get into a good college. In the eyes of many foundations, private high schools played a critical role in children's futures, and the foundations were more inclined to award the schools grants.

Of the foundations that provided grants to elementary schools, many considered alumni donations an important criterion for receiving a grant. Unfortunately, considering our age, it would be years before our alumni could contribute—most of them were still in high school and college. These foundations also wanted all parents and friends to demonstrate their faith in and commitment to the school by making a donation; 100 percent participation was a prerequisite for receiving a grant. In the end, the foundations turned me down.

Then I got a call from the Edwin Gould Foundation for Children. They had reviewed my application and asked if I would make an appointment to meet with them. I was optimistic. Established in 1923 to help underprivileged children, it seemed to me that our organizations had similar goals and intentions. I met with Martha Innes, the secretary of the board of the Foundation. During our conversation, she mentioned having some friends in Brewster named Bella and Mike Meyer. "Bella's my secretary!" I exclaimed. With that, she opened the door behind her and introduced me to Schuyler Meyer, the president. We had a wonderful meeting, and I left sure that Green Chimneys would receive a grant. After several months and many more meetings, what I received was a consulting assignment.

Money was money, however, or so I reasoned at the time. If I could earn enough from the Edwin Gould Foundation and not have to draw a salary from Green Chimneys, that also would help us financially. So in January of 1968, I became the Foundation's Director of Program Development, responsible for vetting applicants for funding opportunities. It would prove to be a unique opportunity and last until 1980, longer than I ever imagined.

The income wasn't enough to solve our financial dilemma, but still I was grateful. We were facing difficult times, and the future according to Carl Andrews, headmaster of the Collegiate School in New York City, was not bright for many private boarding schools. In March 1968 he and other headmasters spoke at the National Association of Independent Schools' annual conference. As *Education News* reported the following month, Andrews opened his remarks by saying, "Some of the schools represented in this room will have ceased to exist by 1978." He then went on to say, "The signs of financial strain are coming with increased intensity. The problem is acute. The future of the independent school is not certain."

Others painted an equally bleak picture. Howard Jones, president of Northfield Mount Hermon School in Massachusetts, told attendees to "expect a five percent compounded increase in costs each year for the next decade." He asked if we were charging enough and making regular increases to meet our costs. Andrews noted that teacher salaries had "increased 50 percent in the last ten years" and would continue to rise, albeit more slowly.

It also was evident that many headmasters were feeling pressure from their public school counterparts, which were making improvements now that state and federal aid was increasing. Edgar Sanford, headmaster of the Charles Wright Academy in Tacoma, Washington, warned that "the public schools will continue to improve greatly" and "may narrow or close completely the gap in superiority—our only reason for existence." As I told the parents in our newsletter the following month, "One cannot help but feel gloomy faced with such thoughts."

If we were entering this period from a position of strength I would have felt better, but we were already operating at a disadvantage. Our highest teacher salary was lower than the starting salary for a teacher with a bachelor's degree at our local public school as well as the surrounding areas, yet many of our teachers held their master's degree. In addition, many of the women who worked in the kitchen, laundry, and dorms were with us because we picked them up in the morning and took them home at night. If these folks had a second car they would have been able to find work at a higher rate of pay.

But salaries were not the only issue. If we were going to continue to be competitive with other private schools, if we wanted the type of program that produced academic results, we needed to reduce the size of some of our classes, which meant hiring more teachers. We had families who needed scholarships if they were going to continue sending their children to Green Chimneys. And we had debts to pay down from previous projects.

I called a meeting of the Board of Trustees to discuss the situation. By this time, the Board had grown. In addition to my father, Adele, Myra, Herman Levine, our accountant, and me, it included Louis Otten, a New York City Family Court judge who owned a second home in Brewster, and Edi Wallach, who was not only the generous sponsor of our annual Independence Day fireworks, but a local investment banker.[1]

In view of our financial straits, the headmasters' predictions, and the poor outcome of our 20th Anniversary Fund Drive, the Board decided to make some changes. For the first time, we instituted annual tuition increases. We began charging parents for the psychiatric or psychological services their children received. We also followed the example set by other schools and billed parents annually $100 for the Development Fund and $50 for the Annual Giving Fund. The Development Fund would provide monies for new buildings and renovations, including equipment. The Annual Giving Fund would provide aid for staff development, library improvements, the awards program, in-school cultural activities, and the athletic program. Naturally, some parents were upset as it created a hardship for them, but most saw that it was necessary and took it in stride.

That was for the years ahead, however. It would not help fund our current list of projects, two of which were underway. I had convinced the Board to begin construction and continue until we ran out of money. I hoped that some progress—even digging a hole in the ground—might encourage more parents and friends to make a donation. The Board agreed, and I authorized the excavation for the classroom building to begin. I also signed a contract for the well and water-storage system. The contractors were not used to doing such work piecemeal, but they agreed. In those days, businesses took the long view and considered more than just the job at hand; they wanted to have us as a customer for years to come.

Again, the results were not what I had hoped for—but they were enough to get us to the next step, which was good enough. Late that spring we received a few gifts earmarked for specific projects, and with those in hand, I went to the bank for everything but the gym-auditorium and the library. Those would have to wait. The bank approved a loan, and the work began in earnest. Later still, a few foundations granted us moderate sums ranging from $250 to $2,000—every little bit helped. Of course, by this time it was apparent that we needed a new maintenance shop and a public-address system. It was a never-ending cycle.

Politics and Policies

Charging for psychiatric and psychological services was not a change we made lightly. By 1968 the number in our care who needed these services had increased dramatically and so did our costs. In addition to a staff psychologist, we now employed two psychiatrists who spent three days a week, and sometimes more, providing individual and group therapy. We simply could no longer afford to provide these services without recouping the expense.

Our reputation for helping children was part of the reason why we had more youngsters who needed these services. Another part was that the children tended to have not just one problem, but several. Times had changed and increasingly parents sent their children to Green Chimneys due to behavioral problems at home and in school. After observing the children, however, we suspected their problems were more complex, and testing usually confirmed our hunches: learning disabilities, emotional disturbances, and neurological disorders were the root causes.

The times, too, played a large role. The 1960s began with John F. Kennedy and a presidential platform that included urban poverty and mental retardation; Kennedy's sister, Rosemary, was mentally challenged, and that spurred his interest in the condition. Under his administration, Congress passed the Juvenile Delinquency and Youth Offenses Control Act, which funded programs to reduce dropout rates, improve reading skills, and counsel low-income students in urban public schools; the Manpower Development and Training Act, which included support for high school vocational education programs; the Maternal and Child Health and Mental Retardation Planning Bill, which funded programs for the mentally challenged; and the Mental Retardation Facilities and Community Mental Health Centers Construction Act, which established the Division of Handicapped Children and Youth under the U.S. Office of Education and funded the construction of new buildings for the disabled.

President Johnson, Kennedy's successor, went further. As part of Johnson's "War on Poverty," his administration worked to increase federal aid to education, and in 1965 Congress passed the Elementary and Secondary Education Act (ESEA). This act granted aid directly to state-operated schools and institutions for the education of children with disabilities. This was considered landmark legislation at the time, because it was the first federal grant program that specifically addressed children with disabilities.

The following year, Congress took the grant program a step further and authorized that the aid be sent directly to local schools rather than to state-operated schools or institutions. In addition, it established the Bureau of Education for the Handicapped (BEH) to administer and monitor the federal program. This aid may have been on Edgar Sanford's mind when he warned us that public schools were improving and might surpass independent and private ones.

Congress didn't stop there. The ESEA amendment of 1968 established a set of programs that supplemented and supported the expansion and improvement of special education services. While these programs were not permanent, Congress has continually ratified and often expanded them. For the first time, public schools could apply for federal grants to improve their educational programs and library resources for disadvantaged students, and to develop innovative solutions to educational problems.

These laws and the discussions around them did much to raise the public's awareness and empathy for children with disabilities. At the same time, the medical and mental health professions' knowledge and understanding of these disabilities was progressing. They had identified more categories of mental, neurological, emotional, and behavioral disorders, and testing methods had improved so doctors, psychiatrists, and psychologists could more accurately diagnose children's disabilities. It was still a long way from where we are today, but it encouraged parents to seek answers for their children's problems.

What was happening simultaneously at the state level, however, had the most dramatic effect on us. In the mid-1960s, New York, New Jersey, and Connecticut legislatures enacted bills that provided grants to families whose children could not be educated in the public school. For parents who knew their children were not learning in public school but could not afford to send them to a private one, this was a promising development. Many other states passed similar legislation as well, but the actions of our own state and those of our neighbors had the most significant effect.

Encouraged by the change, many parents whose children had learning difficulties took them to psychiatrists and psychologists for testing. Due to advances in the field, psychiatrists and psychologists were able to diagnose various emotional, neurological, and psychiatric disorders better than ever before.

New Jersey and Connecticut had fairly streamlined and generous programs. Parents who felt their child was not receiving an appropriate education, with a diagnosis in hand, could appeal to the Board of Education and request approval for their children to attend a private school. If the Board agreed that the public school did not have a suitable program, the state would allocate enough education and welfare dollars to pay the full cost of the child's tuition, room, and board at a private school that could address the child's needs.

New York, on the other hand, did not make it so easy. First, the process parents had to follow to show need for special education at a private school for their child depended on whether they lived in New York City or elsewhere in the state. Second, the public school had to agree that it could not educate a child before the Board of Education would approve placement at a private school. Third, if the Board sanctioned private placement, the state gave parents only a stipend of up to $2,000, which could be used only for school expenses, such as tuition; it could not be used for related expenses, such as room and board. Unfortunately, many parents came to the end of this long and arduous road only to realize that the stipend did not cover the cost of private school; their children would have to stay in public school.

New York City residents had a last recourse: if they felt that they could prove that the incremental cost for private school created an undue hardship, they could sue the Board of Education in family court. If the court agreed, it would authorize that welfare funds be used to pay the remaining expenses. It was an ordeal that deterred even the most persistent of parents. What was more discouraging still was that while parents waded through the red tape, their child sat in public schools, for months and sometimes for years, without the attention they needed or deserved.

We received a fair number of applications from New York parents and referrals from New York City Family Court, but we received far more from New Jersey where the hurdles for receiving state aid were not set so high. I did not think much about it at the time—that so many children had serious problems or that so many of them came from New Jersey. But soon, there was no doubt that we had become a special education school largely for New Jersey children.

As if to underscore that point, in the fall of 1968 I had the pleasure of welcoming one of our earliest students to the Green Chimneys faculty. Ken Wilkoff had first come to Green Chimneys when he was five years old. It was a typical situation for that time: his mother was a single parent who found it impossible to work and raise a child. Ken stayed with us for six years and then returned every summer afterward, first as a camper, and later as a camp counselor and riding instructor, although he did whatever needed to be done. Now he was a college graduate and about to become Green Chimneys' speech teacher. I had explained to Ken that things had changed; the children had problems that they did not have years ago. It did not diminish his enthusiasm in the least; he was ready and willing. As any teacher will attest to, you cannot help but take pride in the achievements of your children, and I was proud of Ken for the many things that he had accomplished, but it is particularly gratifying when they follow in your footsteps.

When one door opens, another one closes. That is how many parents felt during this time. Finally, their child's problems had been diagnosed. Their states had not only acknowledged that their child could not be educated in public school, but agreed to pay, in part or in full, for a private day or boarding school education. After years of battling to get help for their children, parents were on the verge of succeeding only to find that their children were not welcome at many private boarding schools. Headmaster after headmaster would insist that they were not equipped to handle children whose behavior or abilities deviated from the norm.

This was unfortunate, not only for the parents and children, but as it turned out, for the schools as well. At a time when many private boarding schools felt financially strained and rightfully concerned about their futures, they refused to change. Had they been open to expanding their missions and meeting the needs of the market, they might still be in business today. Instead, many found themselves forced to merge or close in the years that followed.

Unlike other headmasters, I had never shied away from accepting children with problems, so we were prepared to help these families. By now, not only did we have experience dealing with special needs children, but we were educated about their disabilities and challenges, and trained to work with them.

I had been sending the faculty and staff to conferences, seminars, and workshops since the school opened; I felt we all had a professional responsibility to stay abreast of the happenings in our field and seek out new ideas, methods, and materials. In recent years, however, as we enrolled more and more troubled children, I expanded the number and types of conferences the faculty and staff attended to include ones sponsored by the Adults and Children with Learning and Developmental Disabilities (ACLD), the Association of New York State Educators of the Emotionally Disturbed (ANYSEED), the Council for Exceptional Children (CEC), and the Mid-Hudson Psychological Association.

Sometimes in connection with these conferences and sometimes independently, I also had the faculty and staff attend seminars and workshops. Again, as our work expanded, so did the range of topics. Now they frequently focused on working with learning-disabled children, counseling and guiding emotionally-disturbed children, diagnosing and reaching perceptually-handicapped children, rehabilitating children at independent boarding schools, handling children with epilepsy, working with brain-damaged children, and the like. In addition, many faculty members were taking graduate courses in special education.

Not everyone could attend everything, of course, so we set up in-service training sessions, and those who attended the conferences, seminars, and workshops shared what they learned with the rest of us. The result was a knowledgeable and enthusiastic faculty and staff.

An Ideal Environment: Therapeutic Milieus

A note from a former student, July 2010

> I hope all is well. Every [day] continues to be productive and [I] wanted to inform you of a wonderful experience which I volunteered for on Monday.
>
> My colleague and I were invited as guest speakers to a place that was similar but stricter than GC [Green Chimneys] and the other places which I have been to. The purpose of this was to try and steer these troubled youth into a more prosperous life than what they are currently faced with.
>
> It went so well and I just wanted to share the experience with you. . .

During this time I also had come to realize that private boarding school was an ideal environment for children with special needs. For years, some education and child care experts had held that far from being simply educational alternatives, private boarding schools were therapeutic milieus. From my own experience, I knew this was true. As we worked over the years with children who had learning disabilities and the emotional, neurological, and psychiatric disturbances that went with them, patterns had emerged, and I realized what it was about boarding school that made such a difference for these children.

Crucial to these children's success was the boarding school daily routine. It included everything they had at home—school, homework, recreation, free time—but was more structured. Meals were served at the same time every day, and everyone always ate together. Homework was a priority, and teachers were always on hand to help, including Myra and me; at least two or three children would find their way to our kitchen table daily with questions on one subject or another. The children also knew that the teachers, Myra, and I would follow up. Did they finish all their math problems? What book did they choose for their book report? Did they want to be quizzed on their vocabulary list? After-school activities ran the gamut from sports and clubs to music and dance lessons. There was something for everyone to do, and everyone did something. Even free time was scheduled into the program—enough for the children to appreciate it, never so much that they grew bored.

The daily routine also included something not every child was used to doing: chores. This was quite evident as many did not know how to do even the simplest of tasks or the names of ordinary implements. I remember finding a child pulling a broom behind him, discouraged that it didn't seem to be working very well but unsure of what to do differently. "Do you know what you have there?" I asked him. He shook his head. "It's a push broom," I continued. "You sweep by pushing it ahead of you." You could see the light go on as he began sweeping correctly.

Some parents were amazed to hear that their children were doing chores. It was another benefit of boarding school: children tended to fall in line. They quickly learned that they could not wheedle their way out of their responsibilities as they had with their parents, and as for the age-old whine—"Why me?"—they couldn't very well use that when all their peers had jobs. In fact, being part of the group was often an incentive; they would do something they didn't like rather than be left out.

We also were not rigid. We didn't have to be. If a child didn't want to slop the pigs, he or she could feed the chickens or goats, muck out the horse stalls, pull weeds in the garden, pick up papers on the grounds, sweep the dining room, set the table, or any number of other tasks that needed to be done. With more than 150 children and adults living together on campus, there was no shortage of chores from which to choose.

We could have hired more staff so the children didn't have any chores to do, but they would have been shortchanged. A former student once recalled, "Two or three of us used to get up every morning at 5:30 to feed the animals. I wasn't keen about getting up at that hour and during the winter it was freezing, but for some reason I always did it. We were doing work that otherwise a staff member would have had to do and I felt they appreciated that. And we were doing something none of the others kids were doing. That made us feel special."

Who would have thought chores would make children feel appreciated and special? But they did. The tasks also improved the children's images of themselves and their self-esteem, which changed their attitudes. Increasingly, children arrived at Green Chimneys apathetic or hostile to learning because they had so many failures. They did not think of themselves as capable of doing anything, and they saw no sense in trying only to fail again. Doing chores taught them otherwise. They realized that there were some things they could do and other things that they could learn. We were careful to gauge the tasks of newcomers so that they experienced some success early on, because once they felt a sense of accomplishment, their anxiety lessened and we could begin working with them on their problems.

I may not have conveyed this to the parents, but in the scheme of things, getting the children to do chores was the easy part. Addressing their problems, on the other hand, was when the real work began.

Either before or after a new child arrived on campus, we gave him or her psychiatric, psychological, and medical evaluations, and academic, I.Q., and speech tests. We did this even if such reports were included in the child's files, for we often found misdiagnoses or discrepancies. We then created a therapeutic strategy for each child, which often included medication as well as group or individual therapy, and an individual academic plan.

Many children were already on medication when they arrived; others started a regimen after being assessed by our psychiatrists. Sometimes it was the only way to help children cope with severe neurological or psychiatric disorders. Other times it was temporary; the medication made them more receptive to therapy, and able to work with the teachers and staff who were trying to help them. As they showed signs of overcoming their difficulties, the psychiatrists reduced the dosage or gradually weaned them off the medication.

Having my father and Adele on campus made providing medication for the children possible, for it not only involved dispensing daily medication to more than one hundred children, but monitoring the effects and reporting back to the respective doctors and psychiatrists. When a drug had negative side effects, the physician would tweak the dosage or choose a new drug. My father and Adele would then carefully compare the effects of the new prescription to the previous one. It was a big job with a lot of responsibility.

When it came to academics, faculty members were allowed to be creative with their teaching methods. Being a private school, we were not required to choose a particular approach and implement it consistently across all grades and all subjects. We had more freedom, so instead I directed the faculty and staff to use whatever techniques and materials best suited each child: adapt traditional methods, experiment with new ones, try combinations of the two. If one textbook does not work, get another. Keep trying until something works. The method and books were not important; helping each child was. I felt we needed to remember that we could be creative, thanks to our independence.

I remember one youngster who had severe emotional problems. Despite the fact that he had an I.Q. of 165, he suffered from "school phobia." He habitually wet his bed at night, refused to do any homework, and wouldn't attend classes. We tried everything—enticing, coaxing, and ordering. Even the fact that all his peers went off to class every morning did not allay his fears or induce him to try. Nothing worked. If we wanted him to come to class, we had to literally carry him—which we did a few times only to realize that really did not work either.

One day I said to him, "You can't continue to sit in your room all day and do nothing. If you're not going to go to school, then I want you to tutor younger children. There are plenty of children here who need help, and I know you can help them." He acquiesced, and the next day he began tutoring. A few weeks later he came to me and asked if he could attend classes.

To this day I am not completely sure why that worked, but it did. There is an old saying that "when one teaches, two learn," and I think that happened here—although in this case the child learned something about himself and about us. He realized that he liked science, math, reading, and history. Tutoring reminded him just how much he enjoyed those and other subjects, and it encouraged him to put his fears aside. At the same time he learned that we were going to insist that he function. Many children who had problems were protected by their families who set no expectations for them and, in fact, made excuses. That was not our way. Our attitude was, "Yes, you have problems, but so what? You have to function somewhere, so it might as well be here." Many of the children were intractable, but eventually they came around. I do not think they ever met so many people so determined to help them reach their potential. That cast adults in a whole new light and laid the foundation for positive adult-child relationships.

Companionship was another benefit of boarding school. As one student recalled years later, "You'd wake up every morning and have twenty kids your age to play with!" It was true; no place else could children experience that environment, but in addition to great fun, it was comforting. For the first time, the children with learning and other problems did not feel as if they were on the outside looking in; they were not segregated from neurotypical children; and they were not alone in their troubles—there were others just like them.

Like other progressive educators at the time, we believed that separating slow learners and disturbed children from their peers was not only unnecessary, but led to social segregation, which was detrimental; the special needs children grew more troubled, and the neurotypical children grew intolerant. Rather, we tried to keep class sizes small so we could give the children the individual attention and extra help they needed. If they required still additional remediation in a particular area such as math, we arranged for that and let them participate normally for other subjects. Everyone benefited when the children were mixed together: the special needs children were stimulated by the neurotypical children, and the neurotypical children learned to be tolerant of others who needed special help.

Today, Green Chimneys has become a school for all special needs youngsters. They function at various levels and have different needs. With a multitude of public programs—the farm, wildlife center, organic garden, and summer camp—Green Chimneys is equipped to prepare its students for a regular public school situation by exposing them to visiting school groups and other outside visitors.

The routine, the chores, the therapy, the academic program, the companionship, the integrated classrooms, and the knowledgeable and persistent staff—it all added up to create a therapeutic milieu. For some children, to receive the greatest benefit from this experience, boarding was the best opportunity. Some psychiatrists, psychologists, and educators were against this. In addition to a general feeling that children should be with their families if at all possible, many felt that the prospect of going away added to children's troubles by making them anxious and apprehensive. It was true; we could see the worry in the children's faces as they arrived on campus for the first time. It was entirely reasonable. They would be living and going to school in unfamiliar surroundings with children and adults they did not know. It was unsettling.

After a little while, however, most youngsters found that boarding school was a lot less pressure and psychological stress than living at home. Recognizing that their parents were relieved to have them in a safe and nurturing place, the children acquiesced and became somewhat willing to give it a try. Free from emotional entanglements, the children were not as balky, and we were able to begin helping them modify their behavior, overcome their learning disabilities, work through their emotional problems, and begin to understand themselves—their feelings, their wants and needs, their relation to others, and how to make intelligent decisions. In essence, it was a therapeutic separation and worked well in many instances.

Our day students likewise benefit from our programs even though they do not have the full boarding school experience. For our day students, it is a carefully blended balance of home, school, and farm programs. For me, it is always a milestone when one of our resident students is able to become a day student. It means the program has worked for that child.

I put together all these thoughts for various speeches and articles, but I found I used them most often to justify our services to school districts. As more parents asked their Boards of Education to approve a private school education for their children, officials wanted to make sure the expenditures were warranted. Time and again I had to explain that the value of our school was not just its academic program, but the combination of academics, group living, socialization, and around-the-clock professional care. The faculty and staff were a team who paid close attention to the development and progress of the whole child so no part fell through the cracks. That was what these children needed. Lose the continuity and you may lose the child.

Some Boards of Education saw the benefits of our program and approved parents' plans to send their children to Green Chimneys. Others wanted a strict comparison between our academic program and their public school's special education classes; they refused to consider that these children's success might depend on more than just academics. So you can imagine that I was pleased and felt somewhat vindicated when in September 1969, *Instructor* magazine recognized us with an Honorable Mention Award, noting, "The award to Green Chimneys was made because it is a nonprofit boarding and day school operating year-round in which normal children live and work with emotionally-disturbed and brain-damaged children, both receiving the special attention they need."

◆◆◆

> C. L., age 10: A boy who no one wanted to be with because he always bugged people was in the dorm because he could not go on the dorm trip. I was allowed to go on the dorm trip and I was happy. I decided

> to spend time with this boy because he did not have any friends. I sat down with him to talk and he was excited to have a friend . . . I was very proud of myself.

Notes

1 As it so happened, Edi lived at 993 Park Avenue, which was where my father had his medical practice for fifteen years. I have always been fascinated by such coincidences.

Chapter VIII

Our Own Children at Green Chimneys

In June 1969, David, Myra's and my oldest child, graduated from eighth grade. As any parent knows, your first child's firsts are momentous occasions, but this event turned out to be particularly poignant.

As in previous years, I asked my father to lead the graduation ceremony and hand out the diplomas, and he accepted. He had done this every year since 1965 when we held our first eighth grade graduation. He was the school's longtime benefactor, and I thought he deserved the honor.

As the students lined up on this June day, however, I realized that this year would be unlike previous ones. I was about to watch my father hand a diploma to my son who was graduating from the school I founded. Indeed, it was a special moment.

It was special for another reason as well. From the time David entered grade school, my father had been taking him to medical conferences, on house calls, and to the hospital. For a long time, Myra and I thought David went along for the ride. Then we learned that David was always full of questions afterward, and my father usually spent the ride home explaining a patient's problem, how the body functioned, or what treatments might be appropriate. David was a bright and curious child, but still my father was surprised by how much he absorbed. Over the years, David's interest grew, and by the time of his graduation, a strong bond had formed between him and my father. So it was with particular pride that my dad presented David with his diploma. Myra and I were not surprised when later, as a senior in high school, David told us that he wanted to become a medical doctor.

As I watched David receive his diploma, it seemed like only yesterday that he had started in the preschool program. Now he was fourteen. Earlier in the year he had his bar mitzvah, and in September he would leave for Loomis Chaffee, a prep school in Windsor, Connecticut. Our children were growing up. Donald would begin seventh grade in the fall and Lisa, fifth.

Myra and I were lucky. We had three healthy, happy, smart, sociable children. They did well in school, had lots of friends, participated in numerous after-school activities, played most sports, and loved spending time at the farm with the animals. To all who knew them, they seemed like well-adjusted children. Any worries we had that they might feel inhibited being the headmaster's children proved unwarranted with a fair amount of frequency.

Some children ask to stay over at a friend's house. For our children, the equivalent was sleeping over in the dorms, and whatever mischief happened on those nights we could usually count on them being part of the group. They and their friends would conspire to raid the refrigerator or hide from the night staff who had the unenviable job of getting the children to bed. On summer nights, the children liked to slip out after lights out and go into the woods. Sometimes they would sneak a smoke or just hang out until they got tired, which given their busy days, was not too long.

The dorms also were where our children went when they were upset with Myra and me, although such departures were usually accompanied by more bluster. When they were particularly unhappy with a decision Myra and I made, they would go up to their rooms, pack their little overnight bags, and come downstairs and announce they were going to sleep in the dorms. During the day, they would sometimes express their displeasure by "running away" to the farm. And if they did not like what Myra was making for dinner, they would tell her that they were going to see what Mommy Mac (their step-grandmother) was cooking.

We took such behavior in stride. If they broke the rules, they were in trouble like anyone else. On the other hand, we couldn't help but be secretly amused that they would figure out their options and get up the gumption to use them.

One day, I asked the three of them to help me clean the outdoor grill in the picnic area. I rounded up four wire brushes and some rags, and we headed off together. They were still young, and it was a hard, tedious task to scrape down this big grill. We had been working only a little while when David said to me:

"Dad, do you own Green Chimneys?"

"No," I said, "I don't own Green Chimneys."

> "Does Grandpa own Green Chimneys?"
>
> "No," I replied, "Grandpa doesn't own Green Chimneys."
>
> "Does Grandma own Green Chimneys?"
>
> "No," I continued, "Grandma doesn't own Green Chimneys."
>
> "Well, who does then?" David asked.
>
> At a loss for how to explain the structure of a nonprofit to a child, I simply said, "The Board of Trustees owns Green Chimneys."
>
> Without missing a beat, David exclaimed, "Then tell them to come out here and clean the grill!"

I had to laugh; it made sense. But there was another way to look at it, I explained. Since we all live on campus and use the facilities, we should all pitch in and help maintain them. I don't think that I convinced him or the other two that day, but somewhere along the line they accepted the idea. And as they got older, all three worked summer vacations and winter breaks at Green Chimneys. David worked in the maintenance department. Donald started in the kitchen and gradually worked his way up to being a cook. Lisa also worked in the kitchen and helped out in the office. Years later during college she worked as an outdoor educator, and after completing college, she came to work at Green Chimneys full time. This was somewhat paradoxical since Lisa was the one who wanted to leave and go to another school.

In the fall of 1969, Lisa began fifth grade and suddenly was no longer happy. She complained that the other children didn't like her, that they said unkind things, that they resented her, and that they were going to hurt her. Myra and I tried to reason with her, but to Lisa everything the other children said and did had menacing overtones. She wanted to go to another school, and with good reason.

I wasn't very sympathetic. There always had been a certain amount of teasing and taunting that went on among the children, and I was sure it was nothing more than the usual. David and Donald had held their own and never complained. Lisa, I thought, could be overly sensitive.

I did not take her seriously until the day she came to me and told me she did not want to go to school because a boy had threatened to punch her. "No one's going to punch you," I assured her. Later that day I learned I was wrong; the boy had indeed hit her.

At Green Chimneys we were doing what we always had done: accepting children who needed our help the most. Increasingly, however, the children arrived with serious behavioral problems in addition to other troubles. Tempers easily flared, and acts of verbal and physical aggression followed. They were angry children who were mad at the world.

The faculty, staff, and I were learning how to deal with such outbursts and working to modify the children's behavior, but it was not something we could change overnight or expect our children to tolerate. In the meantime, Myra and I could see the situation was taking its toll on Lisa. She began to stick close to home. She was increasingly anxious. She often was afraid to walk on campus alone. She had fewer and fewer friends. For the first time, Myra and I considered sending one of our children to another school. For months we discussed the pros and cons. Myra felt we should enroll her elsewhere; I was optimistic that things would work out.

Eventually, we consulted the superintendent of the local public school district; he was a friend of ours and knew Lisa. We explained the situation and told him we were contemplating sending Lisa to the Brewster Central School for sixth grade and then enrolling her for seventh at the Wooster School in Danbury, Connecticut. Wooster was a private prep school for boys, but it had announced that it would admit girls as day students beginning in the fall of 1971.

The superintendent discouraged us; taking the bus to school and being one of thirty children in a class would be too big of an adjustment for her. In addition, he did not think that she would fare any better in public school. As the daughter of a headmaster, she would still be singled out by the other children.

We decided to take his advice and keep Lisa at Green Chimneys for another year. Unfortunately, things did not go according to plan. Wooster postponed the admission of girls, and it was the fall of 1972 before Lisa started; by then she had been at Green Chimneys for sixth and seventh grades, a year longer than we had intended.

In hindsight, we probably shouldn't have waited. When the superintendent dissuaded us from sending her to public school, we should have considered other alternatives for sixth grade. She made it through, but it was not easy and became more difficult when Donald left for prep school the following year. Being home alone was lonely, which added to her unhappiness.

In September 1971 Donald joined David at Loomis Chaffee, although it was not his choice. Unlike David, who had looked forward to prep school, Donald wanted to stay at home and attend the public high school. We did not feel that public school was an option when we evaluated schools for David, and the situation had not changed by the time it was Donald's turn.

Myra and I were busier than ever. The day-to-day challenges of supervising, teaching, and caring for children with serious behavioral problems were great. I sent the faculty and staff for training, but in reality, they were learning on the job and needed constant guidance. At the same time, we were learning how to deal with the agencies and school districts that were sending us these children. By 1970 Myra had stopped teaching and was working full time on admissions to ensure compliance with the agencies' and school districts' reporting requirements, proper help for the children, and a steady enrollment for the school. In addition, complaints from parents were escalating. The teachers, staff, dorms, facilities, food—nothing escaped their criticism.

By this time, for a person who lived and worked at Green Chimneys, I had one heck of a daily commute. I had become much more involved with the Edwin Gould Foundation. In addition to program director, I was now a board member of Edwin Gould Services for Children and Families, which operated the foundation's child care programs, one of which was Lakeside School in Spring Valley, New York, where I was serving as acting director. I often began my days with a 7 a.m. meeting at the Lakeside school located in Spring Valley, New York, and then drove down to the Edwin Gould Foundation in New York City. Then I would head back to Green Chimneys in the afternoons and sometimes go back to Spring Valley in the evenings for a board meeting or a school program.

With all that we were doing, Myra and I did not see how we could send David and later Donald to public school with all that it entailed: driving them to and from sports practice, games, and a myriad of extracurricular activities during the week, and then friends' houses, school functions, and the movies on the weekends. We knew we would not have the time, yet we did not want to shortchange them because of our heavy schedules. Prep school seemed to be a good solution. In addition to a better education and activities that the local public school did not provide, there was no question that they would be able to participate in as much as they liked.

David had settled in quickly at Loomis Chaffee and was enjoying it immensely, so we thought that once Donald got there he would too. In addition, it wasn't that far away. Donald could easily come home for a weekend, and Myra, if not I, was always going up to the school for parents' days, teacher conferences, special programs, and the like. Donald would be fine.

It was optimistic thinking on our part. Because he didn't want to be there, Donald had a hard time adapting. In addition, he probably was reluctant to follow in his brother's footsteps.

For David, everything came easy. He was innately talented, and whatever he attempted he seemed to master on his first try. Donald, on the other hand, had to work at things. He had to study harder to get the same grades and practice longer to be as good a ballplayer, swimmer, or horseback rider, and his heart often wasn't in the activities. Small schools tend to compare brothers and sisters, and it can be difficult for younger siblings to make their own mark.

Donald also found it hard to step out of David's shadow because, in fact, they were similar in so many ways. There was one notable difference, however. Donald was always as neat as a pin. He could be out playing all day, and when he came home he looked the same as when he left. David, on the other hand, was anything but neat. His room was a mess. His clothes were wrinkled. He always looked like he had gotten into everything, even when he had done nothing.

Donald eventually adapted, did well, and made a lot of friends—many of whom he is still close to after all these years. Upon graduation he went to college for hotel management and has pursued his career with admirable focus, hard work, and intelligence; today he is Vice President of Catering, Conventions and Events for Caesars Entertainment in Las Vegas.

Without her big brothers and just a few friends at school, Lisa was a bit unsettled. It was fortunate that there were others around to whom she was close. Adele, her step-grandmother, was one. The two of them spent a lot of time together shopping, cooking, and baking. About once a month, Adele, sometimes along with my father, would take Lisa into the city, where they would have lunch and go to the ballet, a play, the opera, or a museum. Some of the performances wouldn't have been Lisa's choice—she was too young to understand the operas—yet she wouldn't have missed going for the world.

Tante Frieda also played a big part in Lisa's life. Frieda Sparr came to us as a housekeeper and quickly became part of the family. The children loved her and soon began calling her *Tante* Frieda, "*tante*" being German for "aunt." Lisa wasn't in school yet when Frieda first arrived, so of all the children, Lisa spent the most time with her.

To Lisa, everything Frieda did was interesting and fun. Even as young as three, Lisa followed Frieda around the house "helping," whether it was dusting, mopping, or drying the dishes. Some housekeepers would have been impatient with a three-year-old tagging behind them all day, but not Frieda. They sang songs and had a grand time.

Many an afternoon, Myra and I would arrive home to find Frieda and the three children gathered around the big kitchen table. They might have been out picking apples or vegetables from the garden and were then baking a pie or in the midst of preparing dinner. The children were infected by Frieda's love for cooking and were only too glad to help. Sometimes after dinner Myra and I had to go out, and Frieda would stay with the children until we got home, getting them in their pajamas and tucking them into bed. For years Lisa recited a German prayer before going to sleep, one that Frieda had taught her.

David and Donald had left home, but Lisa still had *Tante* Frieda.

There also was Bella, my secretary. Although she was working full time and raising three sons alone, she always found time for Lisa. They, too, spent much time together cooking and baking and shopping, but what Lisa remembers most about her time with Bella is laughing. Bella was and is a fun-loving person, and she was just what Lisa needed, as was Grandpa Mattes.

In the late spring of 1969, Ben Mattes, Myra's father, came to live with us. We had been expecting him and Julia, Myra's mother, to move in with us, and had built an addition to our house for them. A month before the wing was completed, however, Julia passed away. We encouraged Ben to move anyway. He was frequently at Green Chimneys, we pointed out, either working in the garden or on the night shift. There was no sense in driving back and forth; he might as well stay with us. He finally agreed, and after the wing was finished, he moved in.

In many ways, Ben was the opposite of my father. Their difference in size earned them the names Little Grandpa and Big Grandpa, respectively. Whereas my dad had gone to college and medical school and spoke several languages, Ben was an immigrant from Romania who had taught himself how to read and write. And whereas my dad was reserved and proper, Ben was anything but, which, along with his big heart, irreverent manner, and willingness to do anything for a laugh, endeared him to our children and their friends, Lisa particularly. Nothing they did shocked him, but he shocked them plenty with his literal pronunciation of words, his wild, flashy outfits, and his use of their lingo, and they enjoyed it tremendously.

Still, Lisa was anxious to get to Wooster. In September 1972 she started eighth grade as a day student. Luckily, it was a good match for her, and she asked to stay on for high school. During her sophomore year, Wooster announced that girls could board beginning the following fall. Lisa was thrilled, and we enrolled her as a boarder for her junior and senior years. Her friends from Wooster remain some of her closest friends today.

Despite Lisa's few years of troubles, overall I think growing up at Green Chimneys was a positive experience for our children. When I look at them today, I see that they get along with many different people, have many good friends, give to those who are less fortunate, and have respect and empathy for others.

Yet I know it was not easy for them, and there were many disappointments. On more than one occasion we were ready to go on a family vacation when a teacher called in sick. Myra and I would call everyone we knew asking if they could substitute. When we could not find a replacement, we had only two choices: her or me. Either way, it meant canceling our vacation, a big sacrifice for all of us, but particularly for the children.

On many holidays—occasions that the children, perhaps rightly, expected it to be just the family—children from the school stayed with us because they could not go home. Every once in awhile I would hear someone grumble, "Why can't it just be us?" If it had not been a rare event, I am sure it would not have elicited such a reaction. But our daily life was one of constant visitors, calls at all hours, and children staying for weekends or longer.

To get some time with me, the children would ask if they could ride along when I drove the housekeepers home after work, do their homework in my office, or tag along when I went to check the horses. It seemed fine at the time, but now that they are grown, I am not sure I gave them all the time to which they were entitled. Today I watch Donald with his own daughters, and I realize how much I didn't do with my children because I was so busy. Sometimes I wish I was the one who had taught them how to horseback ride or fish rather than an instructor. Today I try to take more time with my granddaughters.

One day when David was young, he said to me, "Dad, if I had problems, would you have time for me?" I was a bit surprised by the question and answered what I thought to be true. "Of course I would!" I said. Looking back, however, I have to admit it was a perceptive question, and his concern was not unfounded. In fact, one might say it was prescience.

◆ ◆ ◆

June of 1973 brought a happy occasion. David graduated from Loomis Chaffee High School. After having four great years there, he was looking forward to college; he had been accepted at Middlebury College in Vermont. His plan for the summer was to work at the Danbury Hospital.

For the last several weeks of his senior year, David had been working at the hospital as part of an independent study project. Loomis required all seniors to do one, and wanting to be a doctor, David chose to do his at the hospital where he used to go with his grandfather. He liked working there, so he applied for a summer job and was hired.

A few days before he was to start, he went in for a routine, preemployment physical. They found a few nodes on his chest and, after examining him further, found a lump on his neck. Myra, David, and I scheduled a consultation with the doctors, and it was then that David told us that he had been having night sweats at school. The doctors recommended surgery, and we all agreed. They removed the lump, a biopsy of which revealed Hodgkin's disease, between the third and fourth stages. We were shocked, incredulous, devastated. Why would a normal, healthy, active youngster develop Hodgkin's? How could this happen? There were no answers, of course, only treatments.

David began chemotherapy, and we called Middlebury College to ask if they would defer his enrollment to the following fall, which they did. To say David was upset was an understatement. Why him? Why now? It was unfathomable.

The therapy was harsh. There were no drugs at that time to mitigate the side effects. Despite its debilitating effects, however, David told us that he wanted to take some freshman courses at Western Connecticut State College. He did not want to fall behind; he wanted to enter Middlebury the following September as a sophomore.

Myra and I did not know what to say. The treatments were taking such a toll that we did not know how he could manage going to class and doing homework. On the other hand, he loved learning and had been looking forward to college so much that perhaps it would help to keep up his spirits.

Some weeks later he surprised us again when he came home with his head shaved. He had gone to Rocco Gesauldi, the school barber, and asked him to shave his head. He told us that he would rather have no hair than have it falling out. I had to admire his determination to continue with his plans as much as he could and his courage to face the unpleasant side effects of the treatments.

Through the fall, winter, and spring, David had multiple surgeries in addition to chemotherapy. He experienced several blockages, one that was so severe we nearly lost him. After he recovered, we surprised him by buying him a set of drums and a pool table; he loved playing the drums and pool was a close second. We set them up in the living room, which meant removing everything else, but they were good outlets for him.

When the spring of 1974 came around, David began to talk about going to Middlebury in the fall. Somehow, despite the treatments and surgeries, he had kept up with his schoolwork. He had passed all his courses at Western Connecticut, and Middlebury agreed that he could start as a sophomore. We were concerned, however. As Myra said at the time, "David, you're sick. How can you go?" But as usual, David was not to be deterred. "What if dad was offered a position in Burlington, Vermont, and we had to move?" he asked. "Well, we'd have to find you a doctor there," Myra replied. "So then find me a doctor," he said.

We found Dr. Jerome Yates, the chief oncologist at the University of Vermont's cancer center in Burlington. After reviewing David's history, he agreed to be his physician. David was thrilled; he would finally be going to college. In September 1974 we packed him up and drove him to school.

Chapter IX

Beneficial Alliance

> The Sheltering Arms Childrens Services was one of the first children's homes to which Edwin and Sarah [Gould] made contributions. . . . Although Edwin derived enormous satisfaction from his contact with the children at Sheltering Arms, it was not until tragedy struck his life that he became so entirely devoted to helping children. His son, Edwin, Jr. was accidentally shot while on a camping trip. At the funeral services, a large basket of roses arrived from the children of Sheltering Arms, one rose from each child at the home. This tender memorial so moved the bereaved father that he determined to devote his fortune and his time in their behalf.
>
> -The Edwin Gould Services for Children and Families Web site, 2007

Edwin Gould and Green Chimneys

I never met Edwin Gould—he died in 1933—but his legacy greatly influenced my life. When I had approached the Edwin Gould Foundation in 1967 for funding, I thought the Foundation's goals and ours were sufficiently similar. The Edwin Gould Foundation had been established to promote the welfare of children, and that is certainly what Green Chimneys was about. When I met with Schuyler Meyer initially, he invited me to the Institute on Administration, a two-week workshop that the Foundation was sponsoring in conjunction with the Harvard Business School. That August, a group of Harvard faculty was scheduled to lecture to child welfare professionals on policy making, determining and implementing objectives, and administration in the field of social welfare.

I accepted the invitation, and although I had no special interest in social welfare at the time, I found myself captivated by the lectures. Coming from a private school background, I had very little knowledge or understanding of the social welfare system; this institute opened my eyes to the inner workings and problems of the system, and the thousands of children who needed help. In hindsight I realize that it probably was here that I caught my first glimpse of Green Chimneys as a child care agency.

That fall, Meyer visited Green Chimneys and afterward offered me a consulting assignment. He liked our operation, and he needed help overseeing the Foundation's interests. He thought I would bring a fresh approach to their programs and be able to bring them up to date with the latest developments in child welfare. He saw a need for good fiscal administration and accountability in his programs, something he felt was often lacking among those trained for social work.

I accepted his offer, and in January 1968 I became the director of Program Development for the Foundation. It was my understanding that eventually Green Chimneys would merge with one of the Foundation's programs, Lakeside School, and I was motivated by this possibility. I had no idea that this assignment would mean that I would hold a second—and sometimes a third—job for the next fourteen years. I readily admit that I am forever grateful I took the consultancy work at that time and did not receive outright funding from them. What I learned on the job at the Foundation would prove to be invaluable to the future of Green Chimneys.

I split my weeks between the Foundation's offices in New York City and Green Chimneys in Brewster. It was a lesson in contrasts. The Foundation was rather formal. It had well-appointed offices. Visitors were ushered into conference rooms. Meetings were arranged and decisions made in a quiet and orderly fashion. Days there were predictable.

This was in sharp contrast to Green Chimneys, and my office in particular, which a reporter for *Education News* once described as "small and crowded. The phone is often ringing, and people wander in and out. . . . Behind a cluttered desk sits Mr. Ross in sport shirt, bubbling over with enthusiasm for what the school has done for children . . . and with ideas for future school programs." As I told that reporter at the time, the Foundation's offices were like a strategy room at the Pentagon, whereas ours were like the advanced command post on the firing line. I liked ours better.

One of the first things I took over was the planning of the institutes. The first one was such a great success that it hadn't ended before talk of a second began. The Harvard faculty taught using the case method and examples from other nonprofit fields as well as the business world, and everyone found it instructive and enlightening. So much so that the Council on Social Work Education began developing two textbooks for schools of social work based on the faculty's lectures and papers; in 1970 it published *Social Work Administration* and *A Casebook on Social Work Administration.*

Between 1968 and 1971, I planned four more institutes and, in the process, received quite an education and met many people in the field, one of whom was Barbara Blum, the commissioner of New York City's Administration for Children's Services. As Blum and I became acquainted, we discovered we had a mutual friend, Judge Louis Otten, who later was to serve on the Board of Trustees for Green Chimneys. He and his wife, Marge, were close friends of Myra's and mine. When he learned that Blum and I had met, he encouraged her to get involved with the school and took every opportunity to bring us together. If I was in the city, he set up lunch. If he was having a party, he invited us both. He did likewise with Justine Wise-Polier, a judge and colleague of his in the family court to whom he had introduced me. Largely due to his encouragement, these two women became instrumental in Green Chimneys' future and good friends of mine.

In addition to the institutes, I oversaw other programs for the Foundation including Lakeside School, which was a union-free school district and child care institution for dependent and neglected youngsters. I also oversaw the Hospital Boarder Project. It was not unusual at the time (and still isn't today) for pregnant women who were poor or addicted to drugs to go to emergency rooms to deliver their babies and then leave, abandoning them. The women knew that the hospitals would care for their babies while their cases worked their way through the social services system, which often took many months. This was expensive for the hospital, however, and tragic for the babies. The purpose of the Hospital Boarder Project was to help find parents who would adopt these newborns or at least take them temporarily.

Another part of my job was to become active in various city, state, and national task forces, committees, organizations, and conferences that dealt with child welfare, social work, education, and other related areas in which the Foundation had interests. The Foundation wanted to encourage change, as its sponsorship of the Institute showed; it wanted to develop a network of organizations and people who could assist the Foundation with its projects; and it wanted to stay abreast of trends and methods. I became the Foundation's catalyst, child care and school network, and industry watcher.

It wasn't long before I was entrenched in the Foundation's various programs and busy with all the meetings, conferences, and travel that my new job required. It made my working day longer, but I survived. It was a challenge juggling my responsibilities at Green Chimneys with those at the foundation and keeping on top of everything, but I learned a great deal and met many interesting people, so I hardly noticed. My family did, however, and as time went on so did some of the staff at Green Chimneys. On both counts, it fell to Myra to make up for my absence and to take on additional responsibility, which she did extremely well.

Of all the Foundation's programs, its Board of Directors was most concerned about Lakeside School. There was infighting between the child care and school staff. There was no budget or encouragement for the faculty and staff to pursue any type of professional education and development. There was an attitude of condescension toward the children rather than respect, concern, and caring. To top it off, even minor suggestions from the Foundation and Lakeside School Board were met with great resistance.

It was clear to the Lakeside School Board that the problems stemmed from the top, and in April 1970 they decided to replace the director. They asked me to step in as acting director and run the school while I looked for a new director and assembled a new administrative team.

To be in charge of two schools simultaneously was a tall order. Change was long overdue at Lakeside, particularly for the sake of the children, and this was an opportunity to put the school on a better path, so I accepted, increasing my workload. I also was supposed to be scouting out new projects and endeavors for the Foundation. Luckily, I had been working on one that I thought fit their goals and would allow me to get Lakeside on a better path.

Project Re-ED and the *Éducateur* Concept

A few years earlier, I had received a mailing from the *Association Nationale des* Éducateurs *de Jeunes Inadaptés* (ANEJI or National Association of Educators for Maladjusted Youth). This was the project I thought would interest the Edwin Gould Foundation. As I reread the literature, two things were clear: éducateurs were not teachers, but a new type of child care professional, and there were enough of them to warrant a professional organization. Intrigued, I learned that the éducateur was a relatively new profession that began in France during World War II. It did not gain wide acceptance until after the war, when thousands of children were left orphaned, homeless, and traumatized. With so many children in need of immediate care, and a shortage of psychiatrists, psychologists, and social workers to attend to them, small residential facilities popped up all over France. The staffs were primarily from the field of education rather than mental health, but they learned how to provide these children of all ages with the mental, emotional, physical, social, and academic support and instruction that they needed.

France was not the only country dealing with displaced and troubled children after the war. As officials from various countries contacted each other, they learned that many of them were facing the same situation. In hopes of finding some solutions, they arranged a meeting to which the French brought representatives of the French association of éducateurs who explained the rapidly spreading éducateur concept. Its success was encouraging to the other countries, and they began to adopt this approach and start their own éducateur organizations. Soon these organizations were meeting annually to share information, ideas, and experiences, and in 1951 they formed the ANEJI, which brought together not only éducateurs, but professionals from other disciplines as well.

By the time I became acquainted with the éducateur model, it had evolved, and éducateurs no longer learned on the job, but were formally trained. Their roles were many: part psychologist, part social worker, part mentor, part parent, part counselor, part coach, and part older sibling. It was, in a way, a holistic approach.

I was fascinated by this concept and discussed it with Norman Lourie, a good friend and the Commissioner of Welfare in Pennsylvania. Norman saw what I did: a model to be emulated, and he suggested we join.

The éducateur model captured the Lakeside School Board's interest, and they pledged their financial support. In 1971 we officially launched the American Association of Workers for Children (AAWC). With the Foundation's backing, I was able to travel and learn even more about the éducateur concept. I made several trips to Europe, visiting institutions and attending various conferences. It was at one of these conferences that I met Dr. Nicholas Hobbs.

In 1961 Hobbs saw the United States in a similar position that ANEJI saw Europe after the war: there were millions of emotionally disturbed or mentally ill children in need of therapeutic care and an insufficient number of psychiatrists, psychologists, social workers, and nurses trained to work with them. Drawing heavily on his own research and experience, as well as that of others, including the new and practical éducateur approach he found in Europe, Hobbs conceived a solution to the problem. He submitted a proposal to the National Institute of Mental Health (NIMH) and received a grant to establish Project Re-ED, a plan for the reeducation of emotionally disturbed children. It was based in Tennessee.

I was impressed with Hobbs, his experience, and his description of his program, and I made several visits to Project Re-ED schools between 1972 and 1973. What I saw was no less than remarkable, and I broached the idea of introducing the program at Lakeside. Hobbs' enthusiasm was contagious and his support, overwhelming. In the ensuing months, he and many others associated with the program came up to Lakeside in Spring Valley to help us make the transition. I was extremely grateful, because almost from the beginning it was clear that we would not have been able to do it without them. It was a radical change, and both the school and child care staffs, who had not kept up with developments in their fields and resisted change, needed a lot of guidance, reinforcement, and constant prodding.

In many ways, I felt I found a kindred spirit in Hobbs. We both believed emotionally disturbed and mentally ill children deserved more and better help than they were receiving at that time; that new approaches were worth trying; and that there were certain basics—continuous education, competency at a task, belonging to a group, traditions and rituals, and fun—that were critical to their reeducation. Most importantly, perhaps, we both believed that reeducation was possible. At the same time, I recognized that Hobbs had more experience with these children than I did. Some of his insights and ideas were brilliant, and I borrowed liberally from his program for Green Chimneys.[1]

I found another like-minded thinker in Dr. Jeannine Guindon who, based on her many years of research and her implementation of the éducateur model, introduced a new field: psychoeducation. Upon hearing that she was giving a workshop at the University of Montréal, I traveled there to attend her lectures and was fascinated by what I heard. Guindon had found that emotionally disturbed and mentally ill children could exercise more control over their illnesses if they were told of their conditions, understood the causes and effects (they might resist taking their medication, for example), and grasped how their illnesses affected their lives and the lives of those around them.

This made so much sense to me that I spoke to Guindon about incorporating some of the principles of psychoeducation into our treatment programs. She was very supportive and mentioned that she used a book by Dr. Michel Lemay as her guide to the éducateur model. Translated from French, its title was *The Functions of the Specialized* "Éducateur" *for Maladjusted Youth*. I tracked down a copy and gave it to Vivian Jarvis, a psychotherapist at Green Chimneys who was fluent in French. Finding it to be insightful and instructive, she volunteered to do the translation, which we then typed and printed for the staff; it became our guide as well.

In addition to Hobbs and Guindon's sensible approaches and successful track records, I was interested in the éducateur, teacher-counselor, and psychoeducator concepts because they emphasized professionalism. I had come to realize that in the United States, those who spent the most time with children—the child care workers—were educated the least, paid the least, and had no professional standing. This resulted in high turnover at many institutions when continuity was what children needed. It was my contention that many child care workers were capable of much more, and if training was made available and encouraged, they could acquire more skills and demand more pay. Their professional stars would rise, and they would not move so quickly out of child care into other areas.

The éducateur, teacher-counselor, and psychoeducator concepts seemed to prove this idea. Formal training was required to be hired for these positions, and ongoing professional development was encouraged, often through the ANEJI for éducateurs. The result was that éducateurs, teacher-counselors, and psychoeducators did not feel they had to become teachers or social workers to have a career, because they now had one in which they took pride. This emphasis on professionalism and pride in child care work would benefit Lakeside as well as Green Chimneys.

Hopefully child care workers and others would begin to see child care as a profession rather than a way station.

Implementing Project Re-ED and the *Éducateur* Model at Green Chimneys and Lakeside

To state that the program at Green Chimneys was always the same would be to deny the constant desire for program improvement as well as meet the shifting needs of our changing populations. Green Chimneys' school program had always emphasized the need for innovation and creativity as well as academic achievement. We were keenly aware that education does not begin and end at the classroom door.

We recognized early on that it was disastrous to provide a very rigid schedule for students who have constantly failed. This would be unfair to all concerned. The school program and its faculty wanted the learning opportunities to motivate and reeducate our students. It was our opinion and practice that everyone deserves a chance to experience success. The idea of reeducation was nothing new, but there were missing pieces, and I sought to find and incorporate them.

The Project Re-ED programs in Tennessee, started by Nicholas Hobbs under a grant from the National Institute of Mental Health in 1961, were evaluated in 1969. The evaluation concluded "that Project Re-Ed represents a conceptually sound, economically feasible, and demonstrably effective approach to helping emotionally disturbed children."[2] Some of the enthusiasm for Project

Re-ED had derived from Campbell Loughmiller's work at Camp Woodlands.[3] Loughmiller and his wife, Lynn, had taken on running the camp for troubled boys in Texas. Campbell developed a philosophy there that emphasized the care of the whole child. The healing came for the boys through the wilderness experience. The Loughmillers were no strangers to Green Chimneys. Campbell had spent time with us on a number of occasions. He was also was able to make some very relevant program suggestions.

Although I liked what I saw in each model—Hobbs' Tennessee Project Re-ED, Guindon's psychoeducation, and the Loughmiller's wilderness camp—I was particularly concerned whether these models were suitable as part of an institutional program to serve urban African-American and Hispanic youngsters and adolescents. I felt that we needed to develop a "New York style." I was fortunate that I was able to encourage two very knowledgeable Project Re-Ed experts to come work for Lakeside. First, I had been very impressed with the principal of the Cumberland House Project Re-ED program, Nell Wheeler. Wheeler became the Lakeside school director and helped us develop the "New York style" we needed to reach our youth.. The second expert was Dr. Laura Weinstein, who was researching the effects of Project Re-ED on residential children in Tennessee. Weinstein was to become the Lakeside school psychologist.

Wheeler seriously questioned the Cumberland House Project Re-ED model with teenagers, as did Weinstein. I felt we needed to address ourselves to the kinds of teenagers we would serve. Wheeler and Weinstein agreed that we could not ignore New York State Social Welfare regulations pertaining to the need for social workers. The more I talked with them, the more I was certain we needed to open up some far reaching conversations with New York City Administration for Children's Services, the New York State Department of Family Assistance, and the legislature. I was also deeply concerned with the cost of development of the program in the context of the New York system of compensation. It seemed to me we would do best to start with a small pilot program with a fairly select group of youngsters. We had identified a number of interested people: an "outside" group, which could become a consortium of consultants, and an "in-house" group, which could become the cadre for carrying out the program change. I questioned whether the entire staff could be reasonably expected to absorb the impact of this program and carry out simultaneously many other necessary changes At Green Chimneys, where a history of child care was built on reeducation, changes were incorporated smoothly; at Lakeview, the changes were more difficult to incorporate. Later I was to find the right people to help me get the job done there too.

For Green Chimneys, Dr. George Olshin of Southern Connecticut State University worked on the development of the éducateur model with us, and he has continued to this day promoting the program and the preparation of workers at his University. The idea of a teacher who is also a counselor has made a very important contribution to our ideas of how to work with special needs children.

◆ ◆ ◆

Staff Notes

> O. T. is nearly 11. A small, sensitive looking boy, he's been at Green Chimneys for eight months. His learning disabilities and severe behavior problems at school were more than his parents could control . . . before Green Chimneys, O. T .had both inpatient and outpatient psychiatric care for seriously aggressive, reckless and self-destructive behavior. But now O. T. loves his job at the Farm and often lingers after hours. The staff describe him as very nurturing and personal with all the animals, treating each as his personal project and responsibility. He works closely with a rabbit named Crystal and the concern he shows is touching. With the animals, O. T. expresses his tender side without fear of rejection, criticism, or scorn.

Notes

1 I recommend his book, *The Troubled and Troubling Child,* which explains the evolution of Project Re-ED to anyone who works with children.

2 Project Re-ED, *New Concepts for Helping Emotionally Disturbed Children,* Nashville: Vanderbilt University, 1967.

3 Campbell Loughmiller, *Wilderness Road.* The Hogg Foundation for Mental Health, Austin: The University of Texas, 1965.

Chapter X

Establishing a Social Services Agency

In addition to my travels for the Edwin Gould Foundation, I was increasing my travel on behalf of Green Chimneys, often giving speeches on visual literacy and year-round education. I felt strongly about these programs and the potential they held for children. Depression, learning disabilities, behavioral problems, emotional disturbances, neurological impairments—these programs had helped children with a range of problems, and I was anxious that other schools and child care institutions give them a try. They also showed respect for the individuality of the child. Implicit in the adoption of these methods was the understanding that it was up to us as teachers to recognize the causes of children's failures, to accept that there was more than one way to learn, and to acknowledge that children's perception and performance was personal.

So I began pursuing what was perhaps my most ambitious project at the time: Ballyhack Children's Services, an agency to provide our Green Chimneys services to welfare children. From time to time, we were asked to take welfare children by New York City's Administration for Children's Services. These were children who had been refused by all other child care agencies. In doing so, I became aware of the number of children who were wards of the city and who needed the kind of nurturing, treatment, and special schooling we provided. I decided to inquire as to how Green Chimneys could receive more of these children. What I learned surprised me. According to our charter with the New York State Board of Regents, the only circumstances under which we were allowed to accept welfare children as residential students was that they needed to have been rejected by all other New York child care agencies. This was because we were a special education school, not an approved child care agency.

Barbara Blum, Justine Wise-Polier, and Lou Otten encouraged me to see what the options were. They knew firsthand that there were many children who would benefit from our program and felt it was an injustice that these children couldn't be sent to us if we were willing to accept them. At their urging, I presented the problem to the New York State Board of Social Welfare, which recommended that I establish a child care agency separate from the school. This was possible. In 1969 my family had purchased a piece of Boni-Bel Farm, which was right next to Green Chimneys. I figured that we could convert the farmhouse into a residence and bus the children to Green Chimneys for school and activities.

We ended up purchasing the Boni-Bel Farm in three stages. The final purchase of thirty-five acres was made in 1992 with a bequest from Rudolf G. and Tulli Sonneborn. I had met Rudolf Sonneborn one summer afternoon. Riding in the back of his chauffeured black Cadillac on his way from Danbury, he pulled up in front of Green Chimneys, watching all the children playing on the front lawn. He was curious about us, and before he had a chance to come and ask questions, the children ran to see the car and peppered him with questions. Sonneborn was a very successful businessman and a major player in the establishment of the State of Israel. He had suffered a major stroke previously and had difficulty speaking clearly. Because of this, he tended to avoid social occasions, but the children's enthusiastic curiosity about him and his car make him feel comfortable, and he chatted with them for a while. Pleased with what he learned about the school, he invited us to his estate to swim in his pool.

Sonneborn remained a good friend to Myra and me and Green Chimneys. I usually met him for lunch at his estate when he was in Danbury for the weekend. He was faithful in attending performances given by the students, and he never ceased to do wonderful things for us. Sonneborn always said he would remember Green Chimneys in his will, and he kept his word. When his wife died, I was named as executor, and Green Chimneys received the bequest.

The will specified that something should be done with the money that would be long lasting, which materialized in the final purchase of the Boni-Bel Farm. The community-supported organic garden is located there, and the open land serves as a nature preserve. That will exist for as long as Green Chimneys operates a campus program.

With that as our plan, we applied to the New York State Board of Social Welfare to establish Ballyhack Children's Services. Named after an abandoned road that cut through the Boni-Bel Farm property, Ballyhack, existing as a separate child care agency, would allow us to launch the organization with minimal effect on the boarding and day school. After the agency began operation, we could evaluate it—and a fair assessment would be possible since it was separate from the school—and determine if this was the course we wanted to pursue. If for some reason we decided not to continue, we could close it.

We plunged ahead, tackling the mounds of paperwork the agency application required, submitting numerous evaluations, and attending frequent meetings. After many, many months of work, the Education Department informed us that there was no guarantee that the youngsters from Ballyhack would be sent to Green Chimneys. It was up to the school district to determine where the children should go. The school district could decide that the children should attend the local public school or Board of Cooperative Educational Services (BOCES), which had been organized to address the special education needs of public school youngsters. According to the Education Department, if we wanted to provide a home and a school for welfare children, we had to establish a child care agency as a separate nonprofit corporation on the same campus as the school. So we would have two separate nonprofit private schools on the same campus. Only then could we be sure that the children from Ballyhack would attend Green Chimneys.

Establishing a social services agency at Boni-Bel Farm was a big step. Establishing an agency on the grounds of Green Chimneys was an even bigger one, for it meant we would no longer be a private school. The Education Department did mention this explicitly, but I knew the two could not exist side by side. Already we were receiving complaints from upper middle-class parents whose daughters and sons were learning, playing, and rooming with tough, inner-city kids from Newark. It was a rough time, and Green Chimneys was not untarnished by its growing pains. The opening quote from a disgruntled parent's letter has been excerpted from a long list of complaints, some of them justified:

> In your literature you maintain that you take some children with "small problems," and that they make up about half of the student body. This may have been true once, but apparently it is just not anymore . . . Why don't you try to make this school as good as it used to be?
>
> -A parent, writing anonymously, 1971

Having been a private day and boarding school for almost twenty-five years, it was hard for me to imagine us as a regulated agency. So much of our approach, our attitude, and our success stemmed from being a young, independent school. We never had to contend with layers of bureaucracy and years of tradition that often meant more of the same year after year, child after child. When it came to academics, extracurricular activities, recreation, chores, treatment, and family participation, we always had taken advantage of our independence to foster an environment that was flexible, innovative, and creative.

If a child's previous school experience was traumatic, we might start him off at the farm rather than in class. If a child was distrustful of adults, we might ask another child to show her the ropes. If a child was a science whiz but had trouble with grammar, we let him advance in science while we tutored him in grammar. If a child was more comfortable outdoors, her therapist could conduct a session while they took a walk. If a child felt particularly emotionally fragile, one of us agreed to take her under our wing. It was the teachers, houseparents, psychologists—those who knew the child—who consulted with each other and determined the best way to help him or her.

I had to wonder, if we became an agency, would we lose this flexibility? Would we have to put children on preset academic tracks rather than work with them as individuals? Would we wind up dividing a child into parts—the academic part, the therapeutic part, the social part—or would we still be able to consider the whole child? Would we be pressured to put children in therapy or on medication when time and care would work as well, albeit more slowly? Would we lose our entrepreneurial spirit that spurred us to find creative and innovative solutions to children's problems?

I also had to admit that operating an agency would be new for me. An independent school—that was something I knew how to run and had some success doing. Our enrollment had grown steadily over the years, our programs had expanded, and we had made major improvements to our facilities. We had a good reputation among family physicians, psychiatrists, psychologists, and more recently, social workers and family court judges. Through my involvement in professional organizations, and through my travel and lectures on behalf of Green Chimneys and the Edwin Gould Foundation, the school was becoming known nationally and internationally. Like any organization we had our problems and our challenges, but overall things were going relatively well.

So why would I change course? How could I justify becoming an agency? Yes, there were plenty of welfare children that could use our help, but I also was responsible for more than 130 employees. They had to be considered as well. How would this affect them? Some would not like the change; others would be unable to adapt. Inevitably, people would leave. What about those that stayed? If we succeeded, it would seem that we chose the right path; if we failed, they would question, and rightly so, why I had turned a viable school into a fledgling agency.

Being a viable school, however, was no guarantee that we would continue as one. This thought continually haunting me. Many private schools had merged or closed, and no one thought the upheaval was over. Our costs were escalating. It was a sacrifice for many families to send their children to Green Chimneys. How much longer would they be willing to pay the price when the quality of a public school education for all children continually improved? So far we had been lucky, but we were not immune. Not changing might be the greater risk to our future.

Another reason to consider becoming an agency was the influx of children from New Jersey institutions; for the first time since we opened the doors, we had more children from New Jersey than New York.

This was partly due to New Jersey's red tape being shorter than New York's so that more parents could take advantage of being able to send their children to special schools. However, New Jersey was also (as were other states) pushing to close government-run institutions and send the residents to private ones. A series of investigative reports in the late 1960s and early 1970s had gradually drawn the public's attention to deplorable conditions at state mental institutions. The most famous of these investigative reports was aired by WABC's *Eyewitness News* in 1972. Geraldo Rivera, a young reporter, made a name for himself when he exposed the appalling conditions at the Willowbrook State School, a New York State facility for the mentally ill on Staten Island. On national television, he showed an overcrowded institution with inadequate sanitary facilities where the residents were neglected and physically abused. This led to a government investigation and, eventually, its closing.

To avoid bad publicity and accusations of poor management, inadequate care and facilities, and improper oversight of taxpayer-funded programs, various states approved measures to close government-run institutions and send the residents to private ones, New Jersey included.

Perhaps if the criticism was limited to the conditions in these state institutions and the treatment of their residents, it could have been addressed and remedied. However, because of the investigations, questions about the very concept of institutionalization were being raised, with many claiming it was dehumanizing, depersonalizing, and counter-rehabilitative.

At the time, Green Chimneys had a working relationship with New Jersey. Since the mid-1960s we had accepted students who, unable to be educated in public school, were approved by the state to attend a private school. Now New Jersey contracted with us to accept children from its state mental hospitals.

Unfortunately, the state was in such a hurry to empty its institutions that the process was slipshod. It often sent us large groups of children and insufficient or no paperwork. Myra worked feverishly first to verify that the children were approved for placement and admit them to the school, and then for weeks afterward interviewing and testing the children to determine why they were institutionalized. The reasons ran the gamut from homelessness and juvenile delinquency to serious psychological, psychiatric, and neurological disturbances—even when the children had all come from the same institution. More amazing was that no one had taken the time to determine if Green Chimneys was the right place for them.

This influx of children from New Jersey's institutions did not escape the notice of the parents of Green Chimneys' students. As many explained to me, it wasn't the peer group they expected when they sent their children to private school. Many also believed, although incorrectly, that they paid more than the state and were picking up the tab for these other children. It was obvious that mixing boarding school children and state placed youngsters would not work. I would have to make a choice.

Discussing these issues with Barbara, Justine, and Lou made me realize something else. My family had put down roots in Brewster intending to be part of the community. My father had been making house calls to local residents for years and had become Putnam County's coroner. I had been a member of the Rotary Club, the Brewster School Board, the Patterson Planning Board, and Temple Beth Elohim. One of the reasons for opening the farm to the public and starting the Edwin Gould Outdoor Education Center was not only to share our enthusiasm for and knowledge of animals and nature with others, but to forge a stronger bond with the local and neighboring communities.

As I had done twenty-five years earlier, I thought to myself, "I can do better." It was clear to me from the various investigative reports of state mental institutions that there was a need for innovative residential facilities for youngsters. After visiting various programs in the United States and abroad, learning about the éducateur, psychoeducator, and Project Re-ED models, and working with children with a range of learning, emotional, and mental disorders, I felt confident that we could provide such a place.

Weighing all these factors, in April 1973 I decided to withdraw our application for Ballyhack and seek a license for a residential child care agency on the campus.

It was a good move.

We had also been experiencing extreme payment delays from New York and New Jersey, so I decided to apply for a $425,000 mortgage to pay off our outstanding debt and give us some working capital. The mortgage was a stopgap measure; we couldn't afford to continually borrow money to pay bills and salaries while we waited for payments from New York. But what was the solution? As a New York State agency, we would no longer worry that our beds would be emptied overnight, but it didn't mean New York would pay us any faster. There seemed to be only one answer: a relationship or merger with a larger agency that had the resources to withstand the delays.

Green Chimneys Children's Services, Inc. was approved by the Board of Social Welfare a few months earlier in May; now we could be one of the first places state and city social services departments asked to take New York welfare children rather than the last. We still maintained Green Chimneys School for Little Folk as a special education school approved by the Division of Handicapped Children and Youth of New York State Education Department.

It was a new chapter in our history that was made even more poignant by my father and Adele's retirement to Marco Island, Florida, and the recording of our first official deficit of $175,000 (about $730,000 in today's dollars). The transition between private dollars and public dollars had drained our resources not only because of late payments, but also because we had to hire additional personnel just to fill out the required forms, document our expenses, and then follow up—a cost I had not anticipated.

Open Houses Bring More and Better Referrals

To mark this new chapter in our history, on June 7, 1975 we held an Open House. In addition to many friends, we invited social workers and administrators from social services departments in New York and New Jersey, and with the help of Lou Otten, judges from New York State Family Court. These were the people who decided where children should be sent—who would determine if children should be sent to us.

We did not have many activities that day; there were no presentations or lengthy speeches. This was intentional, for I wanted our visitors to experience the campus and observe the children and their surroundings. I wanted them to sit in on classes, have lunch in the dining room, and take in the many after-school activities. I wanted them to see the faculty and staff interacting with the children, teaching and guiding them. I wanted them to visit the dorms, recreation facilities, and farm where the children spent their time.

In essence, I wanted our guests to experience a typical day at Green Chimneys and have the opportunity to ask us questions so they would gain a better understanding of the type of children we could help. In turn, I hoped that we would come away with a better understanding of their process and how they matched children to agencies. Above all, I wanted the social workers, administrators, and judges to become comfortable with us.

Preparations for this day had been underway for months—months during which I thought that we would begin to resolve our financial dilemma. When the day arrived, however, we were in even worse shape due to late payments by the very departments we had invited. They were now our future, however, so we put our best foot forward and welcomed them.

Our efforts were rewarded. Throughout the day people stopped me to say how much they appreciated the opportunity to spend time at the agency and the school. For weeks afterward many expressed being pleasantly surprised by our openness, by our willingness to let them wander as they pleased. I knew a good rapport with these folks was important for our and the children's success. Inviting them to campus seemed to have struck the right chord. So we hosted several more Open Houses during the first few years.

It also proved to be an important first step toward improving referrals. For years we had accepted whatever children the states and city sent us; we were grateful that they sent children to us and did not want to seem hard to deal with by turning any away. It was becoming increasingly clear, however, that it would be in the best interest of both the children and agency to match the youngsters' needs with the agency's strengths. I was debating how to broach the issue when the problem began to abate. Apparently by opening the campus to social workers, administrators, and judges, they had been able to see for themselves the type of children who were best suited for us. Gradually we began to receive more appropriate referrals.

I was also somewhat cheered by a call from one of our largest donors. Philip Crystal pledged to cover the entire cost of the new Resource Classroom building. A few days later, the Edwin Gould Foundation sent money for the farm, and the Hayden Foundation notified us that they would fund the completion of several building projects. Donations also continued to come in from parents and friends, and so with great relief on my part, our building plans were proceeding. We had completed a new gym and renovated the old one to become our new library, and plans were underway for an indoor swimming pool, a new dining room and kitchen, an infirmary, a maintenance shop, a science building, and renovations to our dorms. I greatly appreciated their support. We continued to expand the number and types of special events, trips, and activities for the children. The local kennel club put on dog shows, we held science fairs, and on Fridays we shortened the academic day to allow students to take mini-courses—lessons in activities that they hadn't tried or wanted to learn more about.

We introduced a visiting artist program that arranged for an artist from the area to come to the school and work with the children one day a week for a five- or ten-week period. A cartoonist, a children's book writer and illustrator, a poet, and a musician all made several visits. Each was a great success, inspiring the children to try their hand at a new art form.

Taking a Vacation and More Responsibility: Marco Island, Governor Carey, and Lakeside

> Simply stated, Green Chimneys may fold because $100,000 in funds owed for more than a year have not been paid or even scheduled for payment . . . the problem is complicated by the Courts, by the Board of Education in each local community, by the comptrollers or county clerks responsible for paying the costs, by the [court] cases on appeal, and by the need to go through the myriad of steps each year. We have a deficit hanging over our heads from the 1973-1974 fiscal year. We have accounts payable which we cannot catch up with because we are spending more than we are taking in. We have bank obligations which have to be met which stem from our building program and our cash flow problem . . .
>
> Most foundations have not responded to our appeal for help. Parents, staff and donors have helped as much as possible, but their resources are limited. The Ross Family has personally hypothecated stocks, securities and bank books to help the school through this trying period, but we have reached the limit of our resources. Philip Crystal, a trustee of the school, has rescued us over this last year but he, too, has reached the limit of his capacity. No bank will loan us another cent without security and we have no place to turn. We have no endowment and no reserves to fall back on.
>
> -Samuel B. Ross, Jr., Board Presentation, December 1974

It was a trying time. In essence, we were operating hand-to-mouth. On occasion, I even had to ask the staff to hold their paychecks until we received a check from the city or state that would cover them. As mindful as we were, however, sometimes a check still bounced. Myra was in the bank one day when a staff member tried to cash his paycheck and was refused. She came home understandably upset and embarrassed. On one hand, I felt the financial situation was beyond my control and not my fault; we would not be in such a position if the city and states had paid their bills. On the other hand, I was in charge, and therefore, responsible.

As the holidays approached, Myra and I made a trip to Florida with the children to visit my father and Adele. They had retired earlier in the year and now were living on Marco Island. As soon as we saw it, Myra and I could understand why. It was beautiful and tranquil, and we fell in love with it just as they had.

Myra and I talked about visiting more often. After having my father and Adele living and working with us at Green Chimneys for so many years, we and the children missed them terribly. Besides, getting away would give us some badly-needed breaks and time together as a family. But there was the question of where we would stay. A hotel would be expensive, and my father and Adele were getting older; having the five of us as houseguests was not easy for them. We would have to have a place of our own. Yet considering we had pledged all we had to the bank as collateral to keep Green Chimneys afloat, we were in no position to buy anything.

I discussed the situation with my father who suggested buying a house and covering the mortgage through vacation rentals. That seemed like an ideal solution so, with that as the plan, in 1975 we purchased a house on the island. That said, as anyone who has owned rental property knows, it is a lot of work and sometimes stressful. The property must be advertised and tenants scheduled well in advance, especially when the owner is dependent on them to meet the mortgage payments. When one renter leaves there is only a small window in which to ready the house for the next one. The rent must be collected and the keys given to the tenants, and inspections for damage must take place before returning deposits. There are always repairs. And, of course, all of this had to be completed from a distance. Still, it made owning a vacation home possible, and while we never went down as much as we had hoped, we had many wonderful times that the children still remember.

It was a wonderful getaway, a respite from the world, and one that rejuvenated me even when I was not there. Sitting in my office, feeling overwhelmed by the countless problems, I would close my eyes and see fish jumping, pelicans floating on the sea, and gulls flying overhead. After a few minutes, I would open my eyes and could tackle our troubles once again.

The reality was, however, whether we were on Marco Island or anyplace else, Myra and I would be talking about Green Chimneys. I remember evenings that we would walk the beach gathering shells while trying to solve Green Chimneys' financial problems. Our worries were real and relentless, and we felt a personal, total responsibility for the happenings back home.

◆ ◆ ◆

At the same time that our cash-flow problems were forcing us to rethink our spending, the students were forcing us to rethink our program. By this time we had completely transitioned from a more mixed group of students (neurotypical and special needs) to special needs students with behavioral problems. All of the children enrolled in the program at that time had been suspended from public school. All of them were ineligible not only for regular classes, but special ones as well, including BOCES. All of them had increasingly serious mental, neurological, emotional, and learning disabilities. All of them needed an enormous amount of help and constant supervision.

The first thing we did was to make the daily program even more structured. Academics, extracurricular activities, chores, homework, and meals occupied the majority of the day. It was important for the children to have some free time, but not too much. Now more than in the past, the children were prone to getting into trouble, and we had to do all we could to preempt problems. I insisted that the faculty and staff have ideas that they could put in motion at a moment's notice no matter what the age group, weather conditions, or time of day. This took a great deal of preplanning, but I felt that boredom among children—and the resulting mischief—was predictable, and the adults should be prepared. When they heard the children cry, "There's nothing to do!" that was not the time to begin brainstorming, rounding up the necessary equipment or supplies, and scouting out a location. Adults became restless when they had to sit and wait; it was easy to predict how the children would react.

I also was of the mind that the more control the children exercised over their situations, the more cooperative they would be, and the more progress they would make. So every day during the first few minutes of morning classes, the teachers gathered their students together for powwows. At this time, the children reviewed the personal goals they had set the day before, and with the help of their teachers and classmates, they determined if they had reached them. Then they set new personal goals for the current day. In addition, the children voiced any issues or concerns they had, and the teachers made announcements regarding the class and school. At every powwow, a child took notes that were then added to a diary.

Powwows were one of the ideas I borrowed from Nicholas Hobbs at Project Re-ED, and they were so successful that I introduced afternoon and evening powwows as well. We found that the more we involved the children in their progress and happenings in the classrooms and school, the better they did. Having them set their own goals encouraged them to work harder to achieve them. Keeping them in the loop by making frequent announcements reduced their anxiety. Giving them a voice by letting them raise problems improved student-staff relationships. Interestingly, when given the chance, the children often brought up the very issues the staff was anxious to bring to their attention. Asking the children to take notes demonstrated that the powwows were important; their goals and problems were not going to be lost or forgotten.

Individualization of the curriculum was another area on which I placed greater emphasis. Children came with various individual strengths, needs, interests, and abilities. A child may be at a second-grade level in math, a sixth-grade level in science, and a fourth-grade level in social studies. He or she may have advanced reading abilities but poor listening skills. He or she may hardly talk but be highly observant. He or she may breeze through assignments but do careless work, or be so meticulous that the work is always late. I felt it was critical that we design individual lesson plans that take such differences into account.

I also insisted that we inform each child of his or her level in each area, where they should be, and how we planned to help them. It was also important that each child not only work at his or her own level, but also at his or her own pace so as to reduce frustration and increase learning. If a child exhibited a special talent or interest, I wanted us to make sure he or she had time to pursue it, just like adults. Children feel good when they are engaged in something at which they excel, which in turn helps them persevere at tasks they find difficult. Finally, we set some short-term and long-term goals that we not only explained to students, but made sure they understood and accepted. We always encouraged the children by including a few goals that could be met easily.

As a social services agency, I found that we had a responsibility to monitor the family dynamic. Whereas in the past we would bring something to the attention of a child's parents, now I learned that it was our responsibility to assess and, if necessary, actively address problems with a child's home life. If we determined it was not in a child's best interest to remain with his or her family, we had an obligation to explore other options.

Many children came to us after a series of foster homes and adoptions. It was easy to understand why these children had emotional difficulties: moving from home to home not only meant that they had had to adapt to several families, but also that they had had a series of different names and religions. After coming to Green Chimneys, one such child made it clear that he did not want to be sent to another foster or adoptive home; he wanted to live in a group home. Knowing what he had been through, I had to agree. Unfortunately, the social services department insisted that we seek another adoption. Still, new to the system, we did as we were instructed to do. However, as we became more experienced working with the Department of Social Services (DSS), we took it upon ourselves to prevent inappropriate placements, and we went to great lengths to find solutions that were acceptable to both the system and the children.

Merging with Lakeside

Since 1970, with the support of the foundation and the school board, I had been pushing for change at Lakeside. A 1963 study done by the National Study Service found that many of the children at Lakeside would be better off living in their own homes or with adopted or foster families, and attending their local public schools. It pointed out that there were other types of children—specifically, abused, neglected, and disturbed children—who would benefit from Lakeside's institutional care. The study also observed that the administration seemed confused as to where Lakeside fit on the social services continuum and the difference between residential schooling and residential child care. Many of the school's social workers agreed with this assessment, yet nothing had been done to move the school in another direction.

I thought the study made some excellent points and recommendations, so I used it, the boards' directive for better fiscal management, and innovations in child care as a springboard to hire a new executive director and introduce new practices, policies, and programs.

Unfortunately, neither that executive director nor several subsequent directors could handle all that needed to be done. Invariably, they focused on one area and neglected others. One director concentrated on academics while basic needs for the children were disregarded. Another turned his attention to the school's mission, overlooking more pressing day-to-day matters, including that the school was discharging more students than it was enrolling, portending a financial disaster. They all ignored the boards' directive to control costs and operate within a budget.

Unhappy with the school's progress and, after much debate, deciding that the cost for care of abused, neglected, and disturbed children should be a public responsibility and not that of a private charitable organization, in 1974 Edwin Gould Services for Children and Families took the unprecedented step of spinning off one of its programs. On January 1, 1975, Lakeside became a separate residential child care agency. No longer would it be funded by the Edwin Gould Foundation. Rather, like Green Chimneys, it would be reimbursed by the city and state for providing education, care, and treatment to youngsters referred by DSS, family court, and other social service agencies.

Shortly thereafter, the Lakeside Board of Directors and I concluded that the current executive director had not only failed to improve the recreational, residential, and maintenance programs, but had let them continue to deteriorate—the latter to the extent that the Rockland County Department of Health cited Lakeside for serious health and safety violations.

Once again, the Board of Directors asked the executive director to step down. Rather than search for a new director, however, they asked me to take the post. In addition to having to run a boarding school and now a child care agency, the board knew that I understood Lakeside's history and operations.

It was an enormous undertaking given what needed to be done and how much I was already doing. In addition, the climate for child care agencies and institutions had become forbidding. The city and state were implementing rate freezes and budget restrictions, and social services workers were told to reduce placements. Nevertheless, I accepted. I thought Lakeside had great potential for helping troubled children. I was intrigued by the challenge of not only turning around a school and child care facility, but one that was larger than Green Chimneys. I thought it would advance the merger of the two organizations. I saw savings that could be realized simply by sharing facilities and employees. I glimpsed possibilities for broadening each organization's reach by cosponsoring events and programs. And, yes, I was flattered.

One of the first people I hired was Richard Chorney, who was recommended by our mutual colleague and friend, George Olshin. At the time, Olshin was a professor in the Special Education Department at the (then-named) Southern Connecticut State College; Chorney had received his masters from Southern and took several classes with Olshin, who also served as his thesis advisor. Chorney was an administrator at High Meadow, a psychiatric hospital for children in Connecticut.

Myra and I drove to Hamden, Connecticut, to interview Chorney and his wife. After talking for two or three hours, I offered him the job as resident director, and he accepted. In Chorney, I saw a no-nonsense, high-energy, creative administer who wanted to live on the grounds and be part of campus life—in short, just what Lakeside needed. In Lakeside, I think Chorney saw a great challenge, an opportunity to learn, and a chance for professional advancement, but he and I both had very similar personalities, Type A's who loved to laugh and saw humor in everyday things.

Chorney and I were a team from day one, which in hindsight I believe was crucial to our success. Previous executive directors had tried to operate independently and, as a result, could not address all that needed to be done. Chorney and I were in constant contact particularly in the beginning, discussing ideas, problems, priorities, and solutions.

We both agreed that the basics had to come first, which meant addressing the Department of Health's list of violations and concerns. Then we moved on to the improvements required by DSS. Although extensive, they were by no means unreasonable. So much had fallen into a state of disrepair that the

From birth, I was never without an animal companion. Here I am with Terry. We grew up together.

Me at age five at my Grandparent Taub's house, which was my second home. Already I knew the value of "man's best friend."

Indeed, "the child is father to the man." I never lost my love for animals. Spike is my constant companion at home and in the office. Spike is one of the many staff animals at Green Chimneys. An icebreaker for adults and children alike, our companion animals encourage conversation.

My maternal grandfather, Jake Taub, was a second father to me.

Growing Green Chimneys was a family affair. Left to right: That is me next to Adele, my stepmother. Adele is holding Lisa. My father, Barney, is on the end. On the floor are Donald, David, and Myra.

Here I am in Bermuda. I always loved holding the reins, whether in a pony cart or behind a desk.

My mother, Phinie, holding me in the sunshine.

Initially not very fond of animals, Myra became very at ease. As you can see here, she is no longer afraid of animals. Courtesy of Deborah Bernstein.

A student learns about caring for sheep from one of our international interns. Courtesy of Alice Sipple.

The high ropes—teaching trust and self-confidence. Courtesy of Deborah Bernstein.

Joe Whalen, me, and one of our llamas.

Two students enjoying the fruits of their labors. The students have after school and summertime jobs at Boni-Bel, our organic farm. Courtesy of Jason Houston.

Paul Kupchok teaches a young student about hawks. Paul developed our Wildlife Rehabilitation Program and is the creator of our "bird release" that symbolizes a return home for our rehabilitated wildlife as well as our students. Courtesy of Jason Houston.

A happy young photographer in our 1960s pilot visual literacy program.

Here I am a young teacher presenting a French lesson. Since elephants were not on campus, a cardboard cutout had to suffice. Needless to say, the farm staff is glad I have not found a real elephant yet for the farm.

A young intern, Jackie Bookless, works with students in our gardening program. Courtesy of Deborah Bernstein.

Our executive staff members take a moment to pose with some of our animal stars. Left to right: Associate Executive Director of Operations Dr. Duncan Lester; Associate Executive Director of Performance Improvement and Human Resources Dr. Sheila McGuinness; Associate Executive Director of Clinical and Medical Services Dr. Steven Klee; Associate Executive Director of Facilities Paul Agostini; Executive Director Joe Whalen; and Associate Executive Director of Financial Services Angelo Matra.

Feeding a horse in the sunshine is almost as fun as riding. Courtesy of Jason Houston.

Our beautiful granddaughters, Samantha and Sara, with Rosie, an assistance dog, at our 60th Gala. The girls consider Green Chimneys their second home and enjoy Hillside Camp every summer. Courtesy of Arpad Toth.

A staff meeting in our early years. Our dear Bella is in the foreground next to my dad. Mommy Mac stands beside me. Myra, holding her coffee cup, is one of several teachers at the meeting.

Daughter-in-law Mary, son Donald, and daughter Lisa Ross. They continually make Myra and me proud.

Poochy, the headmaster's dog, helped ease my homesickness while I was in Switzerland. It was a success formula I followed throughout my boarding school years. I befriended the animals and offered to be of service to their owners by walking and caring for the animals. I also helped out with the farm animals while in Switzerland.

Myra and I begin a wonderful life together. I could not have imagined a better partner for myself. She truly is my better half.

Canoeing down the river. Learning teamwork and enjoying the beauty of the Great Swamp at the same time.

condition of the campus was deplorable. As it turned out, the improvements required by DSS were to Lakeside's benefit; they enabled us to house more children, which helped us close the gap between expenses and income.

Just as important as revitalizing the campus was the reestablishment of order and safety. Here, Chorney took no time in making his expectations known. On his first night at Lakeside, Chorney walked into a dorm and found girls and boys making out in the hallway. When he asked where their counselor was, they pointed to a closed door. After several knocks, a young man finally came to the door. He was oblivious and seemingly indifferent to what was happening right outside his room. Chorney was incensed and ordered the counselor back on duty immediately.

Chorney also made his expectations clear to the children: there were rules, and if they did not follow them, there would be consequences. He was true to his word. When one student assaulted another, Chorney called the police who arrived, arrested the child, and removed him from the campus. The next day, DSS called; they wanted Lakeside to take the student back. Chorney explained that the student had broken the rules and knew the consequences beforehand. DSS continued to press, but Chorney held his ground, and the student did not return.

Normally, I was not in favor of such tactics, but Lakeside was so thoroughly lacking in civility and order that I had come to believe such measures were the only way to turn it around once and for all. The staff had become demoralized under the previous executive directors and were doing the bare minimum. The teachers did little to engage the children or help those with difficulties, and the recreational staff let the evening and weekend activities flounder between bedlam and chaos; child care, as we just saw, was practically nonexistent. The children took advantage of the situation to do as they pleased. They knew there were no repercussions for bad behavior, whether it was sneaking out at night, skipping class, damaging property, or worse. Luckily, Richard's tactics worked. The students gradually got the message and changed their behavior.

We were less successful in our attempts to forge agreement between the administration, faculty, and staff. I thought that if we all focused on the goal we shared—helping the children—rather than our differences, we could find some common ground. Unfortunately, many years of infighting had caused irreparable damage to so many professional and personal relationships that it was impossible to bring them together. Over the course of the first year or two, Chorney and I presided over an 85 percent turnover in faculty and staff, most of whom we fired. It was hard to let people go, but it was necessary.

After we took care of the basics, we were able to turn our attention to developing quality treatment and educational programs. We upgraded the psychiatric, psychological, and child care staffs to provide around-the-clock treatment. We expanded the school to include secondary grades; previously adolescents had attended the local public school, but given the students' troubles this was no longer suitable. We held training seminars and workshops for administrative and teaching staff members, educating them in the needs of disturbed and learning disabled children. We shifted from an overly academic approach to an experiential and hands-on learning approach. We broadened the outdoor education curriculum so as to make it not only informative, but therapeutic as well. Finally, we required all teachers to get involved outside the classroom. Some worked with their social services and child care colleagues, others with the recreational staff. It was an eye-opener. For the first time, they began to understand and, therefore, appreciate the work of their counterparts, which fostered a collegial and cooperative environment.

The children at Lakeside, however, were the real beneficiaries of the faculty's involvement. When the teachers witnessed how much learning took place beyond the classroom, they found ways to capitalize on the opportunities. Their participation in after-school activities made it possible to broaden the range of sports and extracurricular activities so even those children who were not athletically inclined had plenty to do. Their cooperative spirit with their colleagues led to interdisciplinary meetings, which helped each professional group do a better job. Their presence at meals and recreational and dorm activities made them accessible to the children who sought them out as role models, mentors, and counselors.

We also revamped the Lakeside vocational program, which was bordering on exploitation rather than rehabilitation. The children were employed as kitchen helpers, janitors, and groundskeepers not because of the talents they demonstrated, the interests they voiced, or the skills they could learn, but because these jobs were suitable to their "station." When I discovered this, I was appalled and dumbfounded. How could anyone involved in the care and education of children support or condone such a thing? How could anyone begrudge these children a chance at a better life? How could anyone think this was acceptable?

We sought to do better—much better. For example, there existed a day nursery for staff children that was poorly run. We hired a certified kindergarten teacher and an aide to set up and oversee the program. The teacher and aide taught the students how to care for children of different ages, how to choose appropriate games and stories, how to teach them letters and numbers and manners, and how to deal with various temperaments and actions. For the students, particularly those who were only children, the day nursery provided quite an education. It also went a long way toward improving relationships between students and staff. The students felt honored that the staff trusted them with their children, and in turn, they took their responsibility seriously and began to trust the staff. The day nursery was such a success that eventually we opened the program to the community.

As so much was in those days, the auto repair program was pure happenstance. One day, Chorney learned that a teacher owned an auto repair shop, which gave him an idea: would the teacher create and oversee an auto repair program for the kids? Chorney had worked at a school that had such a program, but he recognized that he did not know enough to get it off the ground. He needed someone with the technical expertise. The teacher agreed and work began. He and the children fixed up a rundown garage on campus, rummaged up some old tools and equipment, and then advertised for donations of old cars.

Little by little, local residents came by and dropped off or towed in their rattletraps; they were happy to get rid of them, and the students were happy to have them. Then the teacher taught the children how to use different tools and equipment, diagnose problems, and determine which cars were worth fixing and which they should sell for parts. Some cars took months to repair and usually involved a much-anticipated excursion to the local junkyard for parts.

After the children fixed the cars, the teacher taught them how to repair the bodies. They banged out dents, replaced rusty fenders and broken mirrors, and stripped and painted the cars. When a car was ready to sell, they did the necessary paperwork, determined the price, advertised it for sale, and negotiated with prospective buyers.

Word spread, more donations came in, and soon they needed more space. With the help of a local contractor, some donated materials, and borrowed equipment, several teachers and many students together they built an eleven-bay garage and body shop. Through donations they equipped it with the kind of professional equipment and tools found in a regular garage: hydraulic lifts, grease guns, air wrenches, a tire changer and wheel balancer, an air compressor, and much more. The children did such a good job that local folks sometimes stopped by looking for cars. All of the proceeds were used to pay the children and buy equipment and supplies.

The auto repair program was such a success that we used the same model to establish other programs. We set up a small snack shop for children who were interested in food service. It, too, thrived and soon began outgrowing its quarters. Following the example of their peers, the teachers and students renovated an abandoned campus garage, solicited donations of furnishings and commercial-grade equipment, and opened a restaurant for the public. A furniture repair and refinishing shop followed next.

These were huge but worthwhile undertakings. The children who were at Lakeside when we developed these programs had a unique experience: they helped build businesses from the ground up. Even the ones after them, however, learned more than the skills of a mechanic, cook, waiter, or cashier. Servicing the public, they learned they had to meet certain expectations and standards as well as think about business issues, such as the cost of materials, price of their goods, and how to attract customers. It was a learning experience that went beyond most vocational programs of the time and one I am sure they remembered.

◆◆◆

Staff Notes

> Just a nice FYI—we have kids do Farm Learn and Earn with Wilfredo—and every child that has worked with him LOVES doing so—they get to do farm maintenance, work with tools etc.
>
> Today was the first day that T. worked with Mr. Ramon this fall.
>
> He was so happy, I just saw him briefly in the barn, and he said, "Thank you so much, Ms. Miyako, for giving me this job!" with such enthusiasm that everyone who were around just smiled. It was such a reminder to me what farms jobs are about. I just want to let you know, he was doing great, and I am glad to see that.

Chapter XI

No Need For Institutions

> The public schools are the kind of institution one cannot really dislike until one gets to know them well. Because adults take the schools so much for granted, they fail to appreciate what grim, joyless places most American schools are, how oppressive and how petty are the rules by which they are governed, how intellectually sterile and aesthetically barren the atmosphere, what an appalling lack of civility obtains on the part of teachers and principals, what contempt they unconsciously display for children as children.[1]
>
> -Charles E. Silberman, 1970

I felt very good about our nature-based and academic programs, and in general we had made great strides at Lakeview and at Green Chimneys. I had experienced for years how much good can be accomplished with a group of passionate, creative, caring people, for children with special needs and challenges in an "institutional" setting. We were immersed daily in creating positive experiences and expecting no less than good results for our students. The children we took care of came to us as a last resort. These positive results had not been able to be accomplished for a variety reasons at home or in foster care, and the 1970s also brought a whole new challenge.

I had been continuing graduate studies all along, and in 1977 I formally entered the graduate program at the Union Institute and, as part of my thesis, began reading and researching the emerging trend toward deinstitutionalization.

My graduate studies made me aware of the public perception of institutions and residential care facilities, and because of my studies, I became hypervigilant to prevent Green Chimneys from ever being remotely associated with providing substandard care.

When we became a child care agency in 1974, we were not used to referring to Green Chimneys as an institution, and it was a very misunderstood term as far as I was concerned, though gradually we accepted the label.

We did not exist because we wanted to be an institution. My original goal was to open a boarding school. Green Chimneys and staff existed solely to help special needs and challenged children heal and reach their best potential. We were looking to break the downward spiral cycle of failure for a child, not keep it going. Anyone who knew Green Chimneys' programs was very much aware how hard we worked toward making our campus a friendly place and a positive experience for children, staff, and animals. Our goal was one of enabling the child to learn to live as effectively as possible within society and social institutions rather than adjusting the student to the restrictive needs and conveniences of what the public perceived happened in an institution. We emphasized integration into mainstream society rather than highlighted the differences between our children and those not faced with special needs and challenges. Our philosophy and practice were very much the opposite of the abuses that were being exposed. I was never interested in "warehousing children."

Kenneth Wooden, a reporter with a keen interest in the welfare of children, in his book, *Weeping in the Playtime of Others: The Plight of Incarcerated Children*,[2] describes a dismaying catalog of indiscriminate dumping of the orphaned, the neglected, the truant, the runaway, "children who fall under the legal form of 'incorrigible,' 'ungovernable,' 'wayward,' or even 'stubborn,'" and the mentally challenged into the same institutions as serious offenders.[3] According to Wooden there were more non-criminal children committed to institutions than serious offenders, and these children served longer terms in New York during 1965.[4] Culling this information from "Child Convicts," an article by Paul Lerman that Wooden cited, this was a pattern apparently repeated across the country.[5] He described intolerable mistreatment and physical abuse; neglect, non-service, non-treatment, non-education; official corruption, greed and misapplication of funds; and exploitation, experimentation and gross misuse of psychoactive drugs. This opposed our goal, which was to provide an enriched program for children who had to be institutionalized. I wanted to offer a secure "home away from home" for children whose parents could not maintain their children at home and could not afford a boarding school.

At one extreme were the state "training schools, which operated in every state, except Massachusetts, which represented a nadir in a class filter system for juvenile malefactors who are picked up by police, arrested, detained in a juvenile hall and eventually sentenced by a judge for rehabilitation."[6] Then there were "private 'hospital,' 'ranches,' 'homes,' which [ran] the gamut from exceedingly good to exceedingly poor; from state-approved and licensed to unsupervised and unevaluated."[7] Wooden brought a broad indictment against the American pattern of incarceration of juvenile offenders, mentally challenged children, and disturbed children in high security institutions.

My education on institutional abuse of children did not begin or end with Wooden's book. I began to find many other books that were required reading, and I began to wonder what I was getting us into and how would we manage to keep our reputation intact during this time. I had to catch up quickly so as not to make mistakes in what we would be doing.

Other resources included Burton Blatt's *Christmas in Purgatory* (1966); Edwin R. Newman's NBC television program *This Child is Rated X*, which focused on the inequities in the juvenile justice system and the consequences; Frederick Wiseman's *Titicut Follies* (1967), a documentary that chronicled the daily lives of prisoners in a mental institution; Thomas S. Szasz's *The Manufacture of Madness: A Comparative Study of the Inquisition and the Mental Health Movement* (1970), which explored the effect of persecution and mental illness; and Blatt's *Exodus from Pandemonium: Human Abuse and a Reformation of Public Policy* (1970). Many others added to the growing documentation of inhumane conditions and treatment in large and small institutions. As newcomers to the social services field, we were concerned what the flood of books and articles would mean to Green Chimneys; I wanted to be very careful how we would be perceived and accepted.

The public exposure of appalling institutional abuses had become coupled with California's growing "Proposition 13 mentality" that saw all social services as overgrown, over-bureaucratized, inefficient, and self-serving. It brought increasing pressure from all sides for "deinstitutionalization" of child care as well as mental institutions. We had not experienced this previously. We were all under close scrutiny because of the trend toward viewing any child in congregate care as being institutionalized. This was a scary way to begin operating a child welfare program.

Of course I was shocked and appalled at the abuses that were being reported, but what I found myself objecting to was the dangerously fast growing belief that all institutions were inherently bad, if not overtly abusive. It was in the midst of this emotionally charged environment that I focused my doctoral studies on presenting a case for the need for good, residential child care. My boarding school experiences would not have made me act otherwise.

In the wake of all this I developed a list based on my studies and on our experiences at Green Chimneys for all staff. We used this list as a starting point for discussion on what makes an institution hinder or help an individual's successful return to living in a normal environment. It was my feeling that the proponents for deinstitutionalization had painted institutions with too broad a stroke, damning the good with the bad, and obscuring the potential that is inherent in a sensitive and rational institutional treatment, residential care, and outpatient system.

Many of the things we established at Green Chimneys stemmed from my years in private school. The socialization of our students with the general public had been key to our program of rehabilitation. That is not to say that all else was less important, but children cannot be isolated and then expected to reenter the real world easily. Our policy was and continues to be operating as an open campus, and we encourage visitors and our neighbors to come up on the weekends and see our campus and farm. At the same time, we have worked hard to train our children how to interact with visitors.

The concept of "normalization" is one that seeks to replicate what a child or adolescent will experience at home, in the community, school, and neighborhood. Children at Green Chimneys do not see Green Chimneys as their home. They know why they are attending the program as a resident or day student. They know that the goal of our program is to *get them home.*

In parallel with the psychological and educational concept of normalization, the legal concept of the "least restrictive alternative" had been introduced by the courts and through legislation to affirm the rights of the disabled to social services, which least intrude upon their personal freedom.[8] The state agencies charged with the care of the disabled were challenged to prove, case by case, that institutional placement was more appropriate than less restrictive alternatives. There remained, then, an implication that institutional placement may, in many cases, be most appropriate.

Too many agencies did not work to prove that institutional placement was more appropriate, and what followed was the precipitous dumping of developmentally challenged children into community residential facilities that were unable to cope with an unprepared public school system. This may have been most inappropriate, however homey it sounded. These children needed more than just a blanket solution to the problems of institutionalization.

The concept of mainstreaming and normalization was introduced. The focus was to integrate special needs children and adults with the other children and adults in the community.

While mainstreaming sought to integrate special needs children with other children, the concept of "normalization" sought to place the disturbed child in a home-like setting, such as a foster care boarding home, therapeutic foster home, or group unit, with "normal" access to community facilities such as libraries, public schools, recreation centers, and theaters, mainstreamed with neurotypical children. But the major impediment to that worthy goal lay in those same community institutions designed by middle-class society to serve their own children. There was no place in them for our students, those the public schools called "uneducable," whom we were expected to educate; those the courts called "incorrigible," whose behaviors we were expected to correct; those the mental health system called "disturbed," whom we were expected to comfort. Our group homes opened at this time because we knew that children who needed residential care could not rely on the community services to meet their needs. As a matter of hard, if deplorable fact, though, when confronted firsthand with the issue, most citizens resisted mainstreaming and would rather have kept the special needs population out of sight and especially out of their "own" schools.

Secondly, it called for retraining public schoolteachers so that they would be able to accept and handle the new role they would play in the teaching of special needs children. Against mounting public resistance, mainstreaming called for funds that would be needed to sustain and expand the effort, which had already been made at the local, state, and federal levels.

There was then and is today a need for residential care. It was seen as part of a child welfare continuum—foster home care, group home care, and residential or institutional treatment. However, the foster care designation for all emotionally troubled children and youth in need of residential care remained highly debatable. The New York Council on Adoptable Children was, by its own claim, "a leading force in the effort to obtain permanent homes (with biological or adoptive parent) for the New York City children who are in 'temporary' foster care,"[9] but by no criteria were all of these children eligible for foster homes or prepared to return to their own parents. During the first six months of 1978, a study[10] of the families of the children in residential treatment at Green Chimneys revealed that:

- in many cases there were viable families to which the children could return;
- the children were in need of help that a residential program could offer;
- the parent(s) had not given up on the child and expected his/her return when feasible;
- the parents did not want to surrender their children to foster parents;
- the parents recognized the value in breaking a pattern of behavior in the family and the help which could be offered jointly to family and child.

In consideration of the problem of appropriate placement, it was dangerous to rely upon conventional labels. For children who had serious developmental needs, it was especially inappropriate to rely upon the old image of the dependent/neglected child. Nationally, according to Irving N. Berlin, M. D., president of the American Academy of Child and Adolescent Psychiatry in 1978, there were "about 2.2 million children (who) require long term intensive care and up to about 30,000 children are so seriously ill that they require in-patient or residential care."[11] That alone raised serious questions about the appropriateness of their placement in foster homes or community group homes lacking the personnel and facilities for the intensive care they so desperately needed.

Green Chimneys' year-round school program had always provided a "total caring environment" for the children in residence with special scheduling for the therapeutic day program. Activities on campus were highly structured in many ways. Social intercourse with the outside was encouraged but controlled, and the children were able depart to visit their families. Visits were always deemed in the child's best interest. Having functioned first as a private school, certain practices were maintained for the betterment of all. These were the experiences I had known.

Nicholas Hobbs had suggested that community and agency work together "to attempt to strengthen traditional sources of family support such as churches and school."[12] Directing efforts to rekindle confidence in our public schools as well as in our state and federal agencies needed to be done also.

The goals of normalization, mainstreaming, providing the least restrictive alternative, and small community living settings have been shown to be achievable, but my experience suggests that there will always be some children who can only be helped by teams of professionals in a total environment.

Dr. Amitai Etzioni has championed the cause for peace in our modern age. He stated his belief that individual rights and aspirations should be protected:

> The lesson is that the social world is complicated above all because people have a variety of needs and capabilities, which require accordingly a variety of responses: some people will continue to require institutionalization, some can live at home. Above all, what we need most is to curb our enthusiasm for over-simplification, and learn to live with, and respond to, the complexities of the world.[13]

At Green Chimneys, we have lived with and responded to the needs of children in our care and adapted to the complexities of the education, social service, and mental health system of which we have been a part since our inception (but heavily since 1974). We are still responding to the changing needs of society, and I imagine those who will keep Green Chimneys alive will face the same challenges. In 2010 we were told that our New York City apartments for adolescents are no longer needed. Where are our older adolescents to go? The decision makers responded, "back to their own homes, be adopted or live with a foster family." However, many of these children, if not all of them, do not have or want that option. Where will they end up?

There will always be a need for residences outside a home environment. What we want to ensure is that they will provide the best quality of care and see to improve the resident's present and future life.

◆◆◆

Staff Notes

> N. L., 18 years old, has been at Green Chimneys Gramercy Residence for one and half years. Passed from house to house as a small child, he had become defiant and hyperactive. His growing attachment to a rare white ferret named Fergie tempers his ups and downs . . . He can still flare up, but recently landed a construction job. He took pains to arrange for and train another resident to take care of Fergie during the day and checks to make sure the care is "A-1 quality" . . . for the first time he meets and greets people with ease, including members of the opposite sex, who show interest in Fergie.

Notes

1 Silberman, Charles E., *Crisis in the Classroom*, New York: Random House, Inc., 1970.

2 Wooden, Kenneth. *Weeping in the Playtime of Others*. US. McGraw-Hill, 1976.

3 Ibid., 32.

4 Ibid., 34

5 Ibid., 34.

6 Ibid., 28.

7 Ibid., 32.

8 Public Law 94-142, the Education for All Handicapped Children Act, as well as Section 504, the non-discrimination clause of the 1973 Vocational Rehabilitation Act, which states, "start with the presumption that everyone has the right to live in normative community settings."

9 Bunin, Sherry, ed., *New York Council on Adoptable Children Newsletter*, vol. IV, no. 4.

10 Nash, George. "The Lakeside and Green Chimneys Families: Results of a First-hand Look," Study. August 1978.

11 Berlin, Irving N., "American Academy of Child and Adolescent Psychiatry," *Psychiatric News*, May 5, 1978.

12 Hobbs, Nicholas, "A Summary of the North American Seminar of the International Association for Child Psychology and the Allied Professions," 6.
13 Etzioni, Amitai. *The Spirit of Community: The Reinvention of American Society.* New York: Crown Publishers, Inc., 1993.

Chapter XII

On a Scale of One to Five

If It Isn't In the Record, It Didn't Happen

> Our experience in developing and using these scales has highlighted the value of an objective instrument in dealing with highly emotionally-laden information . . . we feel we have succeeded in creating a 'small universal language' for reporting a child's progress.
>
> -Myra M. Ross[1]

If you have ever attended a meeting of professionals representing many disciplines you will immediately recognize that every discipline has its own vocabulary and its own way of describing improvement, lack of improvement, and/or concerns. We found ourselves in need of a way to develop a common vocabulary that would provide a better means of communication in order for each participant to provide information on the child and the family.

I suggested to the staff that they seek a way of correcting our lack of a universal language and develop a system of ratings that were objective, not subjective. We needed, I thought, to create a scale for rating the children that all staff would use.

In 1978 Myra took this on as her responsibility, and she worked with staff to begin the process of creating what was to become known as Green Chimneys Longitudinal Assessment Scales (GLAS). It took a great deal of effort on her part, but she made it happen.

The original GLAS were developed with the goal of developing a system that would enable assessment and documentation of a child's functional levels in all aspects of life in a residential program. Scales would also be developed to assess the parent / primary caretaker of the child. We wanted to develop an instrument whereby we could track a resident's progress in treatment from admission to discharge. The GLAS accomplished for us. Once developed, we used the GLAS to gather history, to measure progress, and then, finally, to give a prognosis on the potential for the child and/or family to do well. A major focus was to create a means to provide descriptions of behavior and levels of functioning that would be precise, objective, and easily understood by all disciplines—an instrument that would ultimately be a synopsis of the child's total functioning at specific target dates.

It was hoped that by defining sub-scales in the various categories, all staff would be sensitized to the multiple experiences and pressures that impact a child's life, particularly in a residential program, of his or her strengths and weaknesses, and that use of these scales would facilitate long- and short-term planning. Additionally, it was felt that by having all staff who deal with a child in a residential program input into the assessments, a more comprehensive picture of the child's strengths as well as liabilities would be the result.

For the parent/primary caretaker scales, we looked at and measured as well as we could through observation and questioning the caretaker's overall physical and mental health, parenting skills, social deviations, and psychosocial stress level in order to help us help their child. We also assessed their level of involvement with social workers and the child's treatment to ascertain the family's willingness and openness to treatment. The final evaluation was based on all of the preceding factors and was the social worker's prognosis for the family's potential for change in insufficient areas. It is vital to have a good understanding of the child's family in order to provide the best treatment plan. If it looked like the parent/caregiver was willing to be involved, we wanted to make sure we involved them. On the other hand, if the parent/caregiver was under severe stress or noncooperative, we would encourage their involvement as much as possible, and we would build the child's treatment plan around that factor.

For the child, the GLAS were, of course, much more elaborate. They covered the major areas of a child's life and reflected the various departments that provided care and treatment. For examples, scales that covered physical health and history were listed under Medical/Nursing Scales. There were Activities Scales—our Recreation Department would give the most input on those, and Employment Scales would fall under our Vocational Program. The key was that the actual assessments were well defined and easy to document, no matter which staff member was working with the child, and this held true across the board in almost any imaginable instance.

The GLAS are a rich system that made it possible for diverse practitioners—such as a gym teacher watching a group of children in a pool and a farm educator helping a child learn to milk a goat—to come up with a common language that described the results of their work. The system encouraged diversity within a structured format. We felt that we had developed a system that, in the growing world of complexity in delivering residential treatment to increasingly more challenged children and more families in distress, enabled structure and order to occur.

The children and adolescents arrived at Green Chimneys having experienced failure in prior treatment and special education programs. The records provided little to no evidence of any special abilities. It was important to capture new information and encourage staff to build on each child's areas of strength. The goal was to improve the child's self-image by providing more and more opportunities for success.

Today young people that arrive for care in residential or day programs have documented histories of moderate to severe educational, social, and emotional problems. They still arrive having experienced many failures in prior treatment and special education programs, and can generally be described as fragile, depressed, traumatized, and unresponsive to educational and clinical intervention. With so many disciplines and so many activities going on at Green Chimneys, there is indeed much to capture. With the farm, wildlife center, and garden considered integral components of the total milieu and a focal point in the children's treatment program, it is absolutely imperative that documentation of these program areas be captured and made part of the child's record. Our motto is, "If it isn't in the record, it didn't happen." This held true in the beginning and continues to hold true today.

If it isn't recorded, how can we evaluate our practices? How can we document what special abilities we note? The answers to these questions can only be found if there is written material that can be reviewed. At the present time, we are completing a revision of the scales, which we feel are even less subjective. They are currently being finalized for computerization.

Green Chimneys is indebted to Myra who chaired the development of the GLAS, who has had the responsibility for the use and revision of the scales, and who has been the person who has trained others to understand the importance of these factors.

◆ ◆ ◆

D. A., age 10: Being a Falcon (a leadership club) means making friends, happiness and helping, to me. I feel happy being a Falcon because people like you better when you're nice. I also feel happy because I get extra privileges. Being a Falcon makes me feel special because I worked very hard to get it and I want to keep it for a long time. I have made many new friends.

Notes

1 Ross, Myra M, and Clinical Staff at Green Chimneys. *Green Chimneys Longitudinal Scales.* Published by Green Chimneys. 2002.

Chapter XIII

He Who Has the Gold

> This past year has not been an easy year for everyone. We began the year with a drastic cutback in our resident population as mandated by the State Board of Social Welfare. From a population of 140, we dropped to 88. Not only did this cost us financially, and severely so, but also it cost us in terms of personnel, morale, and an overall deep concern as to whether or not we would survive another year The year has passed. We are still here,
>
> -Richard Hill, resident director, Green Chimneys Annual Report, July 3, 1978.

We had the GLAS in place, we had our programs in place, and we had learned the ins and outs of completing the many forms the state required. Who would have thought that staying a child care agency would prove more difficult than becoming one? But, in fact, that is what happened. That we were paid slowly and our resulting accumulated debt was just the beginning. Our wherewithal and fortitude were being tested at seemingly every turn.

In New York, it was up to the Education Department and the Department of Social Services to determine how much we would be paid per day to educate and care for a child. Every year, they analyzed our services and expenses and established the rates. Unfortunately, neither department ever set the rates for the new fiscal year before the old one came to a close. Very often we were well into the next year before we knew what the rates were.

My initial inclination was to spend at the old rate until the new one was set; that way, we would not spend more than we would be paid. But I soon learned that it was not that simple. This was a time of rapid inflation, and our costs increased quickly. If our food suppliers increased their prices, did we need to change vendors? If a consulting therapist raised her rates, did we need to find someone who charged less? If a child care worker considered another job because it paid better, could we offer him or her a small raise to stay? And exactly how many field trips, extracurricular activities, and sports programs could we afford to offer the children? Not knowing the rates impeded our ability to make basic operating decisions, let alone plans for the school year.

I also risked shortchanging the children. Let me explain by way of an example. Let's say that in 1976 the education rate was $20 a day per child, and we had an average of 130 children enrolled. Given that the children attended school for 220 days a year, we could anticipate that our education revenue would be in the neighborhood of $572,000 and budget accordingly. Now, let's suppose that as 1977 got underway, there was still no word on rates, and 80 days went by before we received the new rate of $25 per day. Had we known the new rate on day one, we could have provided $715,000 worth of educational services to children that year. Instead, because we operated for 80 days at the old rate, we provided only $663,000, a $52,000 difference. That money could have paid for more teachers, more tutors, and a lot more books—all of which would have been of tremendous benefit to the children.

There was another unintended consequence to this approach: it endangered the following year's rate. In government as in many corporations and other organizations, when it comes to budgets, you use them or lose them. If we did not use the monies allotted to us, the following year the department would cut our rate. The fact that we only knew about the new rate for eight months rather than twelve would not be considered.

So as not to lose money for the program, I did what other agencies had long been doing: I not only assumed there would be a rate increase, but also the amount, and at the start of every fiscal year, we began spending accordingly. This, too, had a downside: there wasn't a rate increase every year, and when there was, sometimes it was much smaller than I anticipated. There were several years when we got caught short.

Late rate decisions also delayed our contracts with New York City's Board of Education and Administration for Children's Services, each of which respectively reimbursed us for educating and caring for children from the city. Until the state departments determined their rates, the city could not draw up its contract since its rates were based on theirs. And until we signed a contract, we could not even invoice the city, let alone receive payment.

So every year, for many months, we fed, housed, educated, and treated the children as we waited anxiously for news of our rates. It was nerve-racking.

Another hurdle we faced was New York City's refusal to pay what it was supposed to pay. Every other county in the state honored the mandated rates for care and education, reimbursing us for 220 school days. New York City refused, however, citing the long-standing policy that allowed it to fund only about 90 percent of costs for care and only 180 school days; it expected the rest to be provided by the agencies' religious affiliates.

We were nonsectarian, and this policy was not a major issue when we had only a few children from the city. But as we accepted more and more children, 10 percent became an increasingly large number that caused us distress.

Then there were the audits that retroactively disallowed expenses. On a regular basis, the federal government audited our Medicaid and Title I programs; the Education Department audited our education program; and New York City audited our child care costs.

Common business practice dictates that when a contractor submits a bill, the client reviews it, and the client and contractor discuss any item in question. Depending upon the resolution, the client then pays the original bill or a revised one.

Not so in government. After months and sometimes years of submitting and resubmitting documentation for our invoices, and haggling with comptrollers and clerks in various departments in various counties, we would reach an agreement on the charges and receive payment, only to be audited some years hence and be subjected to another round of scrutiny, after which the accountants would inform us that certain expenses were not allowed even though they had already been paid. We would argue their findings and provide supporting documentation, and sometimes we were successful in convincing them to allow this or that expense. But it was never enough. Generally, in the end, they presented us with a bill—money we owed the government.

Between rate delays, slow payment, the city's partial payments, and then, years later, being informed that we had to return monies, it was no wonder we had trouble balancing our budget. The time and expense we expended just to collect what was due were alone beyond anything I could have predicted.

The most significant difficulties we faced at this time, however, were state mandates for campus renovations, termination of our day program, and a reduction in head count.

Early in 1977, we were notified by the New York State Board of Social Welfare that it would conduct an inspection of the grounds and facility. Technically, we had been granted a temporary license in 1974 to operate as an agency; the inspection was part of the consideration process for a permanent license. I didn't think anything of it. We had completed extensive renovations to become an agency; given that it was only four years later, I was sure we would pass.

I was wrong. That spring, as Board of Social Welfare representatives and engineers walked around the campus, their list of improvements grew quite long, particularly with regard to the dorms. They informed me that the Board had adopted a series of new regulations, and we were no longer in compliance. We needed more sinks, more toilets, and more exits. We needed new doors, new windows, new carpeting, and new tile on the floors. We were to install a sprinkler system in every dorm, which would mean installing several water tanks and a pump house. The rooms, the hallways, the bathrooms—everything needed to be repainted. And that wasn't all.

At the same time, the Board informed me that we had to be strictly residential—we could no longer offer a day school—and we could no longer use several wood-framed buildings as dorms. They were constructed like ordinary houses, and such construction was no longer permitted under the Board's guidelines. In addition, the Board had increased the amount of living space per child; we were now required to provide each child with 120 square feet, which meant that we would have to move walls and reconfigure the rooms.

Between the dorms that no longer met the Board's housing specifications and the additional space needed for each child, the inspectors informed me that we could board only 55 students, 75 less than the 130 currently enrolled.

This was a severe blow. Costly renovations (the Board's estimate was over $200,000) and an enrollment cut of more than half on top of several years of fiscally hard times was something I did not know if we would survive. While to some extent fewer children meant fewer expenses, there were many expenditures that would remain the same no matter how many children were on campus. It cost the same to heat the buildings, run the pool, maintain the grounds—in short, to maintain the infrastructure—whether we had 55 children or 130.

I asked the Board to reconsider their evaluation, but for the most part they remained steadfast in their assessment. Where they were lenient was in the time they gave us to comply, and in light of the fact that we had plans to build a new dorm, they were flexible in how we reconfigured the approved dorms to accommodate additional children. In the end, we were permitted to board eighty-eight children.

Still, with so many fewer children there would have to be budget cuts. We would have to trim expenses and reduce the number of faculty and staff. There would have to be layoffs.

I found this deeply distressing. The faculty and staff were like family. Many had been at Green Chimneys for years. I knew their spouses and their children. How could I tell any one of them I had to let them go?

The answer was I couldn't. I turned to Joe Whalen.

Whalen had joined Green Chimneys in February 1972 as a teacher and was now the Director of Education. I told him the problem and asked him to take the lead on this even though he had been in his administrative position for less than a year.

Whalen quickly realized that there was no simple formula. He could not lay off recent hires, for example, or eliminate a particular function or department and continue to meet the needs of the children. He also wanted to be as fair as possible to the employees. Rather, he undertook the arduous task of considering the talents, skills, interests, and personal situation of each employee—their length of service; job performance; if they were one of a couple working at Green Chimneys; if they were the breadwinner in their household; if they were performing double or triple duty as coaches, club advisors, or residents in the dorms; and if they had the skills or interest to move into a different department or job on campus. He did this as he analyzed the needs of the various academic, extracurricular, and recreational departments plus our operational requirements. Then he matched people to jobs as best he could and came up with a list of those to be released.

Some folks made it easy. They realized that working with such troubled children was not for them and resigned or retired. It was understandable. As Whalen reminded me recently, the children who were enrolled then were angry, destructive, and hard to control. They broke windows, tore out screens, punched holes in walls, toppled tables in the dining room, and threw stones at passing cars. The girls who were living down at Boni-Bel Farm liked to streak across the bridge on spring and summer afternoons, much to the surprise of the locals driving past. Occasionally, a couple of the boys took one of our cars to go joyriding. I had forgotten these things. I tend to remember the children's strengths rather than their weaknesses, what they did right rather than what they did wrong.

While Whalen agonized over the list of people to lay off, morale plummeted. The uncertainty of who was going to lose their jobs and when weighted heavily on all of us. Unfortunately, it continued even after the layoffs were over. Those who remained wondered about our ability to continue and if it was just a matter of time before they, too, might be job hunting. Having to make sudden discharge plans for about fifty children, many of whom we did not consider ready, was disheartening, disturbing, and darkened the already melancholy mood. In the months that followed, fears were fed every time someone resigned, and discouragement spread as we asked others to pick up the slack rather than fill a position.

Looking back, that was a mistake. We were trying to hold the line on expenses, but asking people to do more had other repercussions. When two social workers resigned unexpectedly, their colleagues tried to assume their workloads but simply could not keep up. Reports were filed late, appointments with parents were fewer, and follow-up on discharged students was infrequent. It was no way for a young agency to preserve its reputation with the Department of Social Services or other state and city agencies looking over its shoulder, and it was no way to help the children and their families.

In some cases, our efforts to be thrifty simply backfired. When a couple of child care workers resigned, we determined that day-to-day we still had adequate coverage; should someone call in sick or take vacation, others could work overtime to cover. It wasn't until we submitted our invoices that we realized our error. Our contract permitted reimbursement for hiring additional child care workers. It did not, however, allow for reimbursement of overtime expenses. That was money that had to come out of our own pocket.

There is a saying that "necessity is the mother of invention." That has been true at Green Chimneys often over the years, and it certainly was the case at this point. I was wrestling with the need for more staff, a self-imposed hiring freeze, and thin budgets when the solution hit me: an internship program. We had extra living quarters now that we had few children. The students could live on campus, gain valuable experience, and receive college credit, and we would have additional workers without increasing our expenses.

Myra wrote up a description of the program and the positions we could offer, and we did a mailing to area colleges. That fall we had several undergraduate students from (then-named) Western Connecticut State College, Hunter College, and Fordham University. The students who worked on the farm were tremendous help with the animals, chores, and children. The students in the social work department were less effective. The day and a half they could spend was not enough time to tackle meaningful tasks, and social work required more maturity, particularly with troubled children. The following semester we hired graduate students for social work internships, and it proved to be a worthwhile experience for the students and productive for us.

What we did not expect from the interns was a morale boost. They were hard workers and willing learners who were enjoying this opportunity and looking forward to embarking on their careers. Their energy and enthusiasm was infectious and spread to all corners of the campus. It reminded me why I loved working with young people.

◆ ◆ ◆

> Rollo, his team and his Green Chimneys accomplishment enabled my daughter to intern at Green Chimneys. That experience changed her life. She enrolled in Special Ed in Israel and majored in Animal Assisted Therapy. Rollo not only changes the lives of those in need, but provides others such as my daughter a life changing experience. I'm not sure that even Rollo fully understands the extent of his life long credits!
>
> -An e-mail from the parent of an Israeli intern, August 2010

Notes on Fund-Raising

I think lessons learned from fund-raising are important.

For example, from the very beginning, when turned down for grants or donations, I learned to ask, "Does 'no' mean never or not now?"

I am constantly networking. It is not planned or forced. I did not read a book on how to network. My passion for Green Chimneys just naturally spills over into my conversations. For example, I was lying in a hospital bed in Las Vegas while recovering from a severe bacterial infection—this was 2010 and I was eighty years old—and I fund-raised with the staff there. Doctors (and I had three different ones taking care of me), nurses, technicians, anyone who said "hello" to me and asked me how I was, if they stayed long enough to hear the answer, were sure to hear a bit about my beloved Green Chimneys. I was so touched when one of the kind women who served me my meals handed me $5. What a wonderful thing for her to do. I do not believe you can fund-raise adequately if you are not truly inspired by your cause. I am. I believe in Green Chimneys, our staff, and what we offer to our children and animals. I love the children, and I feel they love me.

Although I am persistent, I understand everyone has his/her own causes. I know not everyone could respond positively to my requests for funding. Making a new friend is very important whether they can financially support us or not.

Luckily I have had the pleasure of knowing people who are willing and able to help us. Donations range from fifty cents to a million dollars or more at one time. I am grateful for all of them. Just like our Green Chimneys Parents' Association in the early days, funding can be hidden and take the form of gifts-in-kind rather than actual dollars. We are the recipients of donated services or goods, these also are appreciated. Our "Days of Caring" by corporate groups encourages us all to give of ourselves. My parents taught me at a young age about the need to give back; I believe Myra and I have taught our children that same message. Recently we were featured on a United Way poster with the words, "We don't just wear the shirt, we live it."

Chapter XIV

Environmental- and Nature-Based Education

By the time I was immersed in Lakeside, I had been reworking the farm and its programs at Green Chimneys. This was to be advantageous to both Green Chimneys and Lakeside. Back in 1970, the farm at Green Chimneys was limping along. We had some animals. We grew a few crops. We had a vegetable garden. Most of the children took to the animals and learned how to feed and care for them; some liked working in the garden or out in the fields. Was that as much as the farm could offer the children? The animals were clearly important to them. When we gave the children cameras and told them that they were free to photograph whatever they wanted, we couldn't help but notice how many took pictures of the animals. We also observed that the more responsibility we gave them for the animals, the more their attitudes, demeanors, and self-esteem seemed to improve. Perhaps we were just scratching the surface.

At the same time, outdoor education seemed to be gaining momentum. Education journals were publishing more articles on it while more professional associations formed; one of them was the New York State Outdoor Education Association, which I joined. In April 1970 an estimated twenty million people nationwide participated in the first Earth Day that formally launched the country's interest in the environment and ecology. Shortly thereafter I was contacted by the Shenandoah National Park and hired as a consultant to help them design an environmental education program. It seemed to me the time was right to expand our farm program.

This was in the back of my mind when one day, while reading the *New Schools Exchange Newsletter*, I saw an advertisement for two teachers who were looking for positions in an alternative school. A married couple, they were both graduates from Cornell University and had teaching and farming experience. Immediately, I called them and invited them to visit the school.

Pat and John Gaines visited February 1971. A wonderful and talented couple, I felt from the beginning that this was a match. Although John was the one with a degree in agriculture, Pat, a Home Economics teacher, had grown up on a farm and was active in 4-H. As we walked around the grounds, I explained that I was looking to advance the farm program. I wanted every child at the school—from kindergarten through eighth grade—to be involved with the farm. I wanted to incorporate the farm into the classroom and have the children learn about animals, crops, and farming in a more formal way. And I wanted to get the community involved.

Pat and John understood my vision and shared my enthusiasm. We were not the alternative school that they were looking for, but I managed to convince them to join us anyway. In June 1971, Pat, John, and their two sons moved into Ross Hall. In addition to John being the farm director and Pat teaching Home Economics (something we began to offer when she joined Green Chimneys), they also were the houseparents for thirty-two boys.

With John on board, the farm began to grow and take shape as a learning center. I put the word out that we were looking for more animals, and donations gradually came in, including ewes, rabbits, ducks—even a donkey and an Angus bull that was made much happier by the arrival of an Angus heifer. John and I worked with the teachers to find ways to incorporate the farm into their daily lessons. We attended conferences and seminars to get ideas, learn what others were doing, and make contacts. We advertised farm tours and invited the local public schools to bring their classes and the community to bring their families.

We also introduced a number of programs for the children. Under the garden program, students could sign up for a plot of land and plant a garden. They got to choose what types of flowers or vegetables to grow, and we taught them how to prepare the ground, plant the seeds, water and weed, and determine when their vegetables were ready to pick. We started the *Farm Journal*, a weekly newsletter written by the students that reported on farm happenings. By this time, the children had taken on the majority of animal care. They mucked out stalls, cleaned cages and pens, and fed and brushed the animals. They worked hard and were knowledgeable about the animals under their care. It seemed to us that they should be given the chance to share what they had learned with others.

We developed the Junior Farm Instructor Program, which taught seventh and eighth graders how to give farm tours. Visiting groups from both urban and rural schools were greeted by trained Green Chimneys student guides and led through a series of activities at the Farm Center. Ideally the guide serves as a role model, sharing his or her confidence and skills in handling animals with the visiting groups. Student leaders can further the major behavioral objective of the program, affecting attitudinal change toward our students in the visitors. The guides have been part of the team that goes out on each Farm-on-the-Moo-ve program.

The program has proved successful for a variety of reasons. Visiting students are better able to relate to people closer to them in age, and thus become more actively involved in the learning process. The guides themselves are rewarded with a more serious and mature demeanor than is normally seen. The opportunity to serve as a role model, to teach other peers something about which they know a great deal, develops feelings of maturity and self-esteem. The responsibility of being able to accomplish various tasks and teach skills, as well as staying on a tight schedule, becomes very rewarding to the students.

In the beginning there were a few raised eyebrows. Teachers especially expected an adult to lead their classes on farm tours. However, when they saw how much the children knew, how successfully they related to their students, and how much their students took away, their concerns disappeared. For our children, it was another confidence-building step.

We also began taking animals on the road. If schools could not come to us, we went to them. We couldn't spare farmhands, but with the help of the guides, Farm-on-the-Moo-ve was possible. The children helped ready supplies for the trip, prepare the animals, and set up the pen when we arrived. Then they talked about the animals as they showed the students how to pet and feed them. Sometimes John did a demonstration on these trips; shearing a sheep was popular.

Seeing the success we were having at Green Chimneys, I began to think about Lakeside and wonder how we could duplicate our efforts there. One of the things that had impressed me about the school was its beautiful 150-acre nature center that included a plant and wildlife sanctuary, a greenhouse, a garden, an apple orchard, a museum, and an historic cemetery. It was open to the public, free of charge, for nature study and walks.

For the school's students, however, access was limited. Students could visit the nature center only as part of a class and supervised by a teacher. On the days that the students had permission to be in the nature center, they had to stay in the designated area, separate from outside visitors.

Coming from Green Chimneys where the grounds were for the children to explore and enjoy, and the students mixed with visitors, I found this startling and unsettling. Why not let the children take walks and hikes? Why not let them sit under trees and watch and listen to the many the sights and sounds? Why not tap the center's potential for experiential learning and recreational and therapeutic activities?

I began in earnest to work with the nature center at Lakeside to broaden its programs and place greater emphasis on creating an outdoor education program for the students. I wanted to take advantage of the center's therapeutic value for the students, to provide opportunities for the resident children to share this resource with visiting parents and siblings, and to allow them to interact with the visitors and the community. This last goal would help to counter already widespread public objections to "closed" child care institutions by giving resident children an opportunity to mingle with and work with other children and adults, as well as to act as a catalyst between the schools and the community—to take down the fences—by bringing in outsiders and leading them and our residents to a better understanding of each other. It was especially important to involve resident children in the public programs in such a way as not to violate their privacy or to display them like fish in a bowl.

At the same time, about a mile from Green Chimneys, a fifty-acre camp was advertised for sale. Owned and operated by the New Rochelle Lions Club, the camp had two winterized dormitories that accommodated seventy people, and a lodge with classrooms, a science lab, and a dining hall that sat one hundred people. It had been on the market for a while, and I had often wished we could afford to buy it; it would complement our facilities.

Then another thought occurred to me: these three venues—the farm at Green Chimneys, Lakeside Nature Center, and the Lions Club property—could each offer a distinct outdoor educational experience for the children, for the public, and for other schools, yet be brought together under one umbrella.

I proposed this to the Edwin Gould Foundation, which the board approved. The Foundation purchased the Lions Club's camp, and we called it "Hillside Outdoor Education Center." We renamed the nature center "Lakeside Outdoor Education Center," and our farm officially became "Green Chimneys Farm Center." In the fall of 1972, we brought them all together by forming a new organization, the "Edwin Gould Outdoor Education Centers," and I became the president and chief administrative officer of this entity.

By the time we were to become an agency, Hillside Outdoor Education Center had been open for two years. The facility had been booked for only twelve weeks a year, but word was beginning to spread, mainly due to our success with the children from Bronx Community School District 8. They had been our first residents.

After the Edwin Gould Foundation purchased the camp but before we opened the doors, Dr. Gene Ezersky and Ken Wilkoff arranged for me to meet District 8's superintendent. Ezersky was an advisor to the Foundation and knew the superintendent through his work at the Educational Facilities Laboratories, a nonprofit organization that helped schools maximize the use of their facilities, among other things. Wilkoff, an alumnus of Green Chimneys, was then a teacher in District 8.

I met with the superintendent and explained my vision for Hillside: it was to be a year-round, residential, outdoor education center where children and adults would explore and experience nature. Admittedly that was a bit vague, but increasingly there was talk of outdoor education in academic circles, and the superintendent already seemed convinced of its value for the children in District 8. He suggested eight, one-week visits over the course of the school year; he would send two classes at a time, and they would stay for five days.

I was thrilled. This was exactly the use of the facility I had envisioned. There was just one glitch: he wanted the first group to arrive in a few weeks, and Hillside was nowhere near ready. We were still in the process of winterizing all the buildings; the New Rochelle Lions Club had operated the camp only during the summer months. We also had to make the buildings suitable for our use. We planned to convert one of the small cottages into an office, create quarters for the staff from an extra bathroom facility, and cut in a driveway. All of these renovations plus many smaller ones were still underway; since the camp had not been used for some time and the buildings had been vandalized, there were dozens of things that had to be repaired or replaced.

I met with the Director Dan Johnson and the Assistant Director Dick Taylor, who had just come on board along with a few counselors. In addition to there being still so much to do, they reminded me, they had yet to develop a program, but being young and optimistic, they were willing to improvise. We cobbled together an outline of projects for the children and then focused on readying the absolute necessities. It was a stretch, and they worked hard right up until the first fifty children and five teachers arrived. Then for a solid week, they kept everyone engaged from the time they got up until the time they went to bed. That the week went as well as it did was a testimony to their energy, creativity, and love of the outdoors, since the program was makeshift at best.

After the classes left, Johnson, Taylor, and the others cleaned up and then got back to the renovations, doing as much as they could before the next group arrived.

That is how it went for the first year, and there was a fair amount of scrambling that went on as a result. Sometimes more children came than expected, and they would call to see if they could borrow extra linens. Sometimes it rained and after exhausting their list of indoor activities, they would call and ask if I could send the Green Chimneys bus to pick them up and bring them to the pool for a swim. Then there were the days when the chef didn't show, which meant that someone from the staff had to step in. I didn't know if they knew how to cook; I never thought to ask when I hired them, but if they didn't, they learned fast and on a big scale. The meals were not fancy, but preparing three per day plus snacks for sixty-plus people is no small undertaking.

After each group left, the staff discussed what went right and what went wrong, and came up with solutions for the latter. Some worked, some didn't. Many problems had to do with managing large groups. Arrivals and departures were chaotic. Gathering sixty people for a hike often seemed like an exercise in futility. There was always one child who couldn't find his shoes or who had to go to the bathroom, again. It had taken time to iron out wrinkles, but after lots of trial and error, things were finally running more smoothly.

In the early 1970s, the intent behind outdoor education was to transform subjects that children might consider boring, tedious, or hard to learn into interesting and memorable lessons; to promote firsthand learning, which helped children become perceptive and observant, and encouraged spontaneity; and to increase children's awareness of nature and conservation. Theoretically, the more children knew about nature, the more they would appreciate it, and the more careful they would be to preserve and conserve it, particularly as they got older.

Given that the program was new and the staff was young, it was a blessing for our first visitors to be from the Bronx. Most of the children had never been outside the city, so everything the counselors did was new and exciting. A walk in the woods took hours as they pointed out different types of trees, showed the children how to identify them, and then talked about their uses. They asked the children look for the various animals and insects that inhabited the trees and taught them how to determine a tree's age by counting rings. Often, they had everyone stop and just listen; children who heard nothing the first morning left able to hear and identify many sounds of the forest.

Rivers and streams were another source of seemingly endless fascination for the children. Fish, frogs, water bugs, snakes, turtles, plants—so many things lived in the water. The counselors discussed their interdependency and their importance to healthy rivers and streams. They would have the children search for paw prints along the riverbank and try to identify the animals to which they belonged. They would talk about the origins of the rivers and streams and their destinations. The children were amazed to learn that the water they drank in the city came from the Croton River in which they were wading.

A trip to the farm was part of every visit and always a big hit. The counselors and children walked the quarter mile down to Green Chimneys, and the farm guides gave them a tour. For many children, it was the first time that they saw horses, donkeys, goats, sheep, cows, pigs, and ducks up close and heard the different sounds they make. The farm guides explained the breed of each animal, what they liked to eat, and how they were fed. They explained how we depend on animals for food and clothing, to help us work, and to have fun. Sometimes the children saw a mother nursing her babies or a Green Chimneys' student nursing a sick animal.

Another popular activity was the archaeological dig. Parts of a local reservoir covered an old mill town, and when the water was low, the foundations of the houses and other buildings were visible. After hiking to the reservoir, the counselors and students would discuss how the mill town came to be flooded. They discussed the soil and rocks. They would take measurements, determine the sizes of houses and buildings, and draw maps. When they found remnants of the townspeople's lives, they wrote up descriptions and drew pictures of them. If many items were found, the children would classify them. It was a geography, social studies, mathematics, English, and art lesson rolled into an exciting outdoor adventure.

Classes that came during the winter had different activities and learning experiences. The counselors taught the children how to make snowshoes, search for signs of animal life, and survive in the wilderness. The latter lesson began indoors with tips on keeping warm in the woods, such as wearing layers of clothing and not sitting on rocks, and ended with an outdoor challenge: in forty-five minutes, the children were asked to build a survival shelter for two using materials found in the woods. As spring approached, they tapped maple trees for sap and learned how to make maple syrup.

None of the outdoor activities required fancy equipment, which we felt was an important lesson in itself. The schoolyard, a park, or a backyard was all a teacher or student needed. We wanted them to understand just how much they could learn by looking, listening, smelling, touching, and on occasion, tasting. They didn't have to travel sixty miles out into the country to learn about the outdoors. They just had to go outside.

I think we convinced the children; the teachers were a harder sell. Some of them had never been in the country and could not bring themselves to touch the animals, wade into streams, or go into the woods at night. Then there were those who felt they were losing valuable class time. As time went on, the staff learned to check with the teachers ahead of time and if asked, create activities that reinforced their lessons plans. If the children were studying the weather, the counselors might teach them how to build simple weather instruments, take readings, convert Fahrenheit to Celsius, chart patterns, and make predictions. If they were studying addition and subtraction, the counselors might take them on a hike to a nearby cemetery where the children calculated people's ages and looked for clues about their lives. Suddenly science, math, and history were interesting.

The staff's willingness to accommodate the teachers paid off. They received high praise, and the district asked us to create a summer camp for their students. They also signed up for another series of eight, one-week visits for the following year.

Word of District 8's programs spread, and soon other districts signed up as well. Unfortunately, hosting New York City schools lasted for only a few years. New York City was in the midst of fiscal crises so severe that it verged on bankruptcy, and eventually it had to reduce its funding to the school districts, which in turn cut funding for the program.

This disappointed the Edwin Gould Foundation. It had agreed to fund the outdoor education centers because their focus, just like the Foundation's, would be New York City children. Now they wondered if those funds would be better spent on another program. I pointed out that there were numerous children living in smaller outlying cities who could benefit from the centers. Outdoor education wasn't part of their curriculum, and nature often wasn't part of their lives.

The Foundation agreed, and we embarked on a series of mass mailings to area schools. We received numerous inquiries, and eventually several schools from New York's Putnam and Westchester counties enrolled as well as a few from nearby Connecticut.

As Hillside developed, so did the Green Chimneys Farm Center. Through personal referrals and announcements in the local newspaper, more visitors came. Parents from the community brought their children whenever we held a weekend farm tour, and kindergarten and elementary schoolteachers from area schools called to arrange visits during the week. One local school district sent all its third graders at seasonal intervals.

Preparation for these events was largely the responsibility of the children, since by this time they were not only caring for the animals, but doing most of the general farm maintenance as well. The younger ones took care of the smaller animals and helped keep the barn orderly; the older children cared for the larger animals, repaired fences and cages, unloaded feed from delivery trucks, and stored baled hay. Several days in advance of visitors, they would begin working to make sure that the barn, paddocks, pens, cages, and animals were all presentable.

◆◆◆

Something that engaged the whole school was the 4-H Youth Fair. Shortly after Pat and John Gaines arrived, Pat suggested getting the children involved in 4-H activities. I called the local 4-H office to seek their input, and within a week, a 4-H agent came to the school. New and enthusiastic, the agent suggested starting a youth fair; he had just launched one in another county and offered to help us.

This was more than Pat, John, or I had in mind, but we loved the idea and got busy. The following July, Green Chimneys was one of the sponsors of the first Putnam County 4-H Fair. For weeks ahead the campus buzzed as the children prepared exhibits that included everything from ceramics and basket weaving, to animal and garden demonstrations. Other area 4-H clubs and local craftsmen demonstrated making pottery, candles, macramé, and leather goods. Games went on constantly—tug-of-war, horseshoe pitching, sack and three-legged races, and egg-throwing and pie-eating contests. It was a wonderful weekend and became an annual event that is now in its thirty-ninth year. Our programs—farm and wildlife rehabilitation, arts and crafts, culinary arts, woodworking, and organic gardening—as well as academics have enabled our children to participate successfully in the Putnam County 4-H Fair, winning ribbons in many different categories.

◆◆◆

As one of the outdoor education centers, I also wanted to see the Green Chimneys Farm Center become a bigger part of the regular curriculum, but I realized that the amount the teachers could do was limited due to logistics. The farm was at one end of the campus and the classrooms at the other, which meant that the teachers had to walk the children down to the farm for part of a lesson, then bring them back to the classroom for the rest. This was less than ideal for several reasons. The barn at the farm wasn't conducive to learning. It was dark and the aisles were narrow; inevitably there were children at the back who couldn't see or hear the teacher at the front. The trip between the classroom and the farm not only disrupted the continuity of the lesson, but wasted time. Then there was the issue of the mud and muck being tracked into the school building; it was quite evident whenever a class had been to the farm. What we needed was a barn that was also a classroom.

I asked John Gaines to call his contacts at Cornell University and see if someone could recommend an architect to design and build such a structure. He did, and one of the professors in the agriculture department recommended an architect nearby. Soon we had a set of plans, and all we needed was the funding.

After sending out dozens of grant applications with no luck, we were finally contacted by the Gannett Foundation. John and I drove to their office for the meeting. On the way, we talked about an article we both happened to see the week before. It discussed the seat of power within organizations and how to know when you are in that environment. According to the author, there was a noticeable difference between the offices of middle management and the executive level. The color of the walls, the type of carpet, the quality of the furniture, the lighting—everything changed when you walked in to the seat of power.

We both had found it fascinating and discussed it for a long time. Then much to our delight, we got to experience it. The receptionist at Gannett directed us to the executive offices, and as we walked down the hallway, we noticed that the color scheme changed. When we walked into the executive reception area, we saw the furniture was nicer and the carpet thicker. When we walked into Tom Dolan's office, the executive with whom we were meeting, and he suggested we sit on the couch, we could hardly contain ourselves. The article had said that if an executive plans to give you the brush-off, he motions to you to sit in a chair by his desk. Being invited to sit on the couch meant Dolan was seriously interested in what we had to say.

It took many months, but eventually Gannett gave us a grant to begin building what came to be called the "teaching barn." Still in use today, it was built with inside pens for sheep, goats, and pigs, and outside pens for chickens, ponies, and other animals. The aisles were made wide enough for a whole class to stand between the pens. Additionally, the classroom had cages for small animals, such as rabbits, guinea pigs, and birds, and was outfitted with various materials and equipment for teaching students about animals and farming. The teaching barn was a real boon to our farm education program.

Hillside Thrives

One of the bright spots during this time was Hillside Outdoor Education Center. It was very successful, attracting over twelve thousand visitors a year. The school program drew children from districts in Putnam and Westchester counties, and Fairfield County, Connecticut. It wasn't only children from New York City who could benefit from outdoor education; even those in the suburbs were losing contact with nature, and more and more schools were trying to address the issue.

One of the things that attracted schools to Hillside was our willingness to tailor programs to fit their academic and social objectives. Some teachers wanted us to create activities that reinforced their lessons or focused on a particular area, such as plants, animals, or insects. Others wanted us to provide the children with new experiences, to do things they normally would not experience. Some schools asked if they could send their students for only a day or overnight, but for three times a year as they wanted the children to experience the same outdoor environment during different seasons. Others requested that their students attend with a class from a different school; they wanted the students to meet new children. Still others wanted to send the children for three or five days so they could bond with their classmates and teachers.

The schools saw us as accommodating; to me it was just common sense. If we wanted their business, it was necessary to adapt to meet their needs and preferences. By being flexible we found that not only were we able to fashion field trips that fit their goals, but their budgets as well. It was good for them, good for the children, and good for us.

By that time, the school program was just one of several offerings. We hosted a summer Environmental Education Day Camp that engaged children in a variety of nature lessons and activities, such as discovering why some plants like the sun and others like the shade, where various animals live and what they like to eat, and why we should be thankful for bugs. They also took swimming, fishing, and map-and-compass-reading lessons, and there were always plenty of arts and crafts.

Throughout the year, Hillside sponsored a variety of special classes and events. There were lessons in basic rock climbing techniques, flat water and white water canoeing, and fly-tying; a fall apple festival had children making apple cider and applesauce, carving apple-head dolls, and bobbing for apples; winter brought family winter sport clinics and a snow sculpture contest. In the spring, the children learned how to tap trees, collect sap, and make maple syrup at the Winter Festival.

The most popular program, however, was "Environmental Excitement." Most Saturday mornings throughout the fall, winter, and spring, Hillside sponsored a nature activity, such as "Art in Nature," where children collected sticks, stones, leaves, grass, feathers, flowers, and berries—natural art materials—and used them to sculpt, draw, paint, and make mobiles; "Symphony of Sounds," where they took hikes and learned to listen to the world around them as well as make music and simple musical instruments from objects they found in the woods; or "Corn Husk Dolls," where they used only corn husks to make an American folk toy.

"Oh, Go Fly a Kite" taught the children how to make and fly kites, and "The Night Sky" introduced them to some well-known constellations and Indian legends. "The Heat is On" demonstrated the power of the sun by having the children experiment with solar cooking and heating; "It's a Small, Small World" asked them to use magnifying glasses to examine insects, worms, leaves, soil, roots, and more; and "Rough or Smooth" had them discover the different textures in nature.

"Wild Cookies" showed the children how to gather wild edibles and make them into cookies, and "The Great Pumpkin" taught them how to carve and cook pumpkins, and roast the seeds. They learned how to make and maintain hiking trails in "Trail Making," and about conservation and recycling in "Paper Making" as they reprocessed used paper into new. In "Heaps of Energy" they built a compost pile.

"Environmental Excitement" was so well received by parents and children that soon we were offering Saturday afternoon sessions as well.

Hillside's initial focus was children ages six to twelve, but we had expanded and were sponsoring a summer "Environmental Studies Camp" for children eleven to fifteen. For two weeks, youngsters studied plants and wildlife in the forest, field, stream, and swamp environments, and took two- and three-day off-site backpacking and canoeing trips. For children eleven to seventeen, we introduced adventure trips, two-week hiking, backpacking, canoeing, caving, and rock climbing expeditions.

Hillside also launched "The Environmental Conference for High School Students," a one-day scientific meeting designed to encourage older students to pursue original, independent scientific research, and learn how to prepare and present scientific papers. In a forum patterned after professional symposiums, students from surrounding public and private schools gathered and presented their research to peers and judges, after which they answered questions. Students could submit projects in any scientific discipline, including biology, chemistry, physics, engineering, computer science, and the environment. Their projects were evaluated by a panel of engineers, scientists, and business professionals from local companies, such as Union Carbide and IBM, and a scholarship was awarded to the winner.

In a real sense, however, every student was a winner. Not only had they been introduced to the process of preparing and presenting scientific research, but many met mentors along the way and received college and career advice and guidance from the professionals who participated as advisors and judges.

The planning and coordination required by this program was extensive, and the following year we looked for a cosponsor, an organization that would not only help organize the conference, but also help attract interest from teachers and students. We found one in the Environmental Science Association of Western Connecticut State University. With its cosponsorship, we attracted more schools and more students every year, and by 1987 over nine hundred students had participated.

None of these events just happened. When budgets for New York City's schools were cut in the early 1970s and the districts could no longer afford to send their children to Hillside, we knew we had to get busy and look elsewhere for business. I encouraged Dick Taylor and the instructors at Hillside to join professional outdoor education organizations, participate in state and local environmental efforts, reach out to schools, and look for ways to involve parents and children of the local community. We needed to keep abreast of what was happening in our field and open ourselves to new ideas, and we needed to network and let people know we existed.

Taylor and the rest of the staff took my suggestions and ran with them. They became active members of the New York State Outdoor Education Association (NYSOEA). They joined the Town of Southeast's Conservation Commission. They sponsored the first Putnam County Environmental Conference. They brought together directors of nature centers to share ideas and information. They opened a recycling center. They developed summer and weekend programs for local children. Additionally, they issued press releases on happenings at Hillside that were picked up by the local newspapers and radio stations.

Their efforts to reach out to schools, however, were the most extensive. To drum up interest in outdoor education, the staff began traveling to schools in the surrounding counties, meeting with teachers, and educating them on how they could use the outdoors to expand the study of all subjects. Outdoor education, the environment, and conservation were hot topics in education circles. Still, the reception was mixed. Those who had a predisposition toward the outdoors or new teaching methods were quick to get on board. Others were less inclined. The staff realized that, as with children, theory only went so far.

They began scheduling day visits to schools, during which they took a teacher and his or her class into a field or woods nearby. This worked. The teachers began to see how to use nature to teach their lessons, and more importantly, they saw the children's excited and engaged reactions.

These outings convinced some teachers to arrange field trips and overnight visits to Hillside. Others tried but were turned down as their schools simply did not have the budget. Ironically, the reason why some schools couldn't afford to send their children on field trips was the very reason that nature, the environment, and conservation were on everyone's mind: the gas crisis. In the 1970s, gas prices skyrocketed, shortages abounded, and it made transporting children costly. The schools could, however, afford an instructor for a day or two.

The Hillside staff was game. If the students couldn't come to us, we would go to them. Unfortunately, we soon realized that it didn't make sense for the staff to travel from school to school while the facility sat empty. It also didn't pay; we needed to bring in more revenue per day than instructors could generate through daily fees. As with Green Chimneys, Hillside had infrastructure to maintain whether or not there were visitors.

Some months later, the Mahopac School District contacted me and asked if we wanted a bus. The district was taking it off the road and was willing to donate the vehicle. "What luck!" I thought. If the schools could not bring the children to us, we would go get them.

However, this, too, proved impractical. We didn't know anything about repairing and maintaining a bus, and it needed a fair amount of work; there was a reason the Mahopac School District had retired the vehicle. We couldn't buy gas for our bus any cheaper than the schools could for theirs. And it was, after all, only one bus.

Eventually, we came up with a more efficient way of getting the word out: teacher workshops. If we could inform even fifty teachers about outdoor education, we might reach as many as one thousand children. That made more sense than having the staff visit a class here and a group of teachers there. It was important for another reason as well. We knew that while we saw hundreds of children a year, it was only for a few days. If what the children learned was going to stick, if their interest in the outdoors was going to grow, it would be up to the teachers. We could jumpstart the process, but it was the classroom follow-up that would make the difference.

Taylor and the staff put together a day-long workshop and mailed flyers to school administrators and teachers. Participants could choose from a dozen or more sessions on topics ranging from mineralogy to composting and gardening, as well as how to begin an outdoor education program and how to plan an outdoor experience for a class.

Part of the inspiration for these workshops came from the staff's participation in the New York State Outdoor Education Association. Every year, teachers from around the state attended the annual conference in hopes of learning how to do math in the outdoors, how to put together a camping experience, how to use the school grounds for an outdoor education program, and the like. Taylor and his staff realized that many teachers were hungry for information; they weren't knowledgeable about the outdoors and didn't know how to construct an outdoor curriculum.

More teachers enrolled than we expected, and they all left with a long list of activities to try and a lot of enthusiasm. The second workshop garnered an even larger response, and soon it was not unusual to have one hundred teachers attend a workshop.

The staff also reached out to colleges and universities, offering to sponsor undergraduate and graduate courses with hands-on experience for education, recreation, and environmental majors. They worked out programs with several institutions, including Ithaca College, San Francisco State University, State University of New York at Plattsburgh, Fairfield University, and Fordham University. The program included courses such as Open Educational Organization and Administration of Environmental, Camping, and Outdoor Education Programs; Outdoor Education Program Planning for the Classroom Teacher; Interpreting the Winter Woods; Elementary School Arts and Crafts; Leadership Development; and Personal Growth through Adventure in an Outdoor Experience. They also established internship programs with several schools. In exchange for college credit, undergraduate students spent a semester at Hillside developing education programs, creating and maintaining hiking trails, designing exhibits and displays, leading children in outdoor activities, and helping with public relations.

I was pleased with Hillside's growth. It still was not self-sufficient, but it had come a long way and was on the right track. That was largely due to staff. They loved nature. They were passionate about helping children and adults understand and enjoy the outdoors. Because of their attitudes, they rose to the occasion time after time and did whatever needed doing. No one ever said, "I'm a naturalist, not a cook," or "I'm an outdoor educator; I don't do public relations." They saw what needed to be done, learned how to do it, and did it; I was proud of them.

◆◆◆

In 1981 Hillside Outdoor Education Center was permanently transferred to Green Chimneys from the Edwin Gould Foundation. My more than fifteen years of work with the Edwin Gould Foundation and Lakeside was supposed to have resulted in a merger with Green Chimneys. The idea had been that Green Chimneys was to continue the tradition of younger children and Lakeside was to remain an adolescent program. So when the Edwin Gould Foundation moved in a completely opposite direction, only those present at that time could grasp the depth of my disappointment. However, it was always like that here. Good things, bad things, I really had to take them in stride and just keep working to make sure the most important pieces were in place. Fortunately, good things did keep happening.

◆ ◆ ◆

In 2008 Green Chimneys merged with Clearpool Education Center in Carmel, New York. Clearpool was founded in 1901 as a summer camp that offered disadvantaged children a temporary escape from inner city New York. In 1990 Clearpool redefined itself to become a year-round second campus for its public school partners as well as other educational and human service organizations. Clearpool was one of the first educational organizations in the country to design a curriculum consisting of multiple-day, residential retreats conducted in a rural setting and coordinated with students' classroom studies. This "dual campus" model is still the cornerstone of our program.

Beginning in the summer of 2009, Clearpool began offering an educational program for youngsters with special needs in addition to camping activities. Having a magnificent 351-acre site with residential and day facilities, the campus was resource for the local community. We extended the Green Chimneys campus farm by remodeling Clearpool's old, unused barn and bringing over some of our animals. In addition to our Hillside Summer Camp, we now offer a second camp at Clearpool with close to two hundred children signed up each session. Clearpool is a welcome addition to our Green Chimneys programs.

◆ ◆ ◆

> J. M.: I like Green Chimneys because they take care of me. When I had chicken pox, the nurses put some white stuff on my dots to stop the itching. They told me to lie down and not scratch. I scratched them anyway. My teacher came to visit me and brought me a book. It is nice here because people take care of you even though you're not their own kid.

Chapter XV

Traditions as Part of the Fabric

While writing this book, I came across a short article that I had saved called "A Recipe for Boys." It was written by Robert L. Lamborn in 1964 when he was headmaster of the all boys at McDonogh School in Maryland. The following is an excerpt:

> We must be ourselves what we would most like our children to be. . . . This is not an easy assignment for us as parents or as teachers. . . . Only as we demand the best of ourselves—in warmth and interest and enthusiasm, in integrity and honor and . . . uprightness. Only when we have demanded this of ourselves can we have reasonable hope that our children will demand it of themselves—and only their demanding is, in the end, significant.

Lamborn's message rings true for all children, boys and girls alike, and it is still as relevant today as it was forty-seven years ago, if not more so. Green Chimneys has become a model for others to follow. We are truly national and international, for the work we do has implications well beyond our local area.

When people ask about our record of success, we reply that we will be judged not by the behavior of the children we serve, but the children of our children. There are no miracle cures in what we do. We just continue what works and look for answers. People may wonder if the cost justifies such a program. Will our teaching, our creativity be long lasting? Will our effort be sufficient to make a difference in the years ahead? We who are conducting the program share the same concerns for: funding, insurance, liability, staff turnover, and it will be many years from now before one can safely say the work was worth the result.

Success is not an accident. It is hard work. From a dream, an idea, a school with one program, we have become an organization with an array of programs. We dropped a pebble into the pond, and each ripple encouraged us to do more. Our first effort was a school for very young children. As we followed the ripples, we developed new ideas and accepted new challenges.

◆ ◆ ◆

I was thrilled as was Joe Whalen about the merger with Clearpool, a wonderful opportunity for growth. The setting is pristine, a perfect site for children, nature, and nurture. It seems to me that our programs, not our purpose, must change as times change, the needs of society change, and the economy ebbs and flows. It is important then that along the way, we create traditions. Events and ways of doing things, even small things, keep us connected.

Our first populations of students spanned all backgrounds and levels, and we worked hard back then to create ways for all of our children to succeed. We used cameras, tape recorders, mobiles, typewriters, art, music, poetry, and physical education. We made sure the children had campus jobs that they could complete. We gave them responsibility for cleaning their rooms, their classrooms, the dining room, and the policing of the grounds. The care of the animals and garden gave them activities and chores to carry out each day. We were able to enrich their lives through trips, artists in residence, musical events, and carnivals and fairs. We gave them the opportunity to appreciate the outdoors. We went on long hikes. We swam in the river across from the main campus. We fished and caught frogs and turtles. We looked for exciting things for them to do. If something worked, we kept it, and it became part of the fabric of Green Chimneys; it became a tradition.

We provided diverse and enjoyable activities. Our offerings kept the children busy and involved in our Green Chimneys community, and gave them an opportunity to give back to the community in which they lived. By contributing, they developed a sense of belonging. Along the way, they learned independence and inter-dependence.

Children and staff celebrated birthdays and holidays together. We all ate together in the dining room. We had picnics for children and staff in the warm weather, and in the cold weather we served hot chocolate for snacks after school. When children were ice skating on the pond or sleigh riding on the hill behind the barn, they really enjoyed the break. Much of this continues today. In fact, many more activities occur. We have off-ground skiing and skating trips in the winter and camping trips in the summer.

Today, most staff continue to eat and say grace with the children in the dining hall for meals. It keeps us connected. The present grace reads, "For this food upon our table and for the animals outside our door / We thank you Heavenly Father / For these things and many more."

Holidays are, of course, a big part of tradition at Green Chimneys. Thanksgiving is an important holiday for us, and my personal favorite. Nondenominational, it is an opportunity for all of us to celebrate together, give thanks for what we have, and remember to give back. Initially, we had our Thanksgiving service on campus, and then it branched out when we were given permission to hold a service in the Old Southeast Church, which was built in 1794. Donald's class was the first to have the Thanksgiving service in the church. The church had no electricity or heat, and it was often cold enough for the windows to fog up inside from our breath while we were there.[1] We would give the children a hot stone to hold to help keep them warm. In the earliest days, we would walk there. The road was not as direct as it is today, and there was much less traffic in years gone by.

The children and staff created the nondenominational services, which include readings, songs, skits, and announcements about charitable collections undertaken by classes. The services end with a moment of silence as the rope to ring the old bell in the belfry is pulled.[2] Because some children rejoin their families over the holidays and some remain on campus, we traditionally hold a Thanksgiving service and luncheon the Tuesday before the holiday so that all students can participate. The children who remain on campus still celebrate the actual holiday with staff. 2009 was the first year in many years that we could not use the Old Southeast Church due to a flu epidemic. Instead, we held the nondenominational service in our Dining Hall as well as our traditional feast. The Dining Hall is transformed with cloth table coverings and china instead of the usual plastic trays. Staff volunteers become the wait staff, and our chef creates a terrific traditional Thanksgiving feast.

The December holidays give rise to caroling, baking, gift making and a special party. Our outdoor education program has sold trees and wreaths over the years. Our neighbors have been wonderful to the children on holidays, providing them with wonderful gifts.

Halloween was always fun and today is a big production. Our recreation staff sends out a list of the costumes to all the classes so the children can choose what they would like to be for Halloween. Because we have been collecting costumes for many years, there are literally hundreds to choose from, some made here, some purchased. If one of the students really wants to be something we do not have, our staff will sew or purchase a costume for them. Last year one dorm unit wanted to be characters from a cartoon show, so staff sewed them each costume. Many staff come dressed in costumes also, and we have a pumpkin roll and the children "trick or treat" right on campus. On Valentine's Day the children distribute fresh flowers that are sent by staff to each other and to the children. It is a mini-internal fundraiser as well. At Easter we hold an egg hunt. All it takes to do these things is a vivid imagination and mobilizing people.

The release of a bird when a child is about to leave is definitely one of our most beautiful and unique traditions, which and was developed twenty years ago by Paul Kupchok, when he was director of the Farm and Wildlife Program. A child who is ready for discharge holds a rehabilitated bird that is also ready for "discharge" and releases it. As the child releases the bird, students and staff gather to offer a short prayer expressing the hope that each will make it home. The message is that the bird is returning to the wild and its natural home after being healed, and the child is returning home or to a less restrictive environment. A beautiful tile mural depicts this event. It is located on the outside wall of the dining room for all to see. Joe Whalen called the mural "Safe Journey Home," which is an appropriate name.

In the summertime we walk along Gage Road, which was originally a dirt road, to the reservoir where we enjoy a picnic lunch. After the picnic, the younger children are picked up by van, and the older children walk back to the campus. Some of the children are allowed to ride bicycles and at times some even ride horses.

Twice a year we visit the Cathedral Church of Saint John the Divine with Farm-on-the-Moo-ve. In the fall we go down for the annual blessing of the animals, which is a big celebration. The children and animals find a warm welcome there, as do our staff, who are encouraged to bring their pets along for the blessing.

On campus, we have a parade of the animals to celebrate special times. The animals are groomed by the children and wear a ribbon or flower, and the children proudly parade them around campus. This past summer, when we dedicated our school as Newman's Own Education Center, was one such occasion where we had an animal parade. Our visitors really enjoyed it.

In autumn we celebrate the inception of Green Chimneys with the Fall Harvest Festival and again in the spring with three days of festivities that we call Little Folk Farm Day. Both events are open to the community, but the primary focus is for preschool children to enjoy our campus and farm. Children come from the entire region to visit the farm, go on hay rides, pony rides, and play games. Also in the spring we have the With Wings and a Prayer Day, a birds of prey event with a whole range of activities at the farm. With Wings and a Prayer Day began over eighteen years ago and now attracts a crowd of over five thousand. Celebrities and wildlife experts attend the event, and we could not manage without the children and staff helping.

Our participation in 4-H is another tradition of which I am especially proud. We were one of the first organizations in Putnam County to participate, and today our children are major presenters. Our students participate in public speaking presentations in the winter, and every student and teacher cooperates in our participation in the Putnam County 4-H Fair at the end of July each summer. Our life skills classes enter baked goods to be judged and sold. Individual students enter art projects. Each class enters a group project with themes from science, social studies, literature, math, horticulture, agriculture, arts and crafts, and technology. Projects run the gamut of butterfly gardens to solar powered model cars, basketry to rocketry, life stages of frogs to the life of Rip Van Winkle. The whole school attends the fair on Friday. Some of our students' projects have been chosen to continue on to the New York State Fair. We are extra proud of their accomplishments, perhaps because our Green Chimneys children come here because they cannot cope in a regular school. Their accomplishments in 4-H are not just about winning—they represents the long, hard journey they took to get there.

One of the activities I particularly enjoy are sing-alongs with the children. My favorite songs are not part of the children's repertoire these days, and I have to admit that what they like to sing is not part of my musical background. However, nowadays I would not try to put on a breech cloth and beat a drum so that we could perform Native American dancing, though there was a time I did that too. Former counselor Rollie Phillips and I put on quite a show. Today Rollie is a practicing surgeon in Cleveland, Ohio, and I doubt he would want to join me in repeating our earlier exhibition.

A number of years ago we developed "We are Family Weekends" for children, families, and staff. We bring children from one unit and their families, including siblings, together with staff to develop an extended "family" so that all members can become acquainted and work together on common goals. The parents make new friends, and it becomes a support group. They sit together at events. They develop a closeness not possible otherwise.

Learn and Earn is another program that is also a tradition. It is a campus career exploration program. Children are introduced to work. Here again we realize that children living away from home and day students experiencing family, neighborhood, and school problems might miss these opportunities, so we provide them here. The children also receive much needed attention and role modeling from staff who have similar interests.

Spring Fling, a week of outdoor activities celebrated after the end of winter and before summer, allows children and staff to enjoy each other. It includes games, competition, and other special events.

Welcoming interns and summer counselors to work in the program always allows our children to meet people from other places, including foreign countries.

Religious instruction has always been included for all children. Years ago we had a bus to take the children to church in Brewster, to the temple on Route 22, and to the Catholic church in Putnam Lake. Everyone went someplace. We sent staff with the children. There were occasional problems, but in general the children were well received. We distributed coins to the children for the collection. Sometimes the coins bought candy instead. It was a chore to see that the children were properly dressed.

Letter writing was always considered a valued activity for children to learn. When children had no one to send letters to, we found pen pals for them. Wish list letters to "Santa" or "Frosty" are followed by thank you notes for gifts received. At Green Chimneys it is customary for children and staff to exchange cards. The practice of giving birthday cards and get well cards are a way for the child to understand that sending letters and cards is a two-way street.

With school in session 210 days a year, much attention is given to keeping the grounds clean, to planting flowers and shrubs, to keeping bedrooms and classrooms clean, and to setting and clearing the tables. It is exactly these daily chores that make us a community. Care for one's environment has to be built into daily living, or it will be overlooked. Groups of students and staff have also often gone to clean the grounds of the Old Southeast Church, where we hold our Thanksgiving service.

It is exciting to watch children compete in athletic events. Some dream about being the superstar of the future. Today we emphasize that athletics must offer intramural as well as interschool competition. We used to have a daily run around the campus before school. The run served two purposes. It gave the students a chance for some exercise before facing the school day. It also provided a chance for the student to burn off a little energy so that the classroom would not suffer from the overacting behavior the child might exhibit.

Running, hiking, fitness programs, swimming, horseback riding, and both high and low ropes courses are all made available to the children on the campus at Green Chimneys and have been encouraged. Non-athletic programs, too, such as poetry, art, music, chorus, and writing continue to play an important role in our school. A literary celebration is held in the winter for everyone, including families. We have published yearbooks and anthologies over the years so that children can have tangible memories of their childhood. Former students who return for a visit like to have us take out the yearbooks so they can sit and remember "back when." Our annual Alumni Day in midsummer becomes a very large "family reunion."

Today we have added the special cultural diversity programs that enrich the lives of the children, including Black History and a Parade of Nations, with the participation of staff and interns from many different countries working at Green Chimneys. We examine what we do for each holiday, lest we find that children look upon the holidays as a day off from school and nothing else.

What are the happy memories children will remember when they leave the program? Which staff member will stand out in their minds and why? What skills will they know they accomplished while away from home? I have always believed that we must fill in for the parents for the times the children are not home to celebrate events.

Recognizing accomplishments is built into every program, and it is a core tradition. At our all-campus meetings that are held the third Wednesday of every month, staff and students are recognized for their achievements. The children also nominate staff for good deeds, and the children receive the same recognition. It is another way of creating that connection to have children and staff together to show their appreciation for each other. When the 4-H awards are handed out to the children, the staff members are all present to applaud their accomplishment.

I have emphasized that if we give consequences to children for poor behavior then we must reward them for good behavior. No child should ever be able to say, "no one ever praised me for what I did well, but they sure pounced on me for anything they felt I did wrong." I think I have learned that lesson, and I believe I have practiced that with the staff as well.

Sharing traditions and special events becomes part of the fabric of the life of the people connected in a community, program, or family. They create a shared history and serve to celebrate the many milestones, large and small, in the children's lives at Green Chimneys. We have emphasized from the beginning that we are here *in loco parentis*, and we have come together and consider ourselves a family, and in a very real sense, we are family.

People are amazed that I answer my own phone, that all of us are friendly, and that we are so responsive to each family's needs. I know, at times, that I have gone overboard to do nice things for people. I know that staff do likewise. It is built into the fabric of who we are. It is also a tradition.

While we value our traditions, we also are innovative, responding to new needs as they are presented. It is not what Green Chimneys does well that counts, but how we respond to people's needs. We want to keep our core program and philosophy intact but only if it truly continues to be of service. More than anything else, Green Chimneys has a long tradition of accepting change. We owe it to the children.

◆ ◆ ◆

> A. A., age 8: Green Chimneys takes us places we have never been before. We go to Squantz Pond, walks and hikes, camping and to a lighthouse. When I go to these new places I feel excited and curious. One time we went to Lake Quassy. My favorite ride was the one that I squished Chris on. I had fun squishing Chris. We went on it two times. First I got squashed then Chris did.

Notes

1 A few years ago, electricity was added; however, the church is still unheated.

2 Nona Starzyk, a beloved teacher for the past twenty years, has traditionally had the honor of ringing the bell.

Chapter XVI

This I Will Never Forget

Certain events I will never forget. There were two children in the first group we served in 1948 who have stayed touch with me. They were a brother and elder sister. A few years ago I heard from the girl who had some personal concerns about which she wanted to speak. In the course of the conversation, she spoke about the two ponies we had when she was at Green Chimneys and wondered if Peaches was still at the farm. I was amazed at what she remembered, and she was amazed that I remembered her and her brother.

In the summer of 2002, one of our first students received a Centennial Award from Western Connecticut State University where he had been a member of the faculty. He had made a name for himself at the Alternative High School in Danbury, and though he is now retired, he remains active with Jane Goodall's "Roots & Shoots" program. A cancer survivor, he has been involved with encouraging running and racing for the physically challenged. His mother, who left him in the care of his childless aunt and uncle, was married to an Iranian physician. They moved to Iran and had little, if any, contact with their son. My wife was able to share the Centennial Award experience with him for she, too, received an award that day. It was the fiftieth anniversary of her graduation from the University where she had earned both an undergraduate and graduate degree. Green Chimneys was well represented as a former board member also received a similar award that day.

Sometimes one has to be very specific with his or her questions. I can remember when suddenly lights appeared in a dormitory room after lights-out. I asked who turned the lights on, and there was silence. Not until I saw a broom standing near the light switch did I change my question to, "Who used the broom handle to turn on the lights?" At that point one of the boys answered that he it was the culprit. "Why didn't you tell me before?" I responded. He replied that I had not asked the right question. That was stretching it a bit, I thought.

One morning the farm staff arrived at the farm to find the cage with the white doves missing. Someone had entered during the night and had made off with them. Before anyone could figure out what had happened or report it to the sheriff's office, a New York City policeman arrived. He and his fellow cop had chased a speeding car that the two men driving ended up crashing into a wall. They found the doves inside the car, which turned out to be car stolen also. When the officers arrested the men, the men explained the presence of doves by saying that they had just bought the doves and needed to get them to their home. The officers explained they do not take birds where they were going. What followed was a conversation between the two officers as to what to do with the birds. One suggested they call the ASPCA. The other said that he had a better idea. He explained that he lived in Westchester County on the border of Putnam County. He told his partner that in order for them to get off duty quicker, he would take the doves to a school in Brewster, New York, which maintains a collection of animals. So, the stolen doves ended back at Green Chimneys before the children even knew they were missing.

Recently, a father of former staff member found out I was writing my memoirs. He wrote a letter reminding me of his experience with Green Chimneys. One spring, in the late 1960s, his daughter and her husband graduated from San Francisco University. They had signed up to go into the Peace Corps in September but needed employment and a place to stay before they left. He suggested they come east and volunteered to find them jobs. His son-in-law had supervised children's playgrounds in San Francisco. The father sat on the camp committee of the Jewish Center of Lake Carmel and proposed they hire the couple. The offer was turned down, and the father was sure it was because they were an interracial couple. On an impulse one Sunday morning after the couple had been rejected, he called me and asked to meet with me. I was just about to leave for a vacation, but he insisted. I agreed. He came to my office, described the couple and their talents, and he was shocked that I immediately said, "They are hired." When he began to explain the husband was black, my instant response was, "Did I ask the color?" More than once he has reminded me that he has genuine respect, gratitude, and admiration for my kindness, lack of prejudice, and my practice of embracing diversity. His other daughter's child has been a camper at Hillside for many years. It was she who encouraged her father to remind me about this incident.

One student showed me that I am not as perfect at my job as I might have thought. He was constantly in motion and his eyes moved from side to side. He would jump up on a piece of furniture and exclaim, "I am hyperactive! I am hyperactive" until you helped him down. He loved to enter my office and read upside down what was on my desk. He used profanity to the extreme. He loved to yell "motherf****r." When admonished one day, he promised to refrain from yelling that expression. The next day I overheard him yelling "twelve." He had found a substitution. Some mornings I would manage the dining room by myself so that the staff could have an early morning meeting. One particular day the children were having trouble quieting down for dismissal. They knew that if they settled down I would take them outside for a few minutes of play before school. Finally they quieted down, and I was about to dismiss them when the door opened and the staff entered. My little friend yelled at the top of his voice, "f****d it up again, Ross," and of course, everyone broke out in laughter.

A student from a very religious Jewish background had an interesting experience one Friday on his way home for a weekend visit. He detoured into Macy's and had a chance to sit on Santa Claus's lap. You can imagine his family's surprise when his picture appeared in the *Daily News*. He's the same student who caught his penis in the door of his clothing cabinet.

Another young man pulled so hard with the bit on a horse's mouth—Mehregan, the Caspian miniature horse from Iran—that the horse fell over backward. The young man's parents sued us because they believed their son could never have children. The case was settled after the boy proved his parents wrong—more than once.

Former students do stay in touch. Occasionally, I get a phone call, and the voice on the other end will say, "I know you won't remember me but . . ." and before they say another word, I ask them a few questions and almost 100 percent of the time I tell them their name, what they looked like, and something special I remember about them. It amazes them, and it amazes my staff.

Some students call to stay in touch, others call for advice, and one in particular calls routinely when drinking to alternately threaten to sue me or tell me how much we helped her. There is the former student who lives in Florida, who suffers from mental illness, and calls me for guidance. Another former student calls to see what is new at Green Chimneys; he says he would like to visit, but he battles with agoraphobia.

Thelonious Monk's daughter, Barbara, and our son, David, were in the same class at Green Chimneys. Barbara died at age thirty-one from cancer, and David died at thirty years old from Hodgkin's disease. Barbara was singing in her brother's band and was doing well. David had graduated with a doctorate in neuropharmacology from the City University of New York and had a medical degree from Stanford University. For Myra and me, that was the most painful time in our lives.

It is always painful to learn that something has happened to a child, whether on campus or after discharge. Once a child was dropped off for camp, and he wandered into the bushes to retrieve something. He accidentally ran into a branch and damaged his eye. Another child was picked up from camp by a neighbor who neglected to check him out of camp. When a second neighbor came to pick up the boy, he was thought by staff to still be on the grounds, and of course, he could not be found. A search by staff, police, and the fire department ended without locating the child. It turned out he was shopping with the first neighbor. A happy ending but a very scary experience for all.

Some children have run away only to be found in New York City. Some of these youngsters were so poorly welcomed at home that they ran back to Green Chimneys on their own. Others have such poor directional skills that they headed north instead of south to reach New York City.

Whenever Myra and I would be awakened in the middle of the night by a knock on the door or the phone ringing, our hearts would begin to pound—and we have been awakened many, many times over the years we have lived on the grounds. Calls have come from anxious parents or from neighbors regarding a problem caused by one of our animals or a complaint about one of our children.

One night we received a phone call from an anxious mother in New York City. Her child was home that weekend and was very agitated. He had locked himself in the bathroom. The mother was afraid of what he would do. I remember driving into New York City unaware that there was a power outage. Why I did not tell her to call the police, I do not know, but the child was calling for me, and I came. I climbed to the seventeenth floor, the child came out of the bathroom, and I brought him back to Green Chimneys.

The uproar relative to our off-campus group homes has been a problem for us all. If the teenagers were members of a family that lived next door, the chance that police would be called for letting the dog run free or for having the garbage cans exposed is doubtful. Since the adolescents who live in these homes are not from the local community, we very often received complaints. I have to be honest and say that the complaints have been valid at times. At other times, the actions of the neighbors have reflected their ambivalence toward the population we served there.

We work very hard to check out our staff backgrounds before hiring. We take seriously our primary responsibility for the safety of the children in our care. We also take care not to react impulsively against the staff person involved. Most accusations have proved to be unfounded.

Over the years we have been faced with drug problems of children, families, and staff. There have been cases of crimes committed by children, families, and staff that have impacted on the program. As an agency, we are drawn into many situations and have to handle the crisis in the best possible manner. We have to conduct an internal investigation and very often we need to involve outside investigators, including police and child protective services.

With police help, we have taken children from a home that was not safe. So many stories, so many outcomes—it took a lot of courage and a lot of support.

I will always remember the pain I felt when we were not able to help a child. Terminating a child's placement is a difficult issue to face. We tend to feel like failures when a child absolutely cannot make it or when family issues are so severe that a positive outcome cannot be expected. It is not realistic to expect that we will be successful with every child, but we do try.

We have a number of students who are in long-term hospitals and a few are in jail. When people ask about the success rate of the program, those cases come to mind. Some of the students in jail write, and some reappear when they are released. Thank goodness some have turned their lives around and are doing well.

We had a young child with limited ability enroll at Green Chimneys and do very well. She remained on with us as a young adult and served as a housekeeper. Her mother and father were divorced and did not have the best of relations. Her father helped by providing funds for us to build her a room on campus, which was to be her permanent home. She became ill with cancer and sadly succumbed to her illness. When she eventually died, he announced he would never do anything more for us in spite of his tremendous wealth. He notified us before he died; he was leaving all his money to a very well-endowed university that he had never attended. Another wealthy parent promised us a substantial sum when he died, but nothing was forthcoming. This was surprising, because he had been generous to us in the past. His son, who was a former student, remains in contact with us but does not have the resources to be of financial help.

For many years, I had regular contact with a woman who visited Green Chimneys, and I made visits to her in nearby Mahopac, New York. She was supposedly wealthy and promised to include Green Chimneys in her will. At the same time, Myra and I met regularly with another quiet, reserved woman who was dedicated to our farm program. She kept predicting that this lady from Mahopac was taking advantage of us, believed that she would never leave us anything, and she was so right. However, this quiet friend did state that she would leave us something. She died in 2009, and her lawyer called to tell me that she had left us a bequest. I thanked him for the information and never asked about the particulars of the bequest. Weeks later, hesitant, but very curious, I called the lawyer and asked if I could know the amount. Imagine my astonishment when he told me the bequest was for a million dollars. This was the largest single donation of that size that we have ever received up until then. Other generous donors have given us more than that over the years, but I used to wonder if we would ever receive a one-time donation of that size, and it did happen.

The children of one of our former social workers, none of whom were students, provided a sizeable contribution after their mother, Susan Abrams, died. They honored her memory by naming the library after her. This was a marvelous way to remember her. She had formed a reading club when she worked for Green Chimneys, and they felt she would be thrilled to know the children will never forget her interest in learning.

If one looks at the members of our workforce, one will find family groups. It has always been that way, beginning with my own family.

Employed at Green Chimneys is the Whalen family. Joe serves as our executive director. Mary, Joe's wife, is not an employee, but she volunteers tirelessly and is a true ambassador for Green Chimneys. It is Mary who creates the beautiful annual *Green Chimneys Magazine* of which the premiere issue was published in 2008. Katie, Joe and Mary's daughter, works in the health center; Karen, his daughter-in-law, works as a nurse; and John Clark, Mary's brother, works in housekeeping.

The Rees family came from Wales to settle in the United States. Riselda (Sylvie) and Dan and their three children all worked at Green Chimneys. Dan had served in the British Navy, and nothing stopped him from coming to work. He would walk to work if the snow was too deep to drive in, and he would sleep on benches in the dining room so that he could be there to cook for the children in the morning. Sylvie eventually became our head housekeeper and kept that position until she retired. The Crapa family, mother and children, worked for us. The children's husbands and wives did as well. Some of the family still work for us today. All of the family members were loyal, hard workers.

Both Eddie Gross and Dick Hill who served in an administrative capacity lived on the grounds. Today Myra and I are the only ones who live in one of the original houses on the grounds. We live in the old tenant farmer's house. Green Chimneys owns three houses across the street. One is an intern house, one is a staff residence, and one is our runaway shelter, which has an apartment downstairs for visitors.

Joe Glass is someone who will always be in my memory. He was a master chef and loved to cook. He loved parties, and he and his wife, Trudy, organized wonderful Oktoberfests in our dining room. We had real German food, alpine horns, dancers, and singers. All of Joe's friends came out to support the activity. It was a tradition over many years. Joe and Trudy have retired to Florida, and although we do not have those German parties anymore, we have plenty of celebrations equally enjoyable. Mark Kaplan, who has been on our staff for over twenty years, followed Joe as the master chef, has continued the tradition of parties, and has taken it a step further by introducing a catering service that gives staff a chance to earn additional money. In the summers and on school vacations, Mark's two sons work here. In June 2003, Mark and his staff catered our fifty-fifth anniversary celebration in a big tent on campus. Our son, Donald, who is in the catering business, flew in from Las Vegas to help.

Many years ago, I was on an airplane with Strachan Donnelley, and he wanted to donate money to Green Chimneys. Since we were both serving on the board of the Union Institute, I told him I would not be able to accept; it would be a conflict of interest. Donnelley told me that he understood, but he would like to "endow the pigs. I laughed, an exchange of letters ensued, and the pigs were endowed. At the same time, we were adopted by his wife, Vivian, and their wonderful daughters and their families. In spring 2011 we dedicated our new student residences in honor of the Strachan Donnelley family.

So many great things have transpired over the years that began inauspiciously. In 1986 when David came home with his medical degree and PhD in neuropharmacology, he was supposed to start his residency; however, David announced to us that it was not to be. He had come to his end and wanted only to enjoy the time he had left with his family. We had just moved into the caretaker's house, which had just become vacant. It was a quieter place for David, and its location was such that much of the noise and bustle of the campus escaped him. He spent his days reading and taking short trips off-grounds. I came into the house one afternoon, and he greeted me with a short note he had read in a magazine: "Read this, Dad! Paul Newman and his partner A. E.Hotchner want to open a camp for terminally ill children.[1] You should call and offer your help. You know what it means to have a terminally ill child, and you know all about running camps."

I took David's suggestion and made a call. I left all my information and wondered if I would hear from anybody. I figured it was a long shot, but what did we have to lose? I went about my routine work, which many times included driving into New York City. My secretary, Bella, caught me in the city one day not too long after my call and told me to drive to the Westport office of Newman's Own; I was having lunch with Paul Newman and A. E. Hotchner. The next thing I knew I was in the car on my way to meet two visionaries. That visit changed my life forever. Newman and Hotchner became great supporters of Green Chimneys, and I was instrumental in giving whatever help and advice I could to the Hole In the Wall Gang Camps, serving on the board for many years. Newman's friendship and spirit meant a great deal to me; he was a very caring person. I will never forget this admonition: "Don't tell me what you think I want to hear. Tell me what I need to know." In 2010 we named our school complex Newman's Own Education Center so all will never forget this giant of a man.

◆◆◆

Student Notes on the passing of our son, David:

> B. H.: I am sorry to hear what happened to your son. I am writing this letter because I am trying to get you out of your sorrow and misery . . . what counts (to me) is the care and the support you are giving me and the rest of the school and I'm not going to forget you. Mrs. Ross . . . because you are the mother of David and if I know that he is your son he has to be a good man.
>
> C. H.: I am sorry what happened to David and if you need anything I am always available if you need me and remember you have Green Chimneys' students as your family who love and care.

Notes

1 The Hole in the Wall Gang Camps are now for "critically ill children," which includes terminally ill as well.

Chapter XVII

International Relations and Rotary

Green Chimneys and Our Soviet Visitors

Some of the most heartwarming experiences of the late 1960s were our visits with the children of the Soviet Mission, the Soviet Union's diplomatic delegation to the United Nations. At the time, almost all members of the United Nations maintained missions in New York City; the missions conducted negotiations on their countries' behalves. Unlike most delegations, however, the Soviet Union's and other Iron Curtain countries kept mainly to themselves due to Cold War hostilities. They socialized among themselves and sent their children to schools operated by their own governments. If they wanted to travel more than twenty-five miles from the city, they had to receive special permission. For diplomats and their families who lived in this country, sometimes for years at a time, theirs was a very small world.

In an effort to make these foreign delegates feel welcome, the New York City Commission for the United Nations, whose purpose was to facilitate positive relationships with the diplomatic community, offered to arrange for the Soviet children to visit American children at their schools. The Soviet Mission thought it a wonderful idea and offered to host the American children as well.

Robert Gottschalk, at the time a consultant to the New York City Commission, was the one responsible for organizing this cultural exchange program. He contacted me and asked Green Chimneys to host the children of the Soviet Mission for a day at the farm. He had heard about our school on a farm and wondered if we would be interested in participating in such a program. I did not hesitate to say yes and arranged to meet him in New York to tell him more about the school.

On March 18, 1967, forty Green Chimneys fifth, sixth, seventh, and eighth graders boarded a bus bound for the Soviet Mission, where they were greeted by one hundred Soviet children. To some extent, I wasn't sure what to expect. I knew a performance was planned to entertain us—the Russian children would sing, dance, and perhaps perform a skit—and this would be followed by lunch. But would the children mix and mingle? Would they introduce themselves? What would they say? Would language be a barrier?

After the program ended, I was relieved when I saw a few Green Chimneys boys sit down next to some Soviet children, but I was appalled when I saw them pull baseball cards from their pockets. I was sure the Soviet children would feel excluded from this game. Much to my surprise, however, the Soviet children knew exactly what the cards were and how to play, and immediately joined in. It turned out to be the perfect icebreaker, and the children became fast friends. As they played, they learned that they liked the same television shows and even rooted for the same baseball team, the New York Mets. The next day, *The New York Times* ran a story on the event and quoted a Russian student as saying, "They do everything we do. Only the language is different."

Less than a month later, the children at Green Chimneys had the chance to return the hospitality. On April 13, over one hundred Soviet, Czechoslovakian, and Hungarian children arrived at the campus. For several hours the children alternated between rides on the hay wagon and merry-go-round, horseback riding, jumping rope, and playing with the animals. Later, our students entertained their visitors with a poetry recital and rock and roll music, and then presented them with gifts of baseball cards, jump ropes, and cans of maple syrup. One particularly memorable moment came during lunch. A usually noisy hour, it was strangely quiet. When an American teacher remarked on this, a Russian teacher explained that the Soviet children were taught to converse quietly during meals. Apparently, our students were following their example. I was proud that the children picked up the clue and hoped that the Soviet's manners might rub off. That was wishful thinking, however. By dinner our students were back to their usual clowning.

When it was time to go, there was a scurry for pens and paper to exchange addresses and even a few tears. Green Chimneys was the farthest the children had been from New York City, and no one was sure when they would see their new friends again.

As it turned out, it was not long. Six months later we were invited back to visit the Soviet children, but this time at their *dacha* (country house) in Upper Brookville on Long Island. Again, *The New York Times* covered the event, and the next day's article noted that this estate had seldom been seen by outsiders. That they opened this estate to their children's new American friends was a warm and generous gesture.

When we arrived at the Soviet's *dacha*, the Russian children greeted us with gifts, and then all the children were off. In no time, the boys had a game of soccer under way, and the girls were happily jumping rope. As I watched I couldn't help but notice how little difference there was among the children—right down to the way they dressed. If I hadn't known the children, I wouldn't have been able to tell the Americans from the Soviets.

That was just one of many important reminders all of us—children and adults—took away from those days, which became annual events at the request of the Soviet Mission. Another was that despite different ideologies and languages, it is possible to find common ground and become friends. We just need to avail ourselves of the opportunity.

Some months later, Myra and I were walking in New York City when we noticed a child pointing at us. When her parents realized we were aware of what was happening, they came over and introduced themselves. They explained that they were from the Soviet Mission and for some reason their daughter insisted that she recognized us. It turned out that she was one of the Russian children who had visited Green Chimneys. We had a wonderful conversation before we continued on our way.

After the Russian children visited us in May 1969, I received a letter from John Loeb, the commissioner of the New York City Commission to the United Nations, in which he said, "I appreciate your continuing interest in the development of friendships between American and Russian children. I am sure that in its quiet way, our effort in this direction will bear fruit some day, benefiting us all." I was sure of it, too.

Today, many years later, we have Russian children at Green Chimneys who have been adopted by families in the United States. We have a Russian teacher who works with the faculty to make sure the children understand the instruction, which is all in English. In recent years our summer staffs have come from all over the world, including Russia and the other countries that were once a part of the USSR. The world is different. Our current allies might have once been our past enemies.

We have developed many international connections over the years through membership in organizations, through our internship program recruits that heavily from outside the United States, through our reputation as a pioneer in animal-assisted therapy, and through the Rotary Club. This international connection has been a good resource for us, and I think we have been a good resource for others.

Our children have had the opportunity to meet people from many cultures. We have had teachers and staff from Brazil, Scotland, Ireland, Wales, Northern Ireland, England, Poland, Japan, Canada, and Nigeria. In the early days, the counselors who worked for the Fresh Air Fund, which was our neighbor, were also recruited from around the globe. They, too, brought much to our children as we all shared time together.

One intern named Miyako left her job in a bank in Japan, came here, and decided to stay. It is great for us because she translates when we have Japanese visitors. In addition to serving as coordinator of our intern program, she is currently also the president of the equine mental health group, which has merged with the North American Riding for the Handicapped Association (NARHA).

Part of our global attraction is the four or more months of training we offer. We accept commuters and those who need housing based on availability of space. We offer a stipend for each candidate. Many are attracted by our human-animal programs. Interns have come from every section of the United States as well as the global community.

Green Chimneys was an organizing member of the American Association of Maladaptive Youth (no longer in existence), the affiliate of the international association. The association organized a tour of institutions in the United Kingdom and Europe in conjunction with the World Congress in Switzerland. I was asked to lead the United States delegation because of my knowledge of French. At that time, Green Chimneys had the éducateur model in place, which used the teacher-counselor system. At Green Chimneys, there were academic teacher-counselors and program teacher-counselors. In terms of child care, Green Chimneys was active in the professionalization of the staff based on this European system. The effort included active involvement with the School of Psychoeducation at the University of Montréal. We have depended on the skills of staff to provide a therapeutic milieu that combined education, recreation, skill development, and group living.

Green Chimney's active relationship with many groups around the globe has resulted in not only many visitors coming to Green Chimneys, but invitations for my wife and I as well as staff to visit programs around the globe. This past year I was invited to Japan, but I felt it would be better if Joe Whalen went. I do my traveling by Skype now. Myra and I have traveled worldwide, presenting workshops in Belgium, France, Switzerland, Spain, Israel, Japan, the Czech Republic, and the United Kingdom.

Staff training has been offered to groups from Holland, Denmark, the United Kingdom, Ecuador, Ireland, Northern Ireland, and Israel. A research effort at Green Chimneys was conducted by the staff at the Université de Franche-Comté in Besançon, France, to study attention in the classroom when animals were present. To our knowledge, Green Chimneys has had its program described in French, German, Japanese, and Spanish books and magazines. Our networking effort has been an important part of our work. Documentaries on the program and television interviews have appeared in Asia, the Middle East, Europe, Canada and the United Kingdom.

Green Chimneys has taken an active role in the International Association of Human-Animal Interaction Organizations (IAHAIO). My wife and I were honored with the distinguished service award by this organization. Green Chimneys has also been involved in the European and the United Kingdom city and country farm movement as well as the Association Nationale pour l'Education de Chiens d'Assistance pour Handicapés (ANECAH), the assistance dog organization in France, for which we have raised dogs.

Another intern, from France, who happened to be trained as an éducateur, after her internship, joined the staff of East Coast Assistance Dogs (ECAD) and is now a trainer on our campus. She teaches the children how to train dogs to be assistance dogs. One of our students finished our program and went on to be both a trainer and a veterinary assistant.

Rotary Club

As active Rotarians, Myra and I have entertained the Rotary Foundation's Group Study Exchange (GSE) visitors, Ambassadorial Fellows, and Youth Exchange students over the years. During the spring of 2000, two teachers from Green Chimneys participated in an exchange to Mexico as part of the GSE program. Their Mexican counterparts visited Green Chimneys. Our latest Rotary visitors in 2010 were from Taiwan. We have been told that the group visit to Green Chimneys is always the highlight of the stay in our Rotary district by any GSE visitors.

For years, the Rotary's commitment to "Service Above Self" has been channeled through the four Avenues of Service, which form the foundation of club activity. The Rotary motto conveys the humanitarian spirit of the organization's more than 1.2 million members. Strong fellowship among Rotarians and meaningful community and international service projects characterize Rotary worldwide.

Everyone has an opportunity to commit to the Avenues of Service. In my case, to be recognized for Vocational Service in 2001 and 2010 is greatly appreciated. Rotary has inspired me over the more than fifty-five years that I have been a member.

◆ ◆ ◆

Student note on Jagger's passing:

> M. L.: Last Thursday a horse died that we all loved. His name was Jagger. He was a very nice horse. He would obey us when we could work with him. Jagger was a very sick horse . . . he had a very hard time breathing. Every time he would try to breathe he would make a wheezing sound. When I heard him doing that I got so scared. But I really feel sorry for Mr. Kupchok because it was his horse. Also I feel sorry for R. D. because Jagger was his project.

Chapter XVIII

Looking Back, It Took Courage

Looking back, I can say that the creation of Green Chimneys took courage. If I were asked today by someone what I was thinking about at the school's inception, or how one might go about starting a place like Green Chimneys, I might hesitate because I would not be sure what to tell them. I wouldn't discourage the idea, but I would certainly have to think back to 1947 and ask myself what I needed to know then to make the dream a reality. What would I have liked to know before Green Chimneys was founded? What was lacking in my knowledge? Would a better understanding of finances have been important?

My background had a great impression on my decision. If not for the idea of Green Chimneys, I probably would have moved away from home again, as I knew I did not want to live in the hotel. In retrospect, what other life could I have considered? I was lucky to have a dream that I had created for myself.

In the beginning there were immediate business operations that required my attention. The first consideration would, of course, involve a discussion of money. How was I going to support myself while waiting for tuition payments? Thank goodness my father was there to help with that problem. I did not understand the difference between for-profit and not-for-profit. As an example, you can rent property and still be a not-for-profit agency. You can, on the other hand, own property and operate just as any other business might. There is more than one way to function. Immediately, I found out that for-profit schools would probably not receive any financial help in terms of donations because there would be no tax advantage to the donor. In some situations, for-profit groups might find it difficult to develop contractual relations with governmental agencies. Parents and referring agencies might wonder if the organization was in business for the money or for the children. We did not investigate not-for-profit status ahead of time, but the lawyers and the accountants put it into place as quickly as possible after we began.

In the early years, when the financial situation required that we borrow money, it was the family stocks and bankbooks that served as collateral. When we became a social service agency, Myra had to resign from the board, as did all the members of our family.

People are confused as to how staff and the administrators get paid in a nonprofit situation. Salaries are set by a governing body, which may or may not permit the founder/administrator to be one of the members of the governing body under the law in the state where the corporation is being formed. Basically, in the case of a nonprofit corporation, no one has stock or receives a profit on the original investment. The way things evolve must satisfy the test that there is an arm's length relationship in every part of the operation. It is probably best to state that legal advice was absolutely critical from the very beginning. None of the family took a salary; instead, we took an allowance as funds became available.

When we began, there were not as many building codes and property regulations as there are today. These new regulations impact our operation. If we were starting out now, we would probably find it impossible to operate. As an example, the disposal of manure from the animals we keep must be carefully handled because of water contamination fears for the nearby streams and the river that flows through our property. Our property happens to be in a region governed by New York City water regulations. Today we pay for the service that hauls the manure away.

Green Chimneys began the second phase of its history when Green Chimneys Children's Services came into being in 1974. The new mission of providing residential child care services as opposed to being a boarding school was undertaken at the same time that institutional and / or out-of-home care was once again being questioned. Additionally, the government questioned children being sent out-of-state for care. Green Chimneys had more out-of-state children than in-state children in the 1970s.

The new mission was an extension of my earlier dream. It was an opportunity to provide underserved New York City children with care in a country setting surrounded by animals. It was a chance to create a model that would build on an earlier history as a private school. It allowed those successful elements to be continued for a new population and their families. In the beginning years, 1948 through 1966, families were responsible for tuition and all other expenses. In later years, 1966 through 1974, families sometimes garnered assistance from government for cost responsibilities. Since 1974, children have become eligible for these services solely at the government's expense. However, we saw no difference. Parents who qualified for aid were able to place their children, and Green Chimneys operated accordingly.

Funding at a Glance

The experience at Green Chimneys in terms of funding and programming is important to understand. The following chart should display an inclusive picture of our operation over the years:

Green Chimneys, Brewster Campus

	1948	1960	Today
Funding	Tuition supported by families	Tuition supported by families and in some cases support by public funds	Tuition for day school and costs of residential programs supported by public funds
Clientele	Middle-class children	Middle-class and children in need.	Middle-class and children in need.
Personnel	Extended family	Stratified with night staff	Stratified with night staff
Turnover	Not a problem	Not a problem	A serious problem
Structure	Interdisciplinary	Interdisciplinary	Interdisciplinary
Orientation	Eclectic and contemporary alternative approaches	Eclectic and contemporary alternative approaches	Eclectic and contemporary alternative approaches
Campus	Structured and open	Structured and open	Great use by public

Our local town, our county, our state, and New York City must agree on everything we do. We are supervised by the local health department as well as various New York State entities, including the Education Department (in terms of our academic programs and our lunch program), the Department of Social

Services, the Office of Children and Family Services, the Office of Mental Health, Administration for Children's Services, and by each county and school district that contracts for our services. Since we do business in Connecticut, we are also supervised by agencies in that state as well. We sought accreditation by the Joint Commission on the Accreditation of Healthcare Organizations (JCAHO), in order to satisfy New York's requirement for agencies that wish to operate a program under Medicaid funds for the Office of Mental Health. Having gained this accreditation, we were eligible for full membership in the Child Welfare League of America (CWLA).

In February 2002, we went through the process of applying for accreditation by the Council on Accreditation (COA). We took this step when we learned that we no longer needed JCAHO accreditation, which was more appropriate for hospitals than a social service agency. We sought and obtained accreditation for our camping program by the American Camping Association and from the North American Riding for the Handicapped Association so that our therapeutic riding programs would meet high standards. In addition, we belong to American Association of Children's Residential Centers as well as numerous other organizations. Some are concerned with matters related to children and families, others are related to animals or plants, or to nature and the environment. It was not always this way, but as we took on more and more programs and interests, these organizational ties developed.

All organizations might do well to find a friendly banker; it is great to have a bank that gets involved.

◆ ◆ ◆

Having read this far, the reader may ask if there is any time to think about and develop the program. The program planning must keep up with the operation planning. The program planning sets the operational needs. In other words, the facilities that will be used must be determined as well as the program organizer and the program recipients. The source of income will guide the planner in determining how the program will be supported. In other words, a budget that shows expenses and incomes must be created. Even with all these parameters in place, income expectations may still not be met or projected expenses may exceed the budget, and a contingency plan will be needed to address these concerns.

In this journey, it has been my experience that sometimes you have to pick up a shovel and begin to dig before you know you have the funds to pour the foundation. You have to have courage to begin a program at any time. It takes a great deal of work and effort, but that is expected from any new venture. That's what makes things exciting. You have to have courage and personal confidence. If everyone who wanted to try something new abandoned the plan before getting underway, the world would be a very different place.

Having spent over sixty-three years nurturing and building Green Chimneys, I feel compelled to tell people what has been most difficult about the experience. If I were only permitted to cite one problem, I would say without the least hesitation that it has been the financial worries. With no reserves and all contingencies supposedly budgeted for, it is stress producing to have a car damaged and require a new vehicle or a find that the furnace must be replaced. Counting on promised income that does not materialize or comes in a much reduced amount can be very devastating. Applying for a grant that has been suggested and encouraged by a funding group, only to have it rejected at the end, can create havoc.

When we counted on a full enrollment and it did not happen, it was upsetting beyond words. The anxiety of meeting expenses became acute—staff must be paid, bills must be paid. We had to face staff and ask for their understanding. We had to share what was happening with our Board and ask for their continued support. We appealed to vendors and asked for patience. In spite of the fact that the business did not belong to us anymore, we still, naturally, took things personally.

People refer to our operation as a school business or part of the child care industry. We think of ourselves as a service to children, families, and animals. I love that part of my work. Aggravation and anxiety are part of the package; hopefully, pleasurable parts outnumber the times that cause pain.

The children make it all worthwhile. They keep us hopping. They keep us young. They are loyal. They have problems, which they realize, but they also have strengths, which, if encouraged, will pull them through. I still love to hear their greeting when we encounter each other. I do not mind having them come to express complaints, though staff should be their first resource for such issues. The children appear to believe that they should go straight to the top when they have an concern to resolve. The problem for me is that I am no longer the top.

Dealing with other people's children is a heavy responsibility. It is not something that can be turned off overnight or on weekends. It requires action on holidays and even when one is away on vacation. These are human beings who depend on us for guidance and care. It is work to be envied.

When my wife and I lost David to Hodgkin's disease, the staff and children were there to comfort and care for us. Returning the favor, they were quick to let us know that we had always been there for them. They, no doubt, wanted us to understand that we could grieve, that life goes on, and that we were very important to their security. One child expressed this sentiment in a condolence card when he wrote about the sad circumstance and then added that Green Chimneys had just won a baseball game. He wanted us to know he was there for us and that Green Chimneys was alive and dependent on our leadership.

Occasionally, I ask myself whether it has all been worthwhile. Would I do it again? I reflect on the many years of time and energy I have spent. I question whether it has been equally good for my family or has it been only I who profited? What if there had never been a Green Chimneys? What if it closed tomorrow? Does it really matter? Maybe it is best not to know all the answers. I know that it has been my determined desire to keep things going. I believe that the program has reached the maturity that makes its existence important to many others besides myself. I had a dream that my father made come true. I must pass that dream to others and have the same faith that my father had when he invested in me. I will always hear his question ringing in my ear, "Who will care for the trees when I am gone?" I understand his anxiety. My concern has always been, "Who will be here to take care of the children when I am gone?"

Part of that is "Founder's Syndrome." In my introduction, I mentioned Thomas A. McLaughlin's book, *Moving Beyond Founder's Syndrome to Nonprofit Success*, and how difficult it may be working with a founder when he or she has "retired." I know it is for me. I struggle to let go, but spending forty-nine years raising my baby before handing over the reins to my successor was very, very difficult. Going from doing it all—creating the vision, ensuring quality, worrying about our fiscal soundness, and overall organizational stability—to watching from the sidelines is not easy. It is difficult for me to share the vision now and see it perhaps go in a different direction.

Myra reminds me over and over that I am not in charge. I know that. I am not trying to be in charge, really. I see things that need doing, I think of new projects, or worse still, old programs that were discarded along the way that I think should be re-introduced. I have not stopped caring simply because I am no longer the executive director. It is the caring that causes me to push a little harder than maybe I should. Do I have faith in Joe Whalen and the other excellent management staff? I hired most of them; of course I have faith in their abilities.

Whalen, a dedicated educator from the beginning when I hired him fresh out of college, really loves the children, and he loves the trees and plants that keep the campus in bloom. I am confident that he will keep the traditions of Green Chimneys in place.

On the Job Training: The Purpose of Life is to Live a Life of Purpose

With the exception of wanting to spend each donation several times over, I have learned and gained some business skills that I totally lacked in 1947.

First, I did not know snow created overtime. I learned this in the winter of 1947, a lesson reinforced every winter since. Unfortunately, I learned it also sometimes happens in the fall or early spring.

I learned about septic tanks and stuffed toilets. I learned about broken windows and frozen pipes. I found out too many lightening storms are bad. I did not know the Croton River could split our campus into two pieces, nor did I know that a severe flood made the road in front of Green Chimneys impassible. I did not realize the East Branch of the Croton River was part of the New York City reservoir and that we would have to follow strict regulations.

I did not own a car in college, so I did not know what havoc owning one car, let alone a fleet of cars, vans, trucks, tractors, and buses, would have on our bottom line. I did not know we would need a separate spot for our maintenance department and a gasoline reserve on campus. I was not aware that oil burners can create very serious problems. I did not know that if an adolescent hid soiled underwear behind the oil burner, the result would be such that we would all have to leave the building until it was filled with fresh air.

What did I know about soiled sheets or clothing? I should have known that all clothing had to be labeled, washed, cleaned, and have buttons replaced. Even zippers had to be changed. Shoes had to be shined. You do not wear sneakers out in the snow, or do you? You wear warm clothing when the temperature is cold. You do not wear layers of clothing so that other students would not take what is yours.

I did not imagine someone would take caterpillars and put them in a can a the dresser to wait to see if a "raccoon" would appear. I did not think that parents would arrive and sleep on beds in the children's rooms.

Life skills such as having a haircut, nails cut, showers taken, teeth brushed, and clean clothes worn seemed something that would happen automatically.

I saw my boarding schools as well-run in spite of the fact there were things I did not like. How did I know they ran well because someone hired the right people for the right jobs? I soon learned there was more to the process. There were salaries, living spaces, and work spaces required. I did my turn sleeping in the dorm with the children. Thank goodness it was not every night.

I found out if you buy something, you should try to get a good price, get a receipt, and not pay taxes since you are tax exempt. And proof is required at all times.

I did not know that we needed permission slips from parents for everything involving the children. Did I know a parent would call a dorm and not be allowed to speak to their child because it was too early or too late? Did I know someone would go home to visit with someone else's clothes? Did I know parents would help themselves to towels and/or other items from the student's room? Did I know that by remaining open twenty-four hours per day, seven days per week that some children would never go home?

I thought a building for which an architect won a prize was a good thing until I learned prizes come with more expensive buildings. I learned that beautiful, big windows add something to the building, but when they are broken, they cost more to repair.

What could I have known about building inspectors, planning and zoning boards, certificates of occupancy, violations, code regulations, health regulations, and safety concerns?

Some reading this, may be wondering if it could all be true. Let me assure you, it is, and there is much more I could add.

If you remember our purchase price was $38,500, you will gasp when I tell you we have to report that our new school buildings, built in 2000, cost millions, and our new residences for eighty-eight children, which are in the final stages as I write this volume, will cost more than twice as much as our school cost in 2000.

And along the way, I learned about deficits.

◆◆◆

In the beginning, our intention was to have a private school and camp for young children. Then I learned that we should refer to ourselves as an independent school. By that time, we spoke about being a year-round school. Then we described ourselves as a special education program. At present we serve children with special needs, and all the state regulations pertaining to our population must be followed.

Child welfare departments have changed their names many times over the years. Every time a new director or a commissioner takes over the department at the city or state level, one can expect a name change.

Titles for staff are important because that is how reimbursement is calculated. Vacation days for students must be monitored to meet regulations and be reported accurately.

Insurance is very important, and I learned that the descriptions that are given to the insurance broker must be such that the carrier can fully understand what we do. Our program has animals, horseback riding, driving, tractors, high and low ropes, and a climbing tower. In addition, we have a pool and gymnasium. Children go on trips and are transported by our vehicles. Drivers must be certified to transport children.

Case records must be locked. The files need to be fireproof. Any publicity must be carefully scrutinized to protect the confidentiality of the children. We try not to use last names of children in any news release.

I must hasten to add that there are many other things I might have written, which at the beginning were unclear, but today are routine. As we continue to offer help to other potential programs, they benefit from our knowledge.

What about the children? Over the years all of us have had to learn an array of ways to describe our students. We speak about intact families; parents who have divorced and some who have remarried; mothers or fathers who had never married; families where one or both parents have died; stepmothers and stepfathers with no children from a previous marriage and those who blended their children together; incarcerated parents; and families where one parent was separated because of work or military service.

I had to learn what made one child gifted and one child weak at grade level. I had to learn about mild retardation, brain injuries, learning disabilities, and physical handicaps. Then I had to learn about foster care, adoption, terminated parental rights, welfare, and poverty.

What about the farm and animals? Gardening I had witnessed from my grandfather, father, and then father-in-law. Animals had always been a big part of my life too. Yet in both cases there was much to learn. Most of my experience with animals had been with dogs, and even that experience was limited to feeding and caring for the dogs I owned. The adults in my life took the dogs for grooming. They made the purchases for them and obtained the licenses. I never owned a horse before coming to Green Chimneys, though I did ride. I loved to ride in horse-drawn wagons. I never dreamed I would have draft horses in my life. I did not think I would have a pony that could be driven and ridden. I had been around mares with their foals and knew what fun that was. I had cleaned stalls, but I had never built fences. I had never tried to corral horses who had escaped from the paddock or got loose when taken from their stalls. There were always adults around to help, but when I became an adult, I learned quickly on the job.

Some Additional Thoughts before We End

> The current national outlook appears to be one of despair. But despite this trend of hyperbole journalism and extreme acts of violence by a segment of our society, there are good people doing good things to counteract the hopelessness. The goals of "Who's Helping America's Children" are to discover and then highlight those adults who are making a positive difference in the lives of children and families in their respective communities.
>
> -Fred Rogers' Heroes: Who's Helping America's Children[1]

In May 1994 we had a visit from Fred Rogers who had selected our program to be one of the segments featured on his forthcoming television special. His week-long visit was inspirational to us and an honor for Green Chimneys.

Animals make no distinction between young people who have been considered failures and those who have always received praise. We find that animals can bring out the best in us. They require constant care. Farm life is labor-intensive. It demands our cooperation and challenges our ability to be responsive to the needs of the creatures who depend on us for care.

Along with the care and concern for the animals comes an equal effort for the environment. The flowerbeds, the trees, the garden, the compost area, the pond, and the extensive green areas require care. The campus serves as a learning place for children and adults. It provides a laboratory experience for all who live or visit. It acts as a place of hope for a better tomorrow. It allows the students a chance to nurture and be nurtured so that they in turn can become stewards of this precious earth. This is something that is difficult to impart to urban children who unfortunately find their neighborhoods in decay.

The land we till is cared for so that it can produce some of the food we consume. The large garden where all crops are produced organically is an excellent model of sustainable agriculture. It not only produces vegetables, herbs, and flowers, but it produces inspired people.

Children, their families, their caregivers, and others find projects that have meaning to all. We have shown that it is possible to take children who are receivers of service and put them into a position where they become service providers.

People enjoy a challenge. If people come together to solve a problem from which they all will benefit, they are more apt to participate. It epitomizes the "WIFM Principle"—what's in it for me? Even the most altruistically intentioned adult wants to know that his/her efforts are going toward their goal. The interdependence on others changes the way we think and act toward others. In a real sense, we find projects that focus on the quality of life for each and everyone involved.

As a society, I firmly believe that we must create opportunities that foster self-esteem and responsibility. We must refocus our schools and communities so that each individual will feel a sense of ownership and pride. It is doable.

An educated public, which is uncaring, uninvolved in the problems of daily living, and unresponsive to the needs of others, will not do very much to improve life for themselves or others. It is frightening to think how, as a society, we deny our children an opportunity to be of service. At Green Chimneys we find that the involvement of our residents in the life on- and off-campus has a significant healing effect on their lives.

I would love to replicate the entire Green Chimneys program in every urban area if it were feasible, but since it is not, it is important to look for ways to take as many elements as possible and provide those opportunities wherever feasible. For instance, children can learn service in the city as easily as in the country. They can be encouraged to give of their time and their talents to help others in need and also to benefit their own group. They can learn care for their environment, no matter how small the space. Ideally, every child should have the opportunity to enjoy a school or a summer camp experience to create an immersion opportunity in nature to instill and permit the goodness in each child to be recognized. We foster this idea through our residential outdoor education program.

The intern program, which invites young people from all around the world, has evolved into an excellent intercultural exchange opportunity. At Green Chimneys the intern can achieve more than one goal. There is the opportunity to learn about the integration of children and animals, but there is the equally important lesson one derives from involvement with a broad range of populations, especially those with special needs. Only lack of housing impedes the number of people who can take advantage of the internship. People who complete the internship are prepared to replicate the program on other sites, and many have done so.

Urban adolescents who are considering a career in veterinary medicine or as a veterinary technician might do well to come to Green Chimneys for an immersion experience. It has been suggested that a series of weekend programs could serve to provide these young people with the practical experiences they might otherwise find hard to locate.

It is our passion to teach those who may have been poorly or inadequately nurtured so that they will be able to pass on the skills of good parenthood. We seek to provide something pleasant to substitute for the violence worldwide, by encouraging the human-animal bond and care of the environment. We seek to improve our students' relationships with one another and all those they will meet. By doing so, we are helping not just the one child at Green Chimneys, but all the lives that child touches.

Green Chimneys has effectively demonstrated over sixty-three years that a "total" environment can be provided for troubled children, which respects their individual humanity, recognizes their families as first-line care givers whenever possible, responds flexibly to the child's needs and aspirations, and hastens their habilitation for reintegration with their families and communities. Green Chimneys encourages the professionalism of the child care worker who spends more or equal time with the children than teachers and social workers.

At Green Chimneys we have argued that residential treatment is a liberating experience for the seriously disturbed and learning disabled child. A person who cannot control his or her own emotions, who cannot order his or her own life in terms compatible with the social order, who cannot make choices based on simple knowledge of himself or herself and understanding of his or her environment, and who has to master basic life skills is not free. Liberation comes with mastery of self in whatever environment; self-mastery is the goal of reeducation, and treatment as it is the goal of a public and/or private education.

The many students who have come back to me years later to thank me for their experience at Green Chimneys have attributed their success in life to attending Green Chimneys. They thank me, but I know it is not just me, but the programs and the staff members who implement those programs that have made it happen.

At Green Chimneys we work with people and animals. We try to develop closeness. We believe that our task is to develop independent, self-starting citizens. We want our children and adolescents to become productive and feel successful.

Three groups love us: those who love children, those who love animals, and those who love children and animals. The people of Green Chimneys—staff, volunteers, and friends—make all the difference.

◆ ◆ ◆

> J. N., age 10: One day while outside my dorm, I was playing football with some friends in Okun [a dorm at Green Chimneys]. I kicked E. G.'s basketball by mistake. He thought I did it on purpose. E. G. threw the ball at me, this got me angry. I was going to hit him back with the ball when the counselor held me back and said: "Calm down, are you Ok?"

Then I went and said I was sorry for kicking his ball. E. G. apologized for throwing the ball at me too. By helping me, the counselor made me feel happy and excited. I knew that we were great friends.

Notes

1 An excerpt from the news release on Fred Rogers' Heroes, a one–hour, prime time special featured on PBS on September 6, 1994.

Chapter XIX

A Personal Note

In spite of all that has transpired over the years, I would do what I have done all over again, only I hope that I would do it better. Hindsight is better than foresight.

Did it take a toll on my family? Yes, of course it did. One day, when our house was bustling with students, when staff were coming in and out to ask this and that, and Myra had a group of students in our kitchen doing homework, our ten-year-old son, David, looked at me and asked if I would have time for him if he had problems. I never forgot that moment, and now that he is gone, I cannot be sure I gave him all the time to which he was entitled. David, though, seemed to have done all right, earning a PhD, becoming a physician, and graduating with honors before he died of Hodgkin's disease at our home.

Donald, our second son, has done well too. He became independent once he began preparatory school. Today he is Vice President of Catering, Conventions and Events for Caesars Entertainment in Las Vegas. Having inherited my personality, high energy level, and enthusiasm, he is a perfect fit for that position. Donald carries on the family tradition of service and concern for others. An exceptional person, he is accustomed to my pressure and frequent requests for help, and help he does.

Some businesses become a father and son operation. Green Chimneys had a father and daughter working together for more than a decade. Our baby, Lisa, was treasured by her grandparents and has pointed out to me that she is my favorite. Girls know how to do that to fathers! Lisa held various positions while at Green Chimneys, and by the time she left, she had held the positions of Director of Quality Improvement and later Associate Executive Director of Quality Improvement and Off- Campus and Community Programs. Working with Lisa at Green Chimneys was great while it lasted and a bit sad for me when it ended, but happiness outweighs working with your father when your heart takes you elsewhere. Lisa's heart took her to Nevada to help with the start up of Touro University Nevada. Today she is Director of Human Resources there. She lives in the same neighborhood as her brother and his family, and they visit each other often.

I would be remiss if I failed to include Mary in the mention of my children. Mary is Donald's wife and the mother of my granddaughters. I could not have asked for a better daughter-in-law. She is all I could want for my son and my grandchildren. From the very beginning, Mary was an ardent and active advocate for Green Chimneys.

We are all close and visit as much as we can. Up until this year, Myra and I would hop flights to Las Vegas to see them and our two beautiful granddaughters. In February 2010 we did just that, and I ended up spending our vacation in a Las Vegas hospital, fighting a viral infection. It wasn't until I was convalescing, finally back on campus several weeks later, that I realized how close a call I had experienced. Myra knew, of course, as did the children.

Myra and I agree, our two granddaughters, who happen to be here visiting us as I write this and attending Hillside Summer Camp as they do every year, have afforded us the kind of pleasure we had not thought possible since the death of our son, David. Lisa, Donald, and Mary have been there for us always, but as only grandparents can know, we consider the presence of Samantha and Sara truly a gift in our lives. Samantha and Sara both like to help out, being quick to offer to bring out the garbage, set the table, and see if we need anything. Samantha has spent some time teaching me card games, none of which I am good at, and she enjoys shopping with her Grandma. Sara likes coming to the office to do what she can to help. She has helped with the editing of this book too. She laughed when she saw I had written about the nursery rhyme "Hey diddle diddle" as I sing it at home to them. Truly the girls have enriched our lives.

The time that we spend together is so precious. I do appreciate, more than they will ever know, the work that Mary, Donald, and Lisa have done to help me. Some things I would not change. I would hope that my wife would marry me again. In August 2010 we celebrated our fifty-sixth wedding anniversary, which is also fifty-six years of working together at Green Chimneys.

Why would I do it all over again? Here are a few reasons:

I love children. I love my own children and other people's children. I have a special love for my two grandchildren. I love being surrounded by animals. The farm staff always hated it whenever I went away, not because they missed me, but because they never knew what I would bring back. I was forever searching for an animal, or maybe a pair, to replace those we may have lost or the animals we always dreamed we would own. Staff can attest that I have been successful in maintaining this enthusiasm.

I take great pleasure when I see staff earn advanced degrees, gain recognition from their peers, and share their new skills and learning with all of us. I am thankful to them for the materials they have helped us publish, which we sell to the public to gain income for our program.

I love to see our students excel at 4-H, to participate in Roots & Shoots, and to accept community service projects. It is easier to do this with the campus population, but at all our sites, our young people and staff are involved.

I am very pleased to see our assistance dog program flourishing. We have completed a training center for the program, which is a wonderful opportunity for the program to expand. It is astonishing to see how our students respond to the program.

I am proud of our community-supported agriculture program at our Boni-Bel Farm site that produces vegetables for the dining room, sells produce through our Country Store to staff and neighbors, and gives our adolescents a chance to learn and earn. The success of the adolescent garden has made it necessary to create a second garden close to the school building for the younger children.

I think our intern program has been a very successful adventure. We have interns with us year-round from all over the world. Most come to learn about our animal programs, but some come to work in the school, in the social work and psychology department, in recreation, and some in the living units. We try to give all our interns a chance to experience the entire program.

The American Society for the Prevention of Cruelty to Animal, the Humane Society of the United States, the American Humane Association, and Green Chimneys have been working together to bring animal awareness and humane education to schools in the urban areas and to conduct humane education conferences on campus.

◆ ◆ ◆

I visited a public school awhile ago, and all over the school were posters stating: "To turn our public school around, / we need to adopt that legendary Noah Principle: / "No more prizes for predicting rain, / Prizes only for building arks."

The message I keep in mind is to remind everyone that animals are indebted to us for all we do. They provide us with unconditional love as long as they feel we treat them with kindness. If we end up needing another ark, I certainly hope to be selected to be on board, but in the meantime, all of us can be the glue that makes the human-animal bond beneficial for all concerned. Along with a sanctuary for humans, we have created a sanctuary for animals. We deserve to be proud of what we do. We must be proud of our students, because they do much to make things run correctly. We have always strived to be our best, and we take that very seriously. I know we must continue with that in mind. When someone talks about my legacy, I feel with the leadership and staff that is in place, I have nothing to worry about, and I do not intend to take credit for all the good that occurs.

◆ ◆ ◆

Green Chimneys has become an oasis amongst a changing landscape. The challenge to preserve the farmland has been one that Green Chimneys has not taken lightly. In fact, the residents of the area have grown to cherish the open space, the opportunity to visit, and the soothing sounds of the animals that graze the open fields. I actually catch my breath when I look at the collection of aerial photographs of our Brewster campus—the barn red buildings with green chimneys and cupolas sprawl over many acres. The farm, trails, and gardens—all are surrounded by woods and pastures. Doansburg Road cuts across, neatly separating our main campus with its multitude of buildings, stable, and upper barn from our Boni-Bel Farm and the Country Store. How we have grown since 1947, and how good we look!

In the fall the campus explodes with the many-colored leaves of the New York autumn that too quickly turns to winter. Snow, when it falls, brings fresh fun for our children and staff. In the spring, trees bloom in front of every building on campus. Flowers are not an exception, but the rule. In between the business office building and the executive offices, it is lush with rose bushes and flowers of every kind. When I leave the office in the early evening, and the roses are in bloom, Spike and I make sure to walk home that way.

Green Chimneys is indeed a beautiful campus, and although I may be prejudiced, many have agreed with me that walking across our campus in any season is restorative.

With the coming of spring 2011, our children will move into our brand new dorms, and although I know we will always be working on some new building or renovation project, the dorms, which offer a private room for each child, make me feel so proud. Soon some of the older buildings that were dorms will be converted to other offices or torn down, new landscaping installed, a new play area, or perhaps a corral for small animals. We are never done, and I do not mind.

The children in residence, the day students, and many local people feel a real sense of ownership of the farm, and this relationship is an essential element for Green Chimneys to encourage.

That is how it is at Green Chimneys.

Appendix

Developing New Programs

We have a very active Board, and they take a dynamic role in the review of proposed programs and/or projects. At present three committees of the Board are involved in the review process.

First the program committee looks at the proposal, then the quality improvement committee performs its review, and finally the fiscal committee looks to see if the budget will allow for the proposal.

This committee approach is appropriate for a large agency or a small one. The time it takes will depend on how soon people can meet and what information is readily available.

- When we begin the review, we always need to determine if we are talking about a new program, program enhancement, or a new project.
- We then indicate the type of service and where the activity will be located.
- We provide a description of the population to be served and indicate the age, sex, and capacity of the service.
- Since licenses and permits are a consideration, we try to be clear if the activity needs to be certified and under whose auspices.
- Next we meet to clearly define the program or project mission and goals. We try to be as clear as we can about expected outcomes.
- Administrative oversight is another concern because we do not want to overload present staff. However, we also know that during start-up we have to be careful about costs.
- The committee review will then answer the following questions:
    - Does the program or project fit the Green Chimneys mission?

- Will the program or project enhance Green Chimneys' status in a community?
- Does the program or project fit into the organizational structure?
- Does it fit into one of the existing divisions?
- Will it fit into the agency's current administrative structure or will it require standing alone?
- Does the program or project enhance the agency's long-range plan?

Financial issues cannot be avoided. Here again are the questions to be answered:

- What is the budget?
- Does it require start-up funds? If so, where will they be obtained?
- Does the program require the use of real property? Must it be owned, or can it be rented? If now rented, is purchase of the property contemplated in the future?
- Who is the paying government agency? If there isn't one, how will expenses be met? How are budget funds paid? Will there be any advances prior to opening for planning and training purposes?
- What will the impact be on the current central office staff? Are additional staff necessary?
- Will the program share in current administrative expense, thereby saving budget dollars?
- Is the program self-sufficient? If not, when does the program break even?
- Does the program diversify the agency's dependence on any one funding source?
- Is cash flow current? Can we expect to receive billings within thirty days? If not, how often are payments made?
- Is the program budget-based or is it reimbursement-based?
- Is the program permanent, or is it founded for only a set number of years? How could unemployment issues be handled if and when the program ended?
- What are the close-down procedures? Are there long-term financial consequences?

-By Samuel B. Ross, Jr., PhD

Chronology

1947 – The Ross family purchases Green Chimneys Farm to use for a school for young children.

1948 – Green Chimneys Farm for Little Folk opens with just eleven students.

1950s – A period of growth and development.

1960s – The program expands to encompass grades pre-kindergarten through eighth. Students come from many countries. The student population served gradually shifts to special needs youngsters.

1966 – Green Chimneys adopts the year-round school plan and provides 223 classroom days.

1970s – The New York State Department of Social Services grants a license to Green Chimneys to operate the residential program as a residential treatment center (RTC) to serve special needs children referred by social service departments. Hillside Outdoor Education Center is added.

Emphasis is placed on the therapeutic integration of children with farm animals, nature, and the environment.

Public farm programs are instituted at Hillside Outdoor Education Center, offering day and resident year-round camping and environmental programs.

1974 – Green Chimneys Children's Services becomes a social service agency.

1980s – Community-based services are added with the acquisition of three group homes in Westchester.

Lesbian, Gay, Bisexual, Transgender, and Questioning (LGBTQ) Youth Program in Manhattan is begun at Gramercy and provides twenty-five bed housing and assistance for lesbian, gay, bisexual, transgender, and questioning youth. Up until 2010, the program included supervised independent living program (SILP) apartments in New York City. Recent cuts by the city have closed SILP. Gramercy remains operational and growing.

The farm now includes a wildlife conservation program. The wildlife rehabilitation center houses a large collection of permanently disabled birds of prey and assorted wildlife.

1987 – Green Chimneys begins a residence program for runaway and homeless teens in Putnam County

1989 – Brewster campus opens a fourteen bed Office of Mental Health Residential Treatment Facility (RTF) and obtains accreditation from the Joint Commission on Accreditation of Healthcare Organizations (JCAHO). This allows Green Chimneys to provide the highest level of care other than in-patient psychiatric hospitalization. The RTF has its own two-classroom school building also.

1990 – Green Chimneys expands into nearby Danbury, Connecticut with supervised living for developmentally challenged adults and three supervised work crews: lawn maintenance service, a restaurant (The Greenery), and a bottle redemption program.

1992 – Danbury asks Green Chimneys to take over Good Friends, a mentoring program for children of single parent homes. Good Friends provides parent training, recreational, and learning opportunities for youth and their families. In 2010 Green Chimneys had to let Good Friends go due to lack of financial support for this program.

Mid-1990s –

An additional group home is opened in Brewster.

RAP/Talk It Out, a runaway and counseling service is added.

Green Chimneys receives international and national recognition for its work in animal-assisted therapy and animal-assisted activities with media coverage in France, Italy, Japan, Belgium, Australia, Spain, and Israel.

Organic garden is certified by Northeast Organic Farming Association.

Rescue program for Premarin™ foals is instituted. The first year six foals were purchased and trained by our residents for future use.

East Coast Assistance Dogs comes on campus, and our students become trainers of assistance dogs for physically challenged people—a perfect complement to the Green Chimneys mission.

A liaison is developed with ASPCA, Center for Animal Care and Control (NYC), and the Wildlife Conservation Society.

Farm-on-the-Moo-ve reaches thousands of children through its mobile educational farm program.

Cooperative relationship with Mercy College of Dobbs Ferry, New York provides courses in animal-assisted therapy, large animal veterinary care, special education, and graduate and undergraduate courses on grounds.

1996 – Samuel B. Ross, Jr., on Founder's Day, October 27, 1996, hands over the reins of executive director to Joseph Whalen. Ross remains managing director and is responsible for The Friends of Green Chimneys, the third not-for-profit corporation.

1998 – Arbor House opens for Putnam County teens across from our main campus, offering shelter for runaways and homeless youth in the area.

1999 – June 1999, ground is broken for our new $12 million school building, and the renovation of the indoor pool and gymnasium begins.

Japanese immersion seminar program is established.

New York City programs are expanded, and new offices are opened in the Sugar Hill section of Harlem.

Arbor House receives a five-year Safe Places grant for after-school programming.

2000 – Our new school with its state-of-the-art classroom facilities is operational.

2001 – Green Chimneys is awarded the first Street Outreach grant, and the Community Outreach Center is opened in downtown Brewster.

2003 – Our riding program gains accreditation and premier status from the North American Riding for the Handicapped Association.

Our first Humane Education Conference is launched.

2005 – Samuel B. Ross, Jr., is named winner of a "Children's Champion Award" from *Child Magazine.*

2006 – Nature's Nursery receives accreditation from National Association for the Education of Young Children and reaccreditation from the Council on Accreditation.

"Quest for Excellence Award" from the School Age Notes Foundation is won by Robin Korson, director of Nature's Nursery.

"Psychologically Healthy Workplace" recognition from the American Psychological Association is bestowed on Green Chimneys.

2007 – Green Chimneys wins a $400,000 challenge grant from the Kresge Foundation, and we work hard to raise the remainder to meet our $1.5 million goal for a new Health and Wellness Center and the construction of a new horse barn.

2008 – National Network for Youth bestows on Green Chimneys its "2008 Agency of the Year Award."

Clearpool Education Center joins the Green Chimneys family.

2009 – The Country Store at Boni-Bel Farm, a new student vocational program, opens.

The Henry J. and Erna D. Leir Health and Wellness Center opens.

A groundbreaking ceremony is held for our new student residences, to be completed in 2011.

2010 – The Extended School Year (ESY) program starts at Clearpool. ESY is a six-week educational program for the prevention of learning loss for students needing remediation, or for enrichment for gifted students.

Our Shark Finatics win *Oceana's 2010 Junior Ocean Heroes* Award.

Dedication of our school complex is held in May, and it is named Newman's Own Education Center.

Further Reading

Internationally recognized, articles and information on Green Chimneys can be found by searching the Internet. We are always happy to answer inquiries about our programs. Go to our Web site, www.GreenChimneys.org, for the most up-to-date contact information. The Web site also contains current events and information as well as links to other Green Chimneys programs. In addition, visit us on www.facebook.com.

Samuel B. Ross, Jr. "My Teachers—The Animals." http://legacysmile.blogspot.com/2010/05/my-teacher-cow.html.

The following publications were printed at Green Chimneys and are currently available for purchase directly through Green Chimneys:

Green Chimneys Staff. *Rain and Shine Activity Book.* 1999.
Green Chimneys Staff and Interns. *City and Country Activities for Children of All Ages.* Edited by Maureen P. Doherty. 2002.
Lemay, Michel. *The Functions of The Specialized* "Éducateur" *for Maladjusted Youth.* Translated by Vivian Jarvis. Third printing, October 2007.
Mallon, Gary, and Debbie MacCarry. *Life Skills Lessons for Little Folk.* 1991.
Ross, Myra, with Green Chimneys Staff. *G.L.A.S.—Green Chimneys Longitudinal Assessment Scales.* 1979. Revised 2002.
Ross, Samuel B., Jr., and Green Chimneys Staff. *A Vision Realized: The Green Chimneys Story.* August 2001.
Senter, Stephanie, with contributions by Samuel B. Ross, Jr., Gary Mallon, and Green Chimneys Farm Staff. *People and Animals—A Therapeutic Animal-Assisted Activities Manual.* 1992.

Printed Material by Samuel B. Ross, Jr.

Mallon, Gerald P., Samuel B. Ross, Jr., and Lisa E. Ross. "Designing and Implementing Animal Assisted Therapy Programs in Health and Mental Health Organizations." *Handbook on Animal-Assisted Therapy*. Edited by Aubrey Fine. London: Academic Press, 2010.

Ross, Samuel B., Jr. "Green Chimneys Commitment to Human-Animal Integration, Horticulture, Nature Study and Environmental Education." *CHANGE by Anthrozoology* in Japan. Newsletter. July 2009.

———. "Making the World a Better Place." *Satya Magazine*. June 2000.

———. "The Correlation between Abuse of Children and Animals." *Citizen News*. May 1999.

———. "The Color Green." *ASPCA Animal Watch*. Winter 1998.

———. "Service is our Task - Now and Forever." *Perceptions* (Association of New York State Educators of the Emotionally Disturbed). Fall 1998.

———. "Future Directions in Serving the Most Troubled Children and Families." A collection of papers for The New York Council of Family and Child Caring Agencies. 1997.

———. "Nurturing with Nature." *Journal of Emotional and Behavioral Problems* 1, no. 4 (Winter 1993).

———. "Thoughts on Serving the Most Troubled Children and Families." Paper presented at the Annual Meeting of the Council of Family and Child Caring Agencies. 1993.

———. "Building Empathy to Reduce Violence to All Living Things." *Journal of the Society for Companion Animal Studies* 1V, no. 1 (Spring 1992).

———. "Children's Best Friends: Human-Animal Interaction." *The Network*, Union Institute 10, no. 2 (1991).

———, et al. "The Ecological Imperative: The Daily Life of One Distressed Child." Children's Environments 11(1): 49-63. Retrieved [date] from http://www.colorado.edu/journals/cye/. 1994.

———, and Myra Ross. "L'Enfant et l'animal Seminar." *Actes du Colloque*. 1994.

Older articles by Samuel B. Ross, Jr.

Ross, Samuel B., Jr. "Children & Animals: Many Benefits – Some Concerns." *The Outdoor Communicator* (Fall-Winter 1989).

———. "Opening Doors to the Community." *Nonprofit World* 4, no. 5 (September/October 1986).

———. "Plants, Pets and People at Green Chimneys." *The Latham Letter* (Fall 1986).

———. "Thoughtful Wisdom on PFT from the Perspective of Green Chimneys." *The Latham* Letter (Fall 1986).

———. "The Effects of Farm Programming with Emotionally Handicapped Children." In R. Anderson, B. Hart, and L. Hart (Eds). *The Pet Connection: Its Influence on our Health and Quality of Life*. Minneapolis: Center to Study Human-Animal Relationships and Environments, University of Minnesota, 1984.

———. "How to Involve the Community in Your Program." *Journal of Experiential Education* (Summer 1984).
———. "The Therapeutic Use of Animals with the Handicapped." *International Child Welfare Review,* no. 56 (March 1983).
———. "Children and Companion Animals: Feelings and Their Medical Significance." Columbus: Ross Labs, 1981.
———. "Outdoor Education Programs Challenge Children's Services." Dutchess County Society for Mental Health, Inc., 1975.
———. "The Farm as a School." Wooster News (1975).
———. "Environmental/Outdoor Education—A Major Priority" *The Communicator* (Journal of The New York State Outdoor Education Association) (Fall/Winter 1974).
———. "Steps Toward Visual Literacy." *School Media Quarterly* (Spring 1973).
———. "Let's be creative with our Independence." *Educational Register* (1972).
———. "Visual Literacy—A New Concept." *Audio Visual Instruction* (May 1972). ERIC Document, no. 060655, July 1972.
———. "A Trip to Europe: A Multi Media Experience." ERIC Document, no. EDO60655, July 1972.
———. "Exploring the Concept of Visual Literacy." *NAIS,* Independent School Bulletin (October 1969).
———. "Setting the Stage for the Lengthened School Year." Association of Children with Learning Disabilities. Selected Papers on Learning Disabilities, Sixth Annual Bulletin (1969).
———. "Rx-Child Care." *The Journal of Learning Disabilities* (June 1969).
———. "The Effective Use of the Extended School Year." Council for Exceptional Children (1969).
———. "Specific Values of a Residential Program for the Learning Disabled Adolescent." Association of Children with Learning Disabilities, Fifth Annual Conference (February 1968). Reprinted ERIC 9—*Educational Resources Information Center Bulletin.*
———. "Therapeutic Value of Boarding School for Disturbed Children." *Feelings & Their Medical Significance* 8, no. 7 (July-August 1966).
———. "You Really Have to Care." Report of First Annual Conference of Association of New York State Educators of the Emotionally Disturbed. 1966.
———. "Why Sex Education in the Schools?" Including a suggested curriculum that was included in a packet of material sent out by the National Association of Independent Schools. 1965.
———. "Parents, Teachers, and Staff—Partners with Children." *Educational Register* (1960).
———. "The Program for the Boarding School for Young Children." Boston: Porter Sargent, 1958.